Praise for Engineering Peace

$1

"Colonel Williams has written a provocative book that gets to the heart of postwar planning. His work identifies lessons from three post–Cold War interventions and offers a framework for addressing postconflict reconstruction. I'd recommend it for anyone undertaking postconflict planning."

GEORGE CASEY
General, U.S. Army

"Anyone who doubts that inadequate planning and staffing for the postconflict phase of interventions abroad can carry high costs need only to read daily reports from Iraq. Problems of postconflict reconstruction are the subject of Colonel Garland Williams's exceptionally timely study that includes detailed chapters on the recent cases of Bosnia, Kosovo, and Afghanistan.

Colonel Williams concludes his fine study with thoughtful recommendations, including about the central role that military engineering battalions should play to reconstruct the physical infrastructure during the period between the end of the conflict and the assumption of authority by international organizations and nongovernmental organizations.

This timely and well-written book is highly recommended for anyone with an interest in improving outcomes in military interventions."

OLE R. HOLSTI
Duke University

D0792630

Engineering Peace

ENGINEERING PEACE

THE MILITARY ROLE
IN POSTCONFLICT RECONSTRUCTION

COLONEL GARLAND H. WILLIAMS

UNITED STATES INSTITUTE OF PEACE PRESS
WASHINGTON, D.C.

The photographs between chapters 2 and 3 and chapters 3 and 4 (Bosnia and Kosovo) were taken by the author or by the Communications Section of the 16th Engineer Batalion, U.S. Army, and are in the public domain. The photographs between Chapters 3 and 4 (Afghanistan) are reproduced with the permission of U.S. Central Command.

The maps presented in this work were modified and reprinted with permission from *Stars and Stripes*, a U.S. Department of Defense publication. © 2005 *Stars and Stripes*.

The views expressed in this book are those of the author alone. They do not necessarily reflect views of the United States Government, the United States Institute of Peace, or the Department of Defense or any of its agencies.

UNITED STATES INSTITUTE OF PEACE
1200 17th Street NW
Washington, DC 20036

First published 2005

Printed in the United States of America

The paper used in this publication meets the minimum requirements of American National Standard for Information Sciences—Permanence of Paper for Printed Library Materials, ANSI Z39.48-1984.

Library of Congress Cataloging-in-Publication Data

Williams, Garland H., 1959-
    Engineering Peace : the military role in postconflict reconstruction / Garland H. Williams
        p. cm.
    Includes bibliographical references and index.
    ISBN 1-929223-57-9 (alk. paper)
    1. Peacekeeping forces—United States. 2. Military engineering—United States—Case studies. 3. Peace-building—Case studies. 4. Postwar reconstruction—Bosnia and Herzegovina. 5. Postwar reconstruction—Serbia and Montenegro—Kosovo (Serbia). 6. Postwar reconstruction—Afghanistan. 7. Yugoslav War, 1991-1995—Destruction and pillage—Bosnia and Herzegovina. 8. Kosovo (Serbia)—History—Civil War, 1998-1999—Destruction and pillage. 9. Afghanistan—History—2001 - I. Title.

U270.W555 2004
355.02'8dc22   2004046084

CONTENTS

LIST OF ILLUSTRATIONS

FIGURES

MAPS

LIST OF TABLES

FOREWORD

S CHOLARS AND PRACTITIONERS OF PEACE OPERATIONS usually
reserve the term "building bridges" for interethnic reconciliation. In Colonel Garland Williams's *Engineering Peace:
The Military Role in Postconflict Reconstruction,* the term is used
in both a literal and a figurative sense. Colonel Williams commanded a U.S. Army engineering battalion in Kosovo and
helped to direct NATO reconstruction efforts in Bosnia, so he
and his combat engineers have bridged many divides during
peace operations in those territories. Building bridges is something that combat engineers do very well—in the midst of war,
they make sure armored and infantry troops can cross any terrain that has been mined or destroyed. As Williams notes in
this work, combat engineers deployed in a peacekeeping mission
also have a vital role to play in rebuilding a war-torn country or
region. Building bridges has relevance in restoring a country's
physical infrastructure, but it also pertains to the kinds of postconflict tasks that many actors in an international intervention
undertake: they must bridge divides among a country's warring
factions and between the populace at large and the country's
governing institutions, such as they are.

When the international community undertakes an intervention in a "failed state" that has been embroiled in internecine
warfare, the military plays a crucial role in halting the fighting. Its involvement usually stops there—no one wants that
"endstate" more than the military itself. Although it has taken
on more complex peacekeeping tasks, the military is essentially
trained to fight wars. "Nation building," as the author notes early
on in this work, is something the military has eschewed, especially since the debacles in Somalia and, earlier, Vietnam. Yet
there is one aspect of an intervention's postconflict tasks that

the military is trained to do well, something that specific units can carry out in wartime or in a peacekeeping mode: reconstruction—specifically, repairing physical infrastructure, everything from roads and bridges and runways to public utilities.

Seasoned observers of multilateral peace operations in the post–Cold War era would argue that those kinds of tasks are usually handled by the myriad nongovernmental organizations (NGOs) that respond instantly to disasters around the world, either natural or man-made, which are typically made more tragic—and deadlier—by the machinations of political or ethnic factions that attempt to capitalize on the chaos of a natural disaster or the loss of a central government's legitimacy. Those observers are right, of course, but NGOs can do only so much in a complex emergency or in the bloody miasma of ethnic conflict: they can feed and clothe refugees and internally displaced persons, they can provide temporary shelter, but they do so under tremendous constraints and peril. Meanwhile, military forces from many countries do the arduous task of trying to quell the fighting, and military engineers accompany peacekeeping contingents to support their maneuverability over terrain that has typically been destroyed (or mined) by the warring factions—or by the international community itself in the service of halting the fighting.

Of course, given more time, these NGOs can rebuild entire countries once the fighting stops; however, their progress is dependent on funds supplied by the international community—usually through donors' conferences—a process that can extend a year or more into the postconflict period. In the meantime, the country or region remains in a perilously ambiguous state: littered with the remnants of bombed-out houses and apartment buildings, factories and farms, electrical grids and water pumping stations, and, in most cases, government offices; the mass violence may have ended, but there are few homes or jobs to return to, and the resentments that may have fueled the fighting in the first place only have an opportunity to fester.

Rather than leave peacekeepers in a peace operation's host country during this period to stanch sporadic violent outbreaks of such resentments, why not also give military peacekeeping forces—especially the engineering and construction battalions—a mandate to blitz the country's infrastructural repair and reconstruction while the international community amasses funds for NGOs to undertake more long-term peacebuilding tasks? If NGOs cannot get major funding for about a year, and if the military is hesitant to take on nation-building tasks, the consequent "reconstruction gap" means that interventions will continue to be long, arduous affairs. It also means that the international community's efforts will continue to be reactive rather than preventive—that is, they will not be directed toward getting the host country's economy moving again by promoting freedom of movement through public works and the rebuilding and repair of the country's economic lifelines: the roadways and shelters and services that support the country's human capital. That task is imperative in establishing durable peace in a war-torn society.

Colonel Williams's solution for closing this gap is surprising, given the military's aversion to nation building. His prescription resides in the nation-building camp, yet it is a tempered proposal that focuses on the immediate postconflict environment and is aimed at extracting the military quickly and efficiently, handing over long-term physical reconstruction tasks to its civilian partners in peace operations. His recommendations for changes in defense and foreign policy planning are grounded in many years of experience not only as a battalion commander but also as an official in the defense bureaucracy, serving as liaison between the assistant secretary of the army for civil works and federal agencies, Congress, and state and local governments. He is also a scholar, holding a doctorate in political science after completing his dissertation on defense reorganization.

The fundamental changes that Colonel Williams proposes for the military's role in postconflict reconstruction raise an equally fundamental question about the foreign policy goals of the major troop-contributing nations in peace operations—particularly the United States. As Colonel Williams aptly demonstrates in the three case studies that follow, the reconstruction of Bosnia and Kosovo seemed to have a predetermined course: restore the network of roads, industrial plant, and public utilities that were mangled in a few short years of ethnic conflict and reintegrate these war-torn venues into the European project. Afghanistan, however, had very little of such infrastructure to begin with prior to its transformation as the first battleground in the War on Terror, one of whose related assumptions is the need to remove the sources of continued poverty and hopelessness that make such countries attractive breeding grounds for terrorists.

So what should be the extent of the military's participation in a peace operation, and how should its success be judged? Critics will view Colonel Williams's recommendations as just more "mission creep" toward the onerous tasks of nation building. In fact, they should be viewed as a way to make international interventions more efficient and to extract most military forces from a peace operation more quickly and more smoothly. If Operation Iraqi Freedom comes to mind as an obvious candidate for the lessons in this book, it should be noted here that senior officials at the Department of Defense requested Colonel Williams to give a presentation on the postconflict reconstruction "template" he details in the final chapter of *Engineering Peace,* and parts of the template were incorporated into the Coalition Provisional Authority's reconstruction plans.

Colonel Williams's study is the most recent installment in a series of monographs published by the United States Institute of Peace on the changing role of the military in peacekeeping operations. It also comes on the heels of another significant work on postconflict environments published by the Institute's Press— Robert Perito's *Where Is the Lone Ranger When We Need Him? America's Search for a Postconflict Stability Force.* Both volumes explore the challenges of stabilizing postconflict environments and the requirements of creating a durable peace, albeit from different perspectives: Perito in the realm of establishing public security in a peace operation's host country, and Williams decidedly "on the ground," looking at the physical things that need to be quickly repaired and rebuilt in order to help make a war-damaged society and country functional again.

RICHARD H. SOLOMON, PRESIDENT
UNITED STATES INSTITUTE OF PEACE

PREFACE

THIS BOOK IS ABOUT POSTCONFLICT RECONSTRUCTION, or more precisely how to execute postconflict reconstruction in the most optimum way to secure long-term peace. These are ideas formed during twenty-two years of military experience: experience gathered during security operations on the inter-German border during the Cold War; multiple peacekeeping deployments in the Balkans; no-notice defense missions in Kuwait; numerous exercises against notional forces in the swamps of Georgia, the deserts of California and Egypt, and the rolling hills of Germany; and almost constant military plan development to prepare for possible missions in places such as Korea, Iraq, Turkey, and Greece. Throughout all of these scenarios, there exists a common thread. After the fighting is done and hostilities have essentially ceased, viable physical infrastructure is essential for a region to develop economic strength, leading to government stability and security. The earlier that the infrastructure can return to normalcy, the better are the chances that the country will grow and that long-term peace will thrive.

Despite the inherent value of infrastructure reconstruction to the long-term peace process, while deployed to Bosnia and Kosovo I experienced significant frustration at the apparent gap between the limits of military infrastructure reconstruction and the beginning of postconflict infrastructure reconstruction by civilian agencies. This frustration later evolved into critical thinking on ways to better execute postconflict reconstruction and to maximize the reconstruction potential of both the military and civilian components, while also maximizing and growing the capabilities of the host country. I developed a comparative study of the experiences of three regions that had significant U.S. forces engaged throughout the three stages of peace operations:

peace enforcement, peacemaking, and peacebuilding. The criteria for my case selection were straightforward:

1. I considered only those peace operations that have occurred since the end of the Cold War. During the Cold War, peace operations had the geopolitical task to ensure that local conflicts did not sufficiently escalate to drag in larger regional neighbors or the two superpowers. The ending of the superpower conflict created a new set of circumstances to which the military and the civilian agencies have had to adjust. Any proposed template for postconflict infrastructure reconstruction must confine itself to the current standard of peace operations and not be sidetracked by Cold War guidelines.

2. I limited my cases to those that had large infusions of U.S. military forces sent to conduct the continuum of military operations from high-intensity conflict to peace operations. Since the end of the Cold War, the United States has sent forces of at least a battalion size or larger to ten conflicts around the world. Table 1 outlines the possible case pool.

3. I limited my case selection to operations that reached the peacebuilding stage and that lasted longer than eighteen months in order to determine what effects the reconstruction gap had on country development. These two stipulations eliminated six cases:

■ Panama—a short operation with no requirement for large infrastructure reconstruction as part of peacebuilding.

■ Somalia—President Clinton terminated the operation when U.S. forces failed to accomplish countrywide peace enforcement. One of the prerequisites for peacebuilding is the establishment of a stable and secure environment. This was never achieved throughout the country.

■ Macedonia—U.S. forces were deployed as part of the United Nations (UN) Preventive Deployment Force. The mission ended on February 28, 1999, and later transitioned to be a part of the Kosovo Force. No infrastructure reconstruction was required in Macedonia and forces were there in a UN observer status only.

Table 1. Major U.S. Peace Operations since 1989

Location	Duration	Peak Number of U.S. Forces
Panama	1989–1990	14,000
Iraq and Kuwait	1991–present	35,000
Somalia	1992–1994	25,800
Macedonia	1993–1999	600
Rwanda	1994	3,600
Haiti	1994–present	21,000
Bosnia	1996–present	26,000
Kosovo	1999–present	7,100
East Timor	1999–present	1,300
Afghanistan	2001–present	7,100

Sources: Nina M. Serafino, *Military Interventions by U.S. Forces from Vietnam to Bosnia: Background, Outcomes,* and *"Lessons Learned" for Kosovo* (Washington, D.C.: Congressional Research Service, May 20, 1999), passim; idem, *Peacekeeping: Issues of U.S. Military Involvement.* CRS Issue Brief (Washington, D.C.: Congressional Research Service, August 1, 2002), 2-3; Congressional Budget Office, *Making Peace While Staying Ready for War: The Challenges of U.S. Military Participation in Peace Operations* (Washington, D.C.: Congressional Budget Office, December 1999), xi; United Nations, Department of Peacekeeping Operations.

■ Rwanda—U.S. forces were not deployed long enough to enter the peacebuilding stage.

■ Haiti—U.S. forces were deployed in large numbers for less than one year, although there are still limited forces in theater.

■ East Timor—short operation; not a sufficient U.S. presence to affect reconstruction.

4. I limited my case selection to infrastructure efforts that required external funding. This eliminated Kuwait, which had the required $14 billion to fully fund the U.S. efforts at reconstruction. Because the United States Army Corps of Engineers fully

reconstructed the country on a reimbursable basis, paid for by the legitimate government of Kuwait, this operation is an aberration from the possible case pool.[1] Most peace operations do not have the luxury of having a fully functioning legitimate government, or one with the wealth of the Kuwaitis.

Therefore, I chose to focus on the remaining cases—Bosnia, Kosovo, and Afghanistan—as the cases for comparison. All three operations meet the proposed criteria and constitute highly visible test opportunities for the international community to mobilize resources and design effective interventions for post-conflict reconstruction and peacebuilding. The findings of these three case studies suggest that even generous, well-intentioned external assistance is not readily available in the critical year after the cessation of hostilities. By demonstrating the problems encountered in each operation with respect to reconstruction, I fully develop a postconflict infrastructure reconstruction template in Chapter 5 to use as a planning guideline for U.S. peace operations in the future.

In the end, the critical determinants of successful peacebuilding and sustainable recovery must be *internal*. This book's focus on *external* resources may overemphasize the role of the military and the international donors in successful postconflict reconstruction. The efforts of the military, with a smooth transition to civil agencies supported by the donor community, cannot substitute for the willingness of local actors to renounce violence and to devote domestic resources to reconstruction. The value of the postconflict reconstruction proposal in the final chapter is that it will help jumpstart the host nation and will give it a rapid start to recovery with a goal of self-sufficiency. A rise in self-sufficiency will subsequently advance the redeployment of the intervening military forces and civilian agencies.

ACKNOWLEDGMENTS

I GRATEFULLY ACKNOWLEDGE the invaluable assistance from persons who consented to be interviewed. They spoke with admirable directness and candor and did not hesitate to give their remarks for attribution. I want to thank those who willingly gave their time to help me hone my ideas and perfect my writing. At the risk of leaving somebody out, I must individually thank a few of my military colleagues such as Lieutenant Colonels Tim Touchette, Dave Carlton, and Ran Garver and Major Eric Niksch, all of whom I served with in the Balkans; Major General Carl Strock who mentored me when I was a young major deployed to Kuwait and then helped me narrow my ideas during the actual writing task; Brigadier General Steve Hawkins, the premier engineer officer for peace operations; and Colonel John Durkin, who not only deserves thanks for help in crafting ideas, but also ran invaluable interference for me in Heidelberg when I was deployed as the task force engineer and engineer battalion commander in Kosovo. I appreciate the advice of Colonel Mike Dooley and his fellow staff at the United States Army Peacekeeping Institute who helped guide my project to completion. And to the soldiers and families of the 16th Armored Engineer Battalion, I owe a debt of gratitude that I can never repay.

I want to thank the United States Institute of Peace for sponsoring me as a Senior Fellow and providing the best work environment possible in which to think and write. The president of the Institute, Ambassador Dick Solomon, my adviser John Crist, my editor Peter Pavilionis, and my research assistant Ryan Sawak—they initially proposed turning my ideas into a book and patiently guided me through the process as a first-time author. I also want to thank Mark Sweberg, Larry Wentz, and Bill Baldwin, each experts in their field, who willingly gave great amounts of their time to read and edit what I wrote in an effort to not only make my writing better, but, more important, to make sure that I got it right.

Finally, I want to thank my family—from my mother who always had words of encouragement, to my brother, Pem, and sisters, Mary and Bobbie, who were very supportive. To my mother-in-law, Rachel, and my brothers- and sisters-in-law—thanks for your encouraging words. But, most important, I must thank my biggest fans—my wife, Kathy, and my daughters, Rebecca and Leah. You gave me the love and encouragement that it took to complete this project. You understood when I would work "a little" on the weekends and would endure the constant barrage of ideas that I would talk about at dinner while I worked my way through to the end.

Dad, I think you would have liked this too. This has been a true pleasure.

LIST OF ACRONYMS

AFSOUTH: Allied Forces Southern Europe (NATO)

ARRC: Allied Command Europe Rapid Reaction Corps (NATO)

ARRC-ENG: Allied Command Europe Rapid Reaction Corps Engineer

CE: Contingency Establishment

CENTCOM: U.S. Central Command

CHLC: Coalition Humanitarian Liaison Cell

CIA: Central Intelligence Agency

CIMIC: Civil-Military Cooperation

CJCIMIC: Combined Joint Civil-Military Cooperation

CJCMOTF: Coalition Joint Civil-Military Operations Task Force

CMOC: Civil-Military Operations Center

CMRWG: Civil-Military Reconstruction Working Group

COMIFOR: Commander of the Implementation Force

DAC: Development Assistance Committee

DAG: Damage Assessment Group

DOD: U.S. Department of Defense

EBRD: European Bank for Reconstruction and Development

EC: European Commission

EOD: Explosive Ordnance Disposal

ERDC: Engineer Research and Development Center

ETRP: Emergency Transport and Reconstruction Project

EU: European Union

FET: Facility Engineer Team

FRY: Federal Republic of Yugoslavia

FYROM: Former Yugoslav Republic of Macedonia

GFAP: General Framework Agreement for Peace (Dayton Accords)

GIS: Geographic Information Systems

GPS: Global Positioning System

H/CA: Humanitarian and Civic Assistance

ICRC: International Committee of the Red Cross

IDP: Internally Displaced Person

IEBL: Inter-Entity Boundary Line (Bosnia)

IFOR: Implementation Force (Bosnia)

IFOR-ENG: Implementation Force Engineer

IO: International Organization

ISAF: International Security Assistance Force (Afghanistan)

KFOR: Kosovo Force

KLA: Kosovo Liberation Army

KPC: Kosovo Protection Corps

MACA: Mine Action Center for Afghanistan

MAPA: Mine Action Program for Afghanistan

MCC: Mine Clearance Center

METL: Mission Essential Task List

MEU: Marine Expeditionary Unit

MMR: Minimum Military Requirement

MNB: Multinational Brigade

MND: Multinational Division

MRE: Maneuver Rehearsal Exercise

MSR: Main Supply Route

MTA: Military Technical Agreement (Kosovo)

NAC: NATO North Atlantic Council

NATO: North Atlantic Treaty Organization

NGO: Nongovernmental Organization

NSC: National Security Council

NSPD: National Security Policy Directive

OECD: Organization for Economic Cooperation and Development

OFDA: Office of U.S. Foreign Disaster Assistance (U.S. Agency for International Development)

OHDCA: Overseas Humanitarian Disaster Civil Aid

OHR: Office of the High Representative (Bosnia)

OSCE: Organization for Security and Cooperation in Europe

PDD: Presidential Decision Directive

POL-MIL: Political-Military

PRRP: Priority Reconstruction and Recovery Program

PRT: Provincial Reconstruction Team

REO: Regional Engineering Office

RMAC: Regional Mine Action Center

SFOR: Stabilization Force (Bosnia)

SHAPE: Supreme Headquarters Allied Powers Europe (NATO)

SNIC: Snow and Ice Clearance

SOF: Special Operations Forces

SRSG: Special Representative of the Secretary-General (United Nations)

TERO: Theater Emergency Recovery Office

TPMO: Theater Project Management Office

UCPMB: Liberation Army of Presevo, Medvedya, and Bujanovac (Kosovo)

UN: United Nations

UNESCO: UN Educational, Scientific, and Cultural Organization

UNHCR: United Nations High Commissioner for Refugees

UNICEF: United Nations Children's Fund

UNMAC: United Nations Mine Action Center

UNMACC: United Nations Mine Action Coordination Center

UNMIK: United Nations Interim Administration in Kosovo

UNPROFOR: United Nations Protection Force

USAID: U.S. Agency for International Development

UXO: Unexploded Ordnance

WFP: World Food Program

ZOS: Zone of Separation (Bosnia)

Engineering Peace

1

THE NEW
SECURITY
ENVIRONMENT

TODAY'S GLOBAL SECURITY ENVIRONMENT is complex and full of unknowns. Peace and stability are constantly threatened by traditional national and ethnic enmities, further retarding many states' economic development and raising the cost of conflict, both in lives and in infrastructure. Ethnic divisions that were suppressed by the Cold War erupted with suddenness and ferocity, as the tragedies in Bosnia and Herzegovina and Kosovo vividly demonstrated. The proliferation of weapons of mass destruction; the threat of terrorism; and the pervasiveness of international crime, drug trafficking, and ethnic cleansing not only grab our newspaper headlines but they also pose a serious danger to global stability.

Within established states, uneven economic development, whether between ethnic groups or simply between the haves and have-nots, will ultimately prolong poverty throughout the world, promoting terrorism, drug-based economies, and ever-increasing instability. The gap between rich and poor societies has expanded dramatically, separating nations and continents into fundamentally different worlds. Transnational threats whose power, influence, and interests cross international borders have transformed global instability from an interstate problem to one that encompasses intrastate divisions. That transformation has removed the management of conflict from the traditional governmental role, which may impart a sense of stability and rationale to the

3

conflict, changing it into one that involves leading actors from various sources.

In contemporary conflicts, it is increasingly difficult to determine who has the reins on the conflict and who can best be influenced to cease hostilities. Recent conflicts have involved nontraditional paramilitary formations that typically do not adhere to the agreed-upon, legally binding rules governing behavior in times of war, unlike professional armies. These nontraditional actors typically define their actions as consistent with their own interpretation of legal conventions. Because the conflict is internal, they argue, their actions fall outside the realm of international law, and because they are challenging another informal faction or a central government they deem illegitimate, their actions fall outside the realm of domestic law as well.[2]

The current and projected environment of international security suggests many potential challenges from either "rogue" or "failed" states, or individuals, constituting "transnational groups" that resort to asymmetrical threats against established powers. Potential foes may devise unique weapons or strategies that strike at bases, diplomatic posts, economic interests, telecommunications, computer networks, or even the American homeland, as was seen on September 11, 2001. Such instability is only compounded by asymmetrical responses and countermeasures, vastly different from the traditional force-on-force encounters that have characterized wars in the past. Without warning, the United States may be forced to conduct simultaneous peace operations, working through the armed forces and the civilian agencies, with little to no reaction time. Why the end of the Cold War brought with it so many intrastate conflicts likely will be a matter of debate for years to come. These conflicts may have been the result of power grabs by ambitious politicians in the post–Cold War reshuffling of regimes and political-administrative boundaries. Even if the debate swings toward the explanation of brewing resentments over the centuries and to long-seething ethnic hatreds unleashed by the end of postcolonial empires, the international community must determine successful methods of intervention in these vulnerable areas if long-term peace is the desired result.

THE POSTCONFLICT RECONSTRUCTION GAP

The proliferation of intrastate conflicts during the post–Cold War era has launched the United Nations (UN), the North Atlantic Treaty Organization (NATO), and the United States, in particular, into a series of complicated peace operations amidst the devastation of sometimes protracted civil war. Though the grim exposure of suffering and humanitarian crises through the international media often propels the urgency of emergency relief and humanitarian operations, the UN, international organizations (IOs), nongovernmental organizations (NGOs), and developmental organizations are left the difficult task of postconflict reconstruction, often with withering resources.

Right after the cessation of hostilities in a protracted conflict, a peace operation's host nation typically finds itself in a precarious position—not only must it reconstitute its governmental and administrative apparatus, but it must also rebuild much of its basic physical infrastructure that was destroyed during the conflict: roads must be rebuilt, public utilities must be restored, and land mines must be removed. Otherwise, such chaotic situations can easily sustain the conditions and mass resentments that led to the conflict in the first place.

Military forces are repeatedly deployed in peace operations, usually with a UN mandate, to put an end to hostilities but are then retained in theater for an indeterminate amount of time without a clear exit strategy and without a clear mandate to execute peace-operation tasks other than to provide security and stability. There is no well-established strategy to make the transition quickly from the military's peacemaking and peacekeeping mission to civilian IOs' and NGOs' longer-term mission of *peacebuilding*—that is, fortifying a postconflict society's institutions to prevent it from lapsing back into conflict—and reconstructing a war-torn nation. The one organization that is uniquely positioned and equipped to take on such postconflict reconstruction tasks immediately is the U.S. military—specifically, its engineering brigades that typically accompany infantry and armored divisions to help them deploy to areas of a peace operation's host country that are cut off from base camps because of destroyed bridges, crater-strewn highways and roads, or vast stretches of land filled with antipersonnel devices. In the initial phases of a peace operation, engineering units must repair such infrastructure to facilitate the movement of peacekeepers; in this way, they also begin the initial phase of the country's or region's crucial reconstruction. Yet going beyond this strictly military limit of rebuilding physical infrastructure in a peace operation presents several formidable obstacles.

First and foremost, U.S. military forces do not have the authority to execute postconflict reconstruction in a peace operation guided by a UN mandate—even though they are already in a theater providing security and stability. Second, even if such authority were granted, U.S. military leaders run the risk of being accused of "nation building," a job they have resisted since the Vietnam era.

But the debate on nation building is still largely framed by its original, pejorative meaning from the Vietnam experience—that is, the attempt to prop up unpopular governments through political support and thus gain the allegiance of the populace toward the central government by redressing grievances that insurgent movements use in their revolutionary agendas. To be sure, nation building is a vague term that, at first blush, means just what it says: an effort to repair and reconstruct a nation (or region) that has been destroyed by war. The effort involves the restoration of practically every social institution in the country. It also includes the targeted country's physical infrastructure, including transportation routes that connect urban centers throughout the country to rural areas and other urban centers and, ultimately, to the capital, to facilitate central governance and administration.

As such, nation building has included a political component with reconstruction tasks in a targeted country. The U.S. experience with nation building from around the beginning of the twentieth century to the post–Cold War era has focused largely on shoring up a state's flagging governing capacity to ward off the popularity of insurgent movements; the extent and commitment of the U.S. nation-building effort was determined by how geopolitically important the targeted state was to U.S. interests. In Vietnam, the commitment was, of course, total, resulting in a pervasive effort of "pacification," defined as

> The military, political, economic, and social process of establishing or re-establishing local government responsive to and involving the participation of the people. It includes the provision of sustained, credible territorial security, the destruction of the enemy's underground government, the assertion or re-assertion of political control and involvement of the people in government, and the initiation of economic and social activity capable of self-sustenance and expansion. The economic element of pacification includes the opening of roads and waterways, and the maintenance of lines of communication important to economic and military activity.[3]

Hence, nation building "is the economic, political, and social activity having an impact nationwide and/or in urban centers." In the Vietnamese experience, it was the foundation of pacification; in the post–Cold War era, nation building sought to reverse the fortunes of failed states to prevent ethnic conflict and "complex emergencies"—humanitarian disasters compounded by factional conflict. In the post–September 11 global security environment, nation building still targets failed states, but the threats it is intended to ward off are now transnational in scope; failed states are magnets for terrorist groups.

In short, nation building contributes to the establishment of a "viable economic and social community."[4] It is an effort to unify the population of a country around a central government—to build a nation through an extensive network of administrative mechanisms that connect all of the country's administrative regions to the capital. Directed by in-country U.S. civilian and military offices working with a bureaucratically creaky South Vietnamese government, the effort was, of course, ultimately self-defeating: no amount of nation building could rally the

South Vietnamese around an indigenous leadership that continued to be unpopular and overshadowed by U.S. civilian and military administrators.

The United States has learned a great deal about intervention since the Vietnam era, and the lessons about overinvolvement of U.S. forces and "mission creep" in peace operations are occasionally reinforced in costly peacekeeping encounters—in Somalia, in particular, where the attempt to provide famine relief turned into a bloody operation to rein in an uncooperative warlord. At the end of the Cold War, Joint Chiefs of Staff Chairman General Colin Powell devised a list of guidelines for the deployment of troops in a new operational environment, requiring a clear mission and, more important, an exit strategy. Yet the post-Somalia experience in military interventions essentially placed so much emphasis on the latter that, in the words of one observer who summed up the Clinton foreign policy legacy, the two requirements were conflated: "the exit strategy became the mission."[5]

Nevertheless, the United States continued with military interventions in the post–Cold War wave of ethnic conflicts, particularly in the Balkans. From the U.S. perspective, these nation-building interventions were distinctly different from the Vietnam example: they were multilateral, usually done through NATO with a UN mandate, but they seemed to put more emphasis on the military's capacity to take on more of the traditional nation-building functions, particularly in light of the reconstruction tasks enshrined in the Dayton Accords. Besides the accords' stipulation that NATO's Implementation Force (IFOR) was to separate warring factions and supervise the withdrawal of heavy weapons in Bosnia, they also authorized IFOR to assist in the implementation of the accords' extensive civilian provisions. Senior U.S. military commanders, including Joint Chiefs of Staff Chairman General John Shalikashvili, drew explicit boundaries around the military's involvement in civilian tasks, but the slowness of the Dayton Accords' civilian implementers to appear obviously meant that in-theater military forces would increasingly come to take on postconflict reconstruction tasks.

Despite its early determination to scale back U.S. troops' involvement in peacekeeping operations, the Bush administration has found itself making the same demands on its military in the War on Terror, particularly in the typical nation-building tasks of reconstituting Afghanistan's and post–Saddam Hussein Iraq's public security forces and reconstructing much of the countries' public utilities and physical infrastructure. These tasks were made all the more difficult not only because of the limited number of troop-contributing nations to help carry out postconflict tasks the U.S. military was forced to do, despite its aversion to nation building, but also because, at least in the case of Iraq, U.S. military planners paid relatively scant attention to what would need to be done after a stellar military campaign to keep the country functioning and facilitate Iraqis' transfer of allegiance to the post–Saddam Hussein provisional authority.

If the strategic purpose of nation building has changed in the post–Cold War era from supporting puppet regimes to reconstituting failed states for the purpose of warding off ethnic conflict, humanitarian disasters, and terrorist havens, the fact is that professional militaries still dislike the essentially nonmilitary heft of nation-building projects that tap ready resources and skills that are devoted to one specific purpose: to fight wars efficiently and with a minimum of casualties. Retired U.S. Marine Corps General Anthony Zinni, the former head of U.S. Central Command (CENTCOM, which is responsible for U.S. military operations in the Middle East and Central Asia) and a veteran commander in Vietnam and in various peacekeeping missions during the 1990s, expressed the tension between expansive peacekeeping mandates and the military's ability to take on more and more essentially nonmilitary duties: "The military probably since Vietnam, maybe before, became more and more saddled with conflict resolution—strange conflict resolution—peacekeeping, humanitarian efforts, nation building. The military has resisted this. They don't like it. They're not trained for it. But there's no one else to do it and it continues to be the mission that confronts us."[6] And, further, on what lessons he learned from all the peace-keeping interventions he commanded, he stated:

> The first thing we learned is the military has limited capability. We obvi-ously bring a lot logistically and we can stabilize a situation very rapidly. We are a good short-term solution. We are a good temporary solution. We can create a condition. We can freeze a condition. We can create a secure environment. We are not a long-term solution. We can go into a humanitar-ian crisis and probably do the immediate required triage and the immedi-ate required care. We can't provide for eliminating the causes of that condi-tion and to rebuild nations, rebuild economies, [and] eliminate a long-term internal strife and squabbling. Then you begin to overlay this with politics, economics, nation building. And that becomes difficult. It's not something our military is very good at doing. It's something that we resist.[7]

The hesitancy of the military to take on these crucial tasks, combined with the paucity of international funding and the subsequent delay of NGOs' arrival in a postconflict environ-ment, means that interventions will continue to be plagued by a "reconstruction gap" that must be filled should the international community expect to achieve a final resolution to the conflict within a reasonable time frame and while significant interna-tional focus still remains on the damaged country. For about one year after the cessation of hostilities, the host nation is in limbo: There is not enough infrastructure to facilitate economic recov-ery, there are practically no internal assets in good enough shape to provide that infrastructure, and there is no external entity that can legally provide the infrastructural help to promote the necessary economic recovery. But why is the required response time about one year? Why can't the response time be shorter, possibly as little as a few months?

The factors that influence the window of opportunity for the international community to take positive action in an interven-tion include basic climate and terrain conditions that hinder military peacekeepers' mobility and maneuverability; the time available to develop a sense in the local nationals that they have a stake in the future of their country before other, usually violent, options are pursued; and the ability of the nationals to endure an extended lack of commercial activity and provision of basic services.

First, military planners carefully account for the effects that weather may have on the former warring factions. Because of harsh winters and terrain that is at times impassable during adverse weather, planners in IFOR and in the Kosovo Force (KFOR), for example, expected seasonal lulls in hostilities during the late fall and winter months but increased their patrols to counter expected military uprisings in the spring, when the weather clears. In addition, the intense heat of mid-summer has a calming effect on hostile actions; reminiscent of historic army campaigns that planned for winter encampments (Washington at Valley Forge and Napoleon during his Russian campaign, for example), formal militaries and paramilitary forces in most underdeveloped countries do not have the technology to carry on significant military operations during weather extremes. This seasonal factor provides the international community with a limited period to execute postconflict operations, and that period depends on what time of the year the international peacekeeping force enters the country. If the force enters in winter, as IFOR did in Bosnia, the initial effort of de-arming and demobilizing armed formations can quell the potential for violence through the first warm season into the second year of operations. If the force enters in the warm months, as KFOR did in Kosovo, the "grace" period may last only until the following spring and summer.

As a second factor, Monica Toft points to the need for the international community to help locals develop a sense of holding stakes in the future of the government to avoid violent power struggles among the factions.[8] The opportunity to reform the government of a rogue or failed state with more representative institutions always exists, but the patience of the nationals to endure either provisional authority or increased anarchy is severely tested if the process is unduly drawn out. Should there be a perception that the international community can reach only limited or no progress, disenfranchised nationals tend to seek alternative methods of governance that may spark renewed confrontations between opposing factions.

Third, the ability of the nationals to endure a severe dropoff in the provision of basic needs and services with no means to earn wages for family support is limited. International agencies have great capabilities to provide food, water, and temporary shelter during a crisis; however, sustaining massive relief for the long term can tax the international community. The emphasis must be on returning basic services to the nationals as quickly as possible to reduce their dependence on outside help. In addition, the international community has to sustain emergency care for prolonged periods without identifiable measures to halt the crisis. Past crisis interventions indicate that international support tends to wane as the immediate humanitarian crisis is averted, forcing nationals to find support from other sources—many of them illicit—when there are no viable, legitimate economic alternatives available.

Under current guidance, all military actions in a peace operation must have a direct impact on the mission. Any infrastructure reconstruction that has civilian-only use has not been covered under recent international mandates, and whatever reconstruction tasks that are implicitly assigned to peacekeeping contingents are typically viewed as "mission creep" and nation building. Two examples aptly demonstrate the military's perception of this kind of flawed decision making.

First, the NATO air campaign in Bosnia destroyed many bridges throughout the country, among which was a two-lane bridge that spanned the Drina River connecting the town of Foca to the main road network leading to Sarajevo. At the beginning of the peace operation, IFOR designated 2,500 kilometers of road as Main Supply Routes (MSRs), opening the NATO funding stream to repair these roads for the support of military operations. The road that was on the other side of the Drina River from Foca was designated as an MSR, but the bridge that connected Foca to the road network was not. Because the bridge was not directly located on the MSR (less than one hundred meters away), NATO could not spend money to rebuild the bridge (which it had initially destroyed in the aerial bombing campaign). The limitation was so restrictive that even employing a temporary bridge was outside of the mandate. Because this policy effectively cut off the town from the Bosnia sector, Foca, a town inhabited mostly by Bosnians, was made even more vulnerable to Serb repression.

Second, again in Bosnia, the United States used four Bailey bridges (temporary "erector set"-type steel girder bridges of World War II vintage) deployed out of war reserve stock to span the gaps that remained when four small bridges were blown up in the NATO air campaign. Unlike the Foca example, these bridges were properly located on a Multinational Brigade North (MNB-North) MSR and fit the criteria allowing the use of U.S. resources on MSRs directly supporting the military mission. However, when the U.S. military shifted its sector to better align with its military mission, the result was a redesignation of the MSRs, and these four bridges were no longer located on a designated MSR. In accordance with U.S. policy, the bridges had to be removed.

The Bailey bridges had been in place for almost a year and had endured numerous crossings by both military and civilian vehicles. Some pieces of the bridges were bent beyond repair, but replacement parts were unavailable because the company that built Bailey bridges had gone out of business long before. NATO issued a formal request to the U.S. Department of State asking that the bridges remain in place, with crossing restrictions because of the bridges' wear and tear, as a gift to Bosnia so that the freedom of civilian movement that had progressed in the year since the cessation of hostilities could continue. The United States refused, first, because the Bailey bridges were to be redeployed to replenish its depleted war stock (even though they were deemed unserviceable upon close inspection) and, second, because leaving the bridges in place would have been considered a violation of the prohibition on nation-building activities.[9] The ultimate solution was to secure nongovernmental funding in the summer of 1997 to replace the Bailey bridges with four new

Mabey-Johnson bridges (basically an updated Bailey bridge made of titanium steel).[10] The result was that additional aid money was spent unnecessarily on four new bridges; the four old bridges were removed, deemed unserviceable, and destroyed; and the outcome of maintaining freedom of movement was attained, but at a much higher cost—precious funds that could have been used in other areas.

These are only two instances, but they are representative of the limitations imposed by a policy of non–nation building on military resources that otherwise could have greatly added to the stability and enhanced security of the theater of operations. This policy causes a significant delay in rebuilding the host country infrastructure and adds to an already considerable list of security concerns. The lack of nation-building authority for the military prolongs the period of instability, uncertainty, and unrest, further extending the military's requirement to remain in theater to provide a safe and secure environment. Given the military's lack of a mandate for addressing such tasks, as well as its aversion to nation building, what is the optimum approach for a postconflict reconstruction mission that will not only jump-start the host country's economy and local governing structures but will also lead to an earlier redeployment of military and civilian interveners?

A MODEL FOR PEACE OPERATIONS

Former UN secretary-general Boutros Boutros-Ghali's *An Agenda for Peace* formally recognizes the peace consolidation activities that take place after a conflict. However, he provides only the following generic definition: "Action to identify and support structures which will tend to strengthen and solidify peace in order to avoid a relapse into conflict."[11] This charge suggests a wide variety of actions that must be undertaken to promote sustainable peace and facilitate the extraction of military forces. Generals George Joulwan and Christopher Shoemaker, two former military officers with considerable peace operations experience, outline the ideal phases that every peacekeeping and peacebuilding operation should pass through: transformation, stabilization, and normalization. In the transformation phase, the terms of the peace agreement are initially translated to on-the-ground operations. There is the urgent task to introduce security forces rapidly to enforce the military aspects of the peace accord, quickly followed by several other steps: establish a legitimate government apparatus; install police, judicial, and penal systems; provide essential social services; and accelerate a return to productive economic activity. The primary thrust in the beginning of this transformation phase is for military or internal security forces to create a secure environment and ensure freedom of movement while longer-term civilian functions are set in motion.[12]

As compliance with the military aspects of the peace accord becomes routine and civilian recovery measures are initiated, the focus shifts from military to civilian implementation and from nationwide strategies to local implementation. The stabilization phase prepares the institutions of the legitimate government to assume their future roles. The legitimate government is charged with maintaining internal stability, establishing a minimum level of military capacity essential for the country's self-defense, re-establishing the economic base, reconstructing an internal police capacity, rebuilding a viable education system, creating legitimate political institutions, and establishing a responsive public health system.[13]

During normalization, external forces and assistance are withdrawn and their responsibilities are turned over to evolving institutions within the country itself. The final transition from conflict to normalcy occurs, clearing the way for the termination of international assistance. Self-sufficiency is the goal. Internal security responsibilities are handled by the local police, the judicial system is competently operated by local judges, basic services are routinely provided by the local government, the economic base is stable, the host nation exercises self-governance, and, finally, international military forces are withdrawn.[14]

Joulwan and Shoemaker's approach presents an ideal scenario—a world in which civilian and military agencies are in
perfect harmony on the path toward normalcy; it depicts a seamless transition from military to civilian implementation during
peacebuilding. It also depicts an intervention in which the extraction of military forces after a short period of time is considered
a normal turn of events. However, a review of the peacebuilding
efforts in Bosnia, Kosovo, and Afghanistan shows that there are
breakdowns and delays in the three-phase approach when local,
tangible factors come into play. There are externally imposed
limitations under which military forces currently operate and
there are recurring delays until the civilian agencies can properly organize, deploy, and operate in postconflict reconstruction.
These delays result in continued instability for the host nation, a
longer military deployment for peacekeeping forces, and greater
outlays of resources for the peace operation's troop-contributing
nations. However, should the mandate allow the military, with
sufficient upfront funding, to engage in postconflict reconstruction immediately upon the cessation of hostilities, the host
nation's economy will be given a significant jumpstart and the
re-establishment of providing basic needs will help secure government legitimacy, enhancing the overall security and shorten-
ing the required deployment for military peacekeepers. The goal
is rapid normalization in the host country with quick military
extraction; the problem is how to make that goal into a reality.

CONDITIONS FOR RECONSTRUCTION

There is no argument: peacebuilding must begin with the
establishment of a secure environment, with a separation of
warring—or potentially warring—parties by the intervening
force in order to maintain peace and security. This remains the
primary focus of a peacekeeping force upon entry into a conflict
scenario. Without secure conditions, neither the military nor
civilian agencies can concentrate on reconstruction effectively.
If the security environment is uncertain, the military must take

the lead. The military not only will be involved in developing and maintaining a secure environment but will also be active in delivering humanitarian assistance or performing emergency civilian police functions, such as the maintenance of law and order. Under current practice the military will repair emergency infrastructure, such as roads and bridges, and perform limited mine clearing, but only to support military operations. The military will enforce arms embargoes and will disarm and demobilize belligerents to enhance the security of the postconflict environment. Only after these basic security conditions are met can the process of reconstruction begin.

Once security is established and maintained, the peace operation moves into the late stages of transition, in which countries emerging from conflict reside in the netherworld between a complete state of war and a complete state of peace, and where the behavior of international actors, the parties to the conflict, and the leaders of civil society directly impacts the outcome of peacebuilding efforts. Often in the wake of war the physical infrastructure of the host nation is in desperate need of repair. Whether because of overt destruction from conflict or from prolonged lack of maintenance, bridges, roads, ports, and airfields are no longer able to provide the support to the economy that a fledgling government requires for self-sustainment, and damaged water and electrical grids cannot handle the demand that the populace requires. To compound the problem, a residual effect of war can be a significant mine threat that not only threatens civilians attempting to proceed with their normal daily lives but also impedes access to the very infrastructure they need to survive.

Thus a rapid infrastructure reconstruction effort becomes the key to peacebuilding, significantly boosting the economy by providing access to markets, employment, and services that promote the social and economic development of the host nation. The host nation's government will steadily gain confidence as basic needs and services are provided on a regular basis. Admittedly, infrastructure reconstruction efforts, though intended to bring a sense of normality back to a conflict-torn land, are not enough to achieve the prevention of violent conflict. The attainment of long-term peace depends on much more than just a successful short-term implementation of a peace accord and the building of a few roads. To be sure, the level of civil participation that individuals can have in their society, even when democratic procedures are available, is greatly constrained by their lack of economic security, and this degree of participation will have a direct effect upon the level of security that can be attained in peace operations. A successful infrastructure reconstruction effort does not guarantee the prevention of deadly conflict, but without reliable infrastructure that serves as the physical integument of a community, long-lasting peace cannot be sustained. Confidence-building measures can be established upon these building blocks and, through verifiable behavior, can demonstrate the willingness of the parties to sustain a long-lasting peace.[15]

THE RUSH TO EXTRACT THE MILITARY

Why should the international community be concerned about leaving the military in place in the world's peace operations? Are there major ramifications if peacekeepers remain deployed for longer periods of time? Is it not fair to say that the international community should consider longer military deployments because they have proven in many instances to establish solidly the security and stability that was lacking prior to deployment? Since 1948, the UN Security Council has authorized fifty-four peacekeeping operations, forty-one of which have been authorized since 1990. The number of deployed international peacekeepers has changed dramatically over the past few years. In June 1993, there were 77,310 soldiers and civilian police deployed in UN operations alone. In January 2002, 47,095 were in UN operations.[16] But combine that with the NATO-led operations in Bosnia (20,000) and Kosovo (50,000), and the number of international peacekeepers reaches an all-time high exceeding 100,000. These numbers show a growing willingness on the part of the international community to conduct peace operations to handle the proliferation of threats to international security.

However, after the unsuccessful UN missions in Croatia and Bosnia (UNPROFOR, 1992–1995) and Somalia (1992–1994), both humanitarian peacekeeping missions that reverted to peace enforcement, there was hesitation to use the United Nations in complex peace operations. The UN was relegated to observing and interpositional peacekeeping (1994–1998), and the number of deployed troops declined. To meet the growing threat to international security, the numbers of international peacekeepers increased in the late 1990s.[17] Overall, the increase in peacekeepers demonstrates an increased confidence in the United Nations' ability to plan and conduct missions, and a belief by the nations of the world that peace operations can succeed if sufficiently supported.

This apparent success, however, comes at a high cost in personnel, equipment, and money. U.S. military forces are deployed in more than 120 countries, preserving peace around the world every day. Yet since 1992, the U.S. military has been cut by more than 700,000. The Army and the Air Force have experienced the largest personnel cuts: 45 percent since 1989. The Navy has reduced itself by 36 percent of its personnel by eliminating vessels and understaffed ships. On the other hand, operational commitments (such as deployments to Kosovo, Bosnia, and Iraq) have increased by 300 percent.[18]

To meet the military's mission to fight and win the nation's wars, the military must have the opportunity to train to maintain its proficiency in high-intensity conflict. Peacekeeping duties, however, do not afford many opportunities to maintain that proficiency. Units alerted for deployment to peacekeeping duties undergo several months of intensive training in peacekeeping tasks, depending on their service (Army, Air Force, Navy, or Marines), branch (for example, Infantry or Engineers), and component (Active Duty, Reserves, or National Guard), capped by an external validation prior to deployment.

Active duty units concentrate on those peacekeeping tasks that are different from their normal war-fighting tasks. Observing the execution of various scenarios that the peacekeepers may face in the theater of operations, external evaluators will certify that a unit is trained for peacekeeping deployment. Reserve and National Guard units, on the other hand, not only have to train for unfamiliar peacekeeping tasks but also must execute their normal postmobilization training in preparation for activation. A RAND study completed in 1998 proposed a brigade training model that would validate a reserve brigade on tactical missions in 92 days and declare it ready to move in 102 days.[19] The study, however, did not consider the additional time needed to train on the specific peacekeeping tasks that are required in peace operations. Units that return from a peacekeeping deployment undergo months of refitting and retraining, in which the emphasis is to return the equipment to the highest maintenance standards, allow personnel to take some needed rest, and then retrain the personnel for high-intensity conflict. This training period is capped by a final training event in which the unit is recertified by external evaluators as proficient in high-intensity conflict. Evaluators recertify active Army units at one of the Army's maneuver training centers; reserve units are recertified during their weekend training and subsequent annual training cycles.

At any given time, a peace operation can involve up to three times the number of troops that are actually deployed.[20] For each unit taking part in an operation, another unit will be preparing as a replacement unit, and a third unit (the unit that was previously deployed) will be recovering from its deployment. (The units that are available to deploy to an operation are referred to as the "rotation base.") Military and civilian leaders have voiced concern about the high operating tempo of military forces in peace operations. Other leaders question that concern, noting that the average number of Army soldiers deployed during 1998, for example, was about 28,000, representing 6 percent of the total active Army, or 9 percent of the deployable Army.[21] However, the reason for the concern about operating tempo becomes clearer when deployments are assessed by unit type. In the Army, large percentages of the high-demand capabilities in the combat-support and combat service–support areas are in the reserve component. Such high-demand/low-density units, such as Military Police, Civil Affairs, and Engineers, are subject to frequent deployments, which have a deleterious effect on morale and retention. In the past, some of those units have repeatedly deployed, either to the same or to consecutive operations. In some cases, nearly all of the active units with a particular support capability have had to deploy to a specific operation. For example, 100 percent of the teams that control movement in and out of air terminals and 75 percent of the petroleum supply companies in the active Army deployed to Somalia.[22]

The Army's experiences in recent peace operations indicate that several units in the active Army have inadequate rotation bases to support extended or continuous peace operations; examples of such units are the quartermaster and transportation units, such as general supply companies and water purification units. Because the Army considers deployments of more than 120 days a year to be a strain on soldiers and their families, the Army needs a rotation base with at least three times as many units as the number deployed.[23] For several types of support capabilities, however, the Army has four or fewer units in its active component, making repeated deployments a usual occurrence and the support for extended operations very difficult.[24] Unlike the Army, the Marine Corps has traditionally incorporated rotation-base requirements into its structure, an approach that allows it to maintain both the regular Marine Expeditionary Unit deployments and the schedule that deploys Marines for six months and then gives them eighteen months at home. Nevertheless, the Marine Corps has also faced personnel shortages in certain specialties because it does not have enough of those forces in its active component. Personnel that have been particularly taxed are those who are expert in dealing with civilian populations: for example, Civil Affairs units, which are entirely in the Marine Corps reserves. In addition, the Marines have faced personnel shortfalls for linguists and joint communications systems specialists.[25]

The current pace also puts a high attrition on vehicles and equipment. In a normal training year, the U.S. Army's M1A1 tank is routinely scheduled to drive 800 to 850 miles. During a year of peacekeeping duties, tanks are driven more than twice that amount. Aircraft limitations on flying hours are exceeded halfway through the fiscal year, causing earlier groundings to conduct required maintenance. Equipment life expectancies are typically halved through overuse, causing additional strain on the supply pipeline to provide replacement parts and then replacement vehicles for overused military equipment. In some cases, the United States is no longer producing replacement vehicles and must rely on equipment overhaul to keep fleets operational. Because there are limited replacements, equipment that is being overhauled is not available to the unit for training and for deployment, degrading the unit's training and equipment readiness. The chairman of the House Committee on National Security argued in 1997 that the pressures of the troop drawdown and "operations other than war" are having "a significant impact on the readiness of U.S. military forces and are placing at risk the decisive military edge that this nation enjoyed at the end of the Cold War. . . . [T]he readiness of our armed forces is suffering."[26]

The strain shows up in the Army's personnel profile. Repeated six-month deployments to the Balkans and Afghanistan cause severe stress for a force that is more than 50 percent married. Soldiers who have recently exited the military cite "operational tempo" and time away from home on peacekeeping deployments as the most common reasons for pursuing another career. General Thomas Schwartz, former commander of the United States Army Forces Command, testified before Congress that "Our soldiers . . . repeatedly tell us that they choose to leave the Army because they cannot raise their family and be constantly deployed."[27] Although the Army easily made its recruiting goal for 2002, critical shortages continue to exist in junior and noncommissioned officers who opt to leave military service once their initial obligation is completed. As the commander of III Corps, then–Lieutenant General Schwartz cited one battalion as an example: The battalion task force of 760 soldiers had to receive 226 personnel from outside the battalion to meet the theater deployment criteria. A second example was from Operation Restore Hope (Somalia), where there was a deployment requirement for ten Military Police companies (1,193 personnel). According to the Time Phased Force Deployment Database, however, these 1,193 personnel actually came from more than fifty different units—forty-one Military Police companies and ten Military Police battalion headquarters.[28] This strain is similarly felt in the reserves and the National Guard; however, the anxiety is compounded by time taken away from their civilian employers in addition to the time taken away from their families.

WHAT SHOULD BE THE MILITARY ENDSTATE?

The strains on peacekeeping personnel, equipment, and funding are further aggravated by the lack of a clearly defined end to military peace operations. There is no tidy sequence of events that will indicate to the military when redeployment will occur. It was clear that the major task confronting the Western powers at the Dayton conference, for instance, was to end the violence in Bosnia, but the Bosnian war was a unique example because a slow, gruesome genocide was televised to a worldwide audience each night. Thus ending the violence was significant not only for the civilians and combatants directly involved in the conflict but also for a wider viewing public. The "CNN effect" clearly and correctly focused attention on ending the carnage; yet the danger of this focus was that the ending of the violence in and of itself was the goal, but the roots of the conflict and the means to create sustainable institutions that would prevent its re-emergence were left unaddressed.

Getting the balance right in such situations is difficult for the actors facilitating the conflict's resolution. There is no possibility that in the midst of ongoing destruction, the warring parties are interested in or able to create the required institutions from the bottom up. Indigenous solutions are impossible to conceive in the wake of genocide and expulsions. A heavy burden is thus placed on the interveners and peacekeepers: they come to the conflict with obligations. Though a noble goal, facilitating the transition from armed conflict to interethnic coexistence cannot be the end in itself. An intervention is judged on the basis of whether the transition to coexistence is a durable one and on how fast the host country can manage its own affairs in a peaceful manner without outside help.

Intervention is also judged by the agreements facilitating an end to hostilities. Some argue, for example, that the Dayton Accords were the best deal that could be made under the circumstances. The realities of an ongoing armed conflict, the political marginalization of a number of key negotiators, the limited patience of the contact states, and the fragile consensus among them compromised the final agreement. The operational result was that the interveners had to create virtually all institutions required for a peaceful coexistence between the former warring parties. The Dayton Accords left unresolved wide disagreements that the international community has little choice but to constantly renegotiate, making a complete withdrawal from Bosnia impossible in the short or medium term.[29]

Empirical Problems with No Defined Endstate

The principal deployment criterion for military forces to Bosnia was specific—all U.S. peacekeepers would remain in theater for one year as part of IFOR. Upon the completion of one year, they would be redeployed back to their peacetime locations. Because of its leadership role in the international system as a whole and within NATO in particular, the U.S. position became the bellwether for the commitment of the entire international community. From the beginning of the operation, the United States made it clear that its commitment was neither open-ended nor permanent, and the rest of the players in Bosnia took their lead from the U.S. position.

The plans articulated by the United States during IFOR's term of service were shaped by the U.S. presidential elections and by mounting public concern about the United States' role in Bosnia. Domestic opposition to U.S. involvement might have been greater had U.S. forces sustained casualties. Even in the absence of casualties, it was clear that U.S. commitment was tenuous, and the international community—particularly America's European allies—watched very carefully for signs of an eroding U.S. resolve. This apprehension created major problems for the forces on the ground: daily interactions with the former warring parties were influenced by the possibility that the United States would not see the process of reconciliation and reconstruction through to its conclusion.

In the fall of 1996, NATO confronted the reality that the conditions allowing military forces to be withdrawn did not exist, and that there was little prospect of such conditions being created in the foreseeable future. Nearing the end of the year, and the day immediately after the U.S. presidential election, President Bill Clinton extended the operation's mandate for another year to allow additional time for the peace process to continue, committing American forces to IFOR's follow-on force—the Stabilization Force (SFOR). This mandate has been extended eight times and still there is not a viable plan for full extraction of all U.S. peacekeepers. To be sure, in the first months of the Dayton Accords' implementation, the presence of overwhelming military force was instrumental in keeping the peace. But the daunting challenges of building the kinds of institutions and processes that are required to support the Dayton agreement and, indeed, that are at the heart of conflict prevention are far beyond the abilities of the military. The military can bring about the absence of war; the civilian agencies have the expertise to reconstruct the country's institutions for an enduring peace. But until those civilian agencies can become operational in the theater, there is a gap in capability and authority.

In comparison to Bosnia, it is still early to determine which of the institutions discussed during negotiations at Rambouillet and Paris in February and March 1999 will be implemented in Kosovo under NATO control; however, Rambouillet provides a second example in which the international community charted an agreement to end a conflict in the former Yugoslavia and provided a territory with a new institutional framework. In this case, the representatives of the state in which Kosovo lies—that is, Yugoslavia and Serbia—negotiated the agreements with the representatives of the province's major ethnic group, the Albanians.[30]

Within the agreement for Kosovo, the proposed constitution took a more prominent place than the constitution had in the case of Bosnia. In general, the proposed constitution is more detailed and elaborate than the six-page constitution for Bosnia. The document, however, falls short and does not define the people enacting the legal text, and in no way determines the composition of Kosovo. It refrains from clearly dividing institutions between Albanians and Serbians. As opposed to the main challenge at Dayton, which was to map out the relationship between the groups within their respective entity of predominance, the challenge of the negotiations at Rambouillet lay in codifying the relations between the province and the state, Serbia or Yugoslavia.[31] The Rambouillet proposals remain vague on contentious issues such as the degree of bilingualism in Kosovo, especially in education and in official institutions.

Recognizing that no two peace operations are alike, President Clinton introduced American peacekeepers into Kosovo under NATO command without a time-based endstate as in Bosnia but, rather, with an endstate to be developed as peace operations progressed. The initial reaction was to deploy ground troops into Kosovo immediately after the aerial bombing campaign to put a halt to the ethnic cleansing. However, once entry was accomplished, the military, as in Bosnia, faced the same lack of defined criteria upon which to base withdrawal. The approach of an event-based deployment fits better into the military's operational scheme; however, no criteria for extraction of U.S. forces from Kosovo have been fully developed to date.

Unlike conventional military operations such as Operation Desert Storm, peace operations are assigned to the military with little strategic political-military clarity. There is no "unconditional surrender" that can be demanded, signaling the end of conflict and the end of American military engagement. Peace operations require a full analysis of the crisis situation in order to fully understand the totality of the problem and its symptoms, becoming the prerequisite for the United States to define the limits of its involvement. There must be a thorough strategic assessment of the crisis, a calculation of a realistic mission event table (to include entry, transition, and exit strategy), and the development of courses of action so that senior leaders can make informed strategic decisions. As can be seen in Bosnia and Kosovo, strategic ambiguity creates tactical uncertainty. Compressed timetables, artificial exit dates, and general confusion as to the purpose of the mission place leaders in a reaction mode to unforeseen changes, as opposed to the execution of a thorough, well-developed plan.

When a peace accord contains strategic statements of a mission and its objectives, those statements must be translated into specific missions and objectives for the forces, institutions, and organizations that will implement the accord. They must include specific tasks to be assigned to the organizations and institutions undertaking the intervention, including the conditions under which these tasks are to be performed, and the standards by which progress can be measured. The list must be broad enough to cover the entire spectrum of relevant activities: military, political, social, economic, psychological, and informational. Once compiled, these tasks should be thoroughly examined to discern where they overlap, complement, or conflict with one another. The task list also helps refine the number of organizations required for the accomplishment of the peace mission. Diplomats, political leaders, NGO officials, and military commanders all must take part in determining what is required to accomplish the assigned missions. Once tasks and subtasks have been identified, it becomes far easier to judge whether the participation of other organizations is necessary or desirable in the first place, or whether the participation of a specific organization is no longer required.

Event-Based Exit Criteria

Since the end of the Cold War, interstate wars stemming from strategic and geopolitical rivalries and ambitions have become less frequent, whereas intrastate wars stemming from cultural and ethnic antipathies (that usually spread, involving other states) have multiplied. The organized, technologically managed warfare of nation-states has been replaced by primal violence. In light of this shift in the origins and course of mass violence, there are certain tasks in proposed peace operations that only a military force can successfully accomplish—tasks that also suggest an outline of event-based exit criteria for military forces.

First, the "CNN effect" establishes a high priority to solve the immediate problem of insecurity and violence. Instant, up-to-the-minute news coverage through the lens of television brings the cruelty and intense violence of conflict into the home of the average American. Public opinion can quickly form with a call for America to "do something" to end the violence. Many argue that peacemaking can be successfully accomplished without involving the military. Peacemaking programs, for example, are specifically designed to bring potential and former combatants together to manage their differences through negotiation, mediation, and reconciliation. Lawyers, diplomats, and social scientists who are trained as mediators believe that with training and assistance people can work through their problems, reach compromises, and manage their conflicts more constructively.[32] But a cost is incurred while negotiation and mediation are taking place: lives are being lost in violent conflict. In simple terms, when a hostile situation exists, only the military has the capability to forcefully separate warring parties at the beginning of a peace operation. If the government is sufficiently swayed to take action, military forces are the only option for bringing a quick end to the violence and immediately saving lives. Military forces can be quickly inserted to separate warring factions and establish a forceful end to the internal violence that has plagued the host country. Military intervention allows the factions to gain a respite from fighting and allows the factions to focus on other problems rather than the immediate problem of waging war. Military intervention also serves to offer "face-saving" ways for belligerents to step back from the brink of conflict.

This task includes not only the separation of belligerent factions, but also the initial execution of routine police functions and the restoration of the rule of law, including the establishment of an interim court system and penal system to give clout to the internal police. Should the military leave without handing off this task, a return to conflict will most likely occur. Therefore, as part of the transition from stabilization to normalization, the host nation must be able to maintain all aspects of internal security, allowing the former combatants time to re-establish bonds of trust across ethnic and cultural lines. For the military to exit the country, the public security responsibilities, which the military assumed upon entry into the host country, must be gradually handed over to local police—whether it be an interim police task force established by a civilian agency, or a police capability operated by the host country. Regardless, the function of internal security must be established and continually exercised by a legitimate authority immediately from the cessation of hostilities through normalization.

Second, military intervention provides a minimum level of military capacity to defend the host nation from external attack while the host country reorganizes into a peaceful state. Upon the cessation of hostilities, belligerents are disarmed and demobilized to quickly establish peace between the separated combatants. Arms embargoes are enforced and peacekeepers supervise compliance with any imposed arms control measures. The successful completion of this task, however, produces an immediate power vacuum in the region that must be filled by the intervening military until the host country can re-establish legitimate capacity to defend itself. Otherwise, neighboring states may feel compelled to take advantage of the opportunity to enlarge their influence and fill the existing power void with their own forces or with "fifth columns" of competing internal forces that may step into the vacuum in a power grab on the legitimate authority. Once the host country can train and establish a minimum level of military capacity essential for the country's self-defense or internal security, the military peacekeepers can withdraw from the host country while maintaining a residual capacity to keep the peace with rapid deployment forces located outside the country. If the survival of the host country is vital to the peace operation, this minimum level of self-defense must be maintained throughout the process from peace enforcement stabilization to normalization.

Subsequently, it is more productive for combatants to work jointly on the technical and economic problems of reconstruction and reconciliation, allowing the development of relationships and civil society to follow from these indirect and more impersonal problem-solving efforts. Such peacebuilding activities can contribute to the construction of civic institutions and identities. Focusing previous combatants on the issues of rebuilding the country's damaged infrastructure and rebuilding its economic base provides paths along which confidence and security can grow. Once combatants are no longer engaged in warfare, they must have something constructive to occupy their time; otherwise they may return to conflict or illegal activities. Economic reconstruction and recovery provide hope and jobs.

Because domestic market and export capacities are limited, major sources of growth and employment generation in the initial stages of recovery will come from construction-related activities. It is critical that reconstruction projects employ local nationals and companies, and that any emergency food aid that comes from external sources does not hamper the recovery of agricultural production and the creation of jobs in the rural areas. Equally important in this initial stage of economic recovery is the early adoption by the authorities of a set of measures that can immediately facilitate economic restructuring. These include measures that promote internal as well as external trade and help reactivate functioning productive assets.

But there is a stumbling block that the military must help overcome until civilian agencies arrive: significant infrastructure damage physically impedes economic recovery. An important focus of the economic recovery program will be job creation and the reconstruction of transport, telecommunications, energy, and other infrastructure damaged by the war, without which it will be impossible to restart production and trade on any significant scale. In parallel, the program must repair water, sewage, and health facilities (without which there will be a continued threat to public health); rehabilitate farms to improve the supply of food; and reconstruct housing to relieve acute shelter shortages. Reintegrating demobilized soldiers and the unemployed into the economy is not only an economic necessity but is essential to maintaining a long-term peace, and certainly a strong reconstruction effort that quickly rebuilds the host country's economic capacities is crucial in that effort.

As the peace operation's host nation has experienced an economic collapse, financing for these security and reconstruction efforts will have to come mostly from abroad, and as the institutions of civil society have broken down, the organizational initiative to spearhead these efforts must also come from the outside. At the point that this effort must begin, immediately upon the cessation of hostilities, the military is the only viable institutional entity deployed in the theater. Therefore, the military must become the executive agent for this reconstruction until the various international aid agencies and NGOs can take over. Only economic progress that visibly improves peoples' lives will demonstrate that peace and reintegration bring more benefits than war, and not until a sufficient level of infrastructure has been reconstructed can a transition in growth strategy be considered. Any delay drives up the possibility for a re-emergence of conflict; thus the military, as the only viable agent in the theater, must tackle postconflict infrastructure reconstruction to facilitate economic recovery. Only when this function can be handed over to civilian agencies, either international or local, can the military withdraw.

There are many governmental institutions that military forces are not designed to reconstruct (banking, social welfare, and educational systems, to name just a few), but the provision of the three basic functions detailed above—internal security, minimal self-defense from outside threats, and a sound economic base—will allow the government to develop the other required institutions necessary for long-term peace with civilian agency assistance. The tasks associated with the provision of these basic functions should be the tenets upon which the declared military endstate should be designed. By mandating the military to focus its work in these three areas, the military mission is clarified and strengthened, the economy will receive a jump start leading to quicker economic revitalization and enhanced security, and confidence in the legitimate government will be strengthened. The accomplishment of all of these will facilitate a quicker military withdrawal.

COMPLEMENTARY CAPABILITIES

Recent peace operations have become so complex and multifaceted that the capabilities each organization brings to the problem can become complementary as long as the capabilities can be focused around a common solution. The stage on which these organizations and forces must operate is typically crowded, not only with warring factions and hard-pressed local populations but also with a cast of external actors: other military forces from a variety of countries, IOs, and NGOs; diplomats and aid workers from national governments; and private individuals and foundations. Despite similar objectives, however, cooperation among these third parties is by no means inevitable. Establishing cooperative relations among the various external players in a peace operation remains one of the most challenging aspects of the international response to conflict and disaster.[33]

Exactly who, if anyone, is responsible for coordinating the work of various players varies from operation to operation. In UN missions, for example, the organization often appoints a special representative of the secretary-general (SRSG) either to head the entire operation or to manage its political and administrative elements. The SRSG's authority, however, is usually limited and is typically given little room for maneuvering by UN headquarters, which is itself constrained by the need to maintain the support of interested major powers; although SRSGs generally have control over the components of the mandated mission, they do not control the aid agencies, the military, or the NGOs. NGOs, which may number more than 100 and may have been on the scene long before a mission is launched, may have already formed their own network to coordinate activities and may not want to change their practices to accommodate the SRSG.

In short, most peace operations are complex activities in which no one is completely in charge, making it all the more important to ensure that all players function cohesively. The various players in an operation may regard one another warily, preferring where possible to be in charge or to function independently. Almost as if they were different countries, they speak different languages, sprinkling their documents and conversations with terms and acronyms that mean little or nothing to the others. Each type of intervener comes to a peace operation with its own philosophy, method of operation, and organizational culture—and these may not merely differ but actually clash. Despite the differences or the complexity of the operation, it is important to remember that each player is involved because it has been mandated to act by some authority or because it wants to help.

If we descend a few levels from this bird's-eye view of an intervention and get closer to the operational arena, we find that the military and the civilian agencies are not really working at contrary purposes, but have complementary abilities that can be meshed together into a well-designed effort of postconflict reconstruction. Those aspects of the reconstruction effort that the military is not specifically trained to accomplish are well filled by the various civilian agencies. On the other hand, the military brings a level of responsiveness and organization that the agencies do not inherently have at the beginning of a peace operation. Six criteria help to define the complementary nature of the military and the civilian agencies: organization, deployability and logistics, security, planning, training, and funding. The challenge lies in the ability to coordinate these criteria among the military, IOs, and NGOs for the benefit of the host nation.

The Military Arm

The military brings certain characteristics to a peace operation that cannot be replicated immediately by the civilian agencies. The overall advantage that military forces have lies in their ability for quick response and decisive action. The common factor found in each of the comparative criteria listed above is that, regardless of the operation, these characteristics already fully exist in a military organization. Although the United States uses a formal certification process for peace implementation forces, military forces do not need a significant preparation phase to bring enforcement and stabilization to bear in a conflict situation. To rapidly respond to a humanitarian crisis or mass violence abroad, the government can choose to deploy its military, which can have an immediate effect on the situation; long-term effects, however, must be realized through a variety of other methods. So let us examine how the military meets these comparative criteria for all actors in a peace operation.

Organization. The military brings an established and ready command-and-control structure and hierarchical organization to the peace operation. It is a highly structured organization that places value on chain of command, unit specialization, and teamwork built through habitual command relationships. Although at times complex, this chain of command runs from the highest elected official to the lowest-ranking soldier. There is little question about who is in charge of the military in a peace operation, resulting in a single, focused continuity of direction operationalized through the commander's stated vision and intent. To be clear, U.S. military forces work for their civilian leaders, who state the desired strategic result of a peace operation; however, the operational details of how to realize the military endstate are developed and reinforced by the military commanders and their staffs. Commanders have broad authority to accomplish the missions assigned; they can organize and employ forces, assign tasks, designate objectives, and give direction over all aspects of military operations and joint training.[34]

To support the commander, subordinate forces are organized into coherent units based on functionality. Through a flexible and adaptable force generation process, a commander's force for deployment is designed and tailored on the basis of the specifically assigned mission in the peace operation. Units are organized to be able to provide all functions required of the mission, whether the requirement is for Infantry and Armor units to work in a peace enforcement role, or for Engineering and Civil Affairs units to work at reconstruction and recovery. The military has the ability to tailor its force for the mission quickly. The result is a unit whose performance as a whole is greater than the sum of the individual efforts of its members, and that can deploy into a peace operation already formed as a cohesive organization without devoting valuable time to developing successful relationships. Because the former warring parties typically pursue their own agendas during a peace operation, the military's emphasis on planning and predictability is heavily informed by the need for flexibility and adaptability to meet all contingencies. Without a doubt, the military is mission-oriented, but that mission can change daily.

Deployability and Logistics. The United States has transformed its logistics structure to reflect the new post–Cold War environment. According to former Army Chief of Staff Dennis J. Reimer: "The brute force logistics of the past, where the military stockpiled massive amounts of supplies, is inadequate for the military operations of the future—we can no longer afford the large amount of equipment that we traditionally moved from one place to the other during the Cold War. We must be able to move quickly around the world and provide our troops with the supplies and repair parts they need in a timely manner."[35] The military has the inherent ability to deploy rapidly and place forces on the ground at the desired time through a variety of methods: Army and Marine war stocks pre-positioned around the globe, air and sea insertion on moderately prepared ports or air strips, forward-staged air and sea deployment nodes that are well designed and highly functional, and creation of debarkation and embarkation nodes in areas of the world where none previously existed. When General John M. Shalikashvili was the chairman of the Joint Chiefs of Staff, he stated the level of importance he placed on this capability: "We are more and more an expeditionary force; strategic air and sealift, complemented by our pre-positioning initiatives, must be our number-one priority."[36]

In light of General Shalikashvili's guidance, the U.S. military, following Operation Desert Storm, concentrated on the deployment of its ground forces and consolidated all Army war reserve stocks, including former theater reserves, into five regional material stockpiles: Continental United States, Europe, Pacific, Southwest Asia, and Afloat. This consolidation in support of the military's Global Pre-positioning Strategy takes advantage of the strategic mobility triad of airlift, sealift, and global pre-positioning. This effort significantly decreases the amount of time required to deploy and position ground troops into a conflict situation, reflecting a strategy designed to fit the changing international environment of the post–Cold War era. In addition, a Mobility Requirements Study Bottom-Up Review concluded that the military could increase its deployability through expanded sealift, airlift, and transportation infrastructure. As a result, in 1999 the Air Force established Air Expeditionary Units that deploy under a predictable rotation system in an attempt to enhance air responsiveness, reduce the stresses of deployment to enforce no-fly zones over northern and southern Iraq, and meet other disaster and humanitarian assistance demands as they arise.[37] Logistically, the Air Force has securely pre-positioned logistics support packages to reduce the degree of logistics that an Air Expeditionary Force would be required to deploy. Using different "flexbasing" deployment categories (48-, 96-, and

144-hour deployment standards), the Air Force can build in flexibility to execute operations in any theater.[38]

The Marine Corps, as the smallest service, pre-positions its heaviest equipment in locations around the world to minimize travel time during deployment. For example, a large portion of the Corps' heavy equipment is located in Diego Garcia, in the Indian Ocean. To be responsive to impending crises, the Corps has a Marine Expeditionary Unit (MEU) on deployment at all times (using a normal six-month rotation system), enabling a Marine force to be deployed to sea with its full complement of equipment. The Navy also uses a rotation system to ensure that a sufficient number of its ten carrier battle groups are stationed in international waters in accordance with perceived threats. Normally employing four carrier battle groups at one time (allowing the other groups to conduct periodic maintenance and stand down), Navy operations have the capability to move battle groups expeditiously around the globe.

As the service that provides the bulk of the forces in peace operations, the Army developed the Strategic Mobility Program, a military transportation capability that can provide a crisis response force of up to corps size (five and one-third divisions) from the United States and forward-presence locations overseas.[39] Under the mobility program umbrella, the Army developed an equipment afloat pre-positioning program to accommodate a combat brigade as well as common equipment and supplies that facilitate rapid deployment. Included in the afloat pre-positioning package are transportation and port-opening equipment that is critical to reception, staging, off-loading, and onward movement of deploying units. The Army Pre-positioned Afloat Program provides the combatant commander with deployment flexibility and increased capability to respond to a crisis or contingency with a credible force. The purpose of a pre-positioned afloat operation is to project a heavy force in the early stages of a crisis that is capable of complementing other early arriving forces; to rapidly reinforce a lodgment established by early entry forces; to protect key objectives (ports and airfields);

and to be prepared to conduct subsequent tasks across the range of military operations.[40]

Supported by the Navy, afloat operations range from the employment of one ship in support of a humanitarian assistance mission to the employment of all afloat vessels to support the combatant commander's campaign plan. An afloat operation carries critical weapons systems, equipment, and supplies common to all theaters, but it is a force package that is mobile and can be quickly positioned in response to a crisis anywhere in the world. This type of program allows the early deployment of an Army heavy brigade force to support the needs of the combatant commander, minimizing the initial requirement for the strategic lift. In view of global operations, the pre-positioning system provides the flexibility to conduct operations across the entire range of military operations. The Army's project will continue to expand, working toward a goal of two million square feet of pre-positioning capacity called for in the 1992 Mobility Requirements Study.[41]

In an effort to deploy even faster, former Army Chief of Staff General Eric K. Shinseki announced in October 1999 a massive transformation of the U.S. Army. At the completion of the transformation, General Shinseki claimed, "We will develop the capability to put combat force anywhere in the world in 96 hours after liftoff—in brigade combat teams for both stability and support operations and for war-fighting. We will build that capability into a momentum that generates a war-fighting division on the ground in 120 hours and five divisions in 30 days."[42]

Should prepared embarkation and debarkation points be unavailable, U.S. forces have the ability to create suitable airstrips in theater and to provide logistics-over-the-shore where port facilities are nonexistent. The combination of all of these initiatives puts almost any scenario throughout the globe within fast reach of the U.S. military should the U.S. government need to respond quickly to a conflict situation.

Once deployed, the military is self-sustaining—a great asset that is often overlooked when deciding which avenue to pursue in peace operations. The military is designed to provide its own logistics capability when no other support is available and can remain in theater for indefinite periods of time. Military-focused logistics fuses information, logistics, and transportation technologies to provide rapid crisis response, to track and shift assets even while en route, and to deliver tailored logistics packages and sustainment directly at the strategic, operational, and tactical level of operations. In Bosnia, the rules of engagement allowed the United States to enforce peace; yet at the same time, the military was logistically prepared to go to war in a moment's notice, if required. The military can make a quick transition from nonlethal to lethal means and can deploy those capabilities on the battlefield.

Security. The primary mission in peace operations is to create a climate of stability and security to achieve a durable and lasting political settlement that prevents more bloodshed. The first of these objectives is strictly military in nature; according to Thomas Mockaitis, "Peace operations to end civil conflict are by their very nature enforcement operations requiring the deployment in a timely manner of a sufficiently large combat contingent adequately armed to stop the fighting with the use of force if necessary."[44] It is really that simple. Military forces have the ability to tailor their forces to the perceived threat in order to intervene in hostile situations, prevent additional conflict, and demonstrate enough potential firepower to thwart any reemergence of conflict. They are able to provide their own force protection and are able to shift into a combat role quickly should the situation deteriorate into hostile conflict. Civilian agencies do not have this capability.

Military forces plan for the worst-case scenario. This allows the potential pitfalls of each situation to be factored into planning, not only enhancing the prospects for success of the mission but also determining the level of protection required for the participating troops. Peace operations can change quickly, often with little or no warning. In situations where religious or political divisions are long-standing, hostility runs very deep and violence can erupt at a moment's notice. Warring parties may target their wrath in all directions; their attacks may spread beyond their traditional enemies to include "outsiders," regardless of whether they are civilians or soldiers. Peacekeepers may be required to demonstrate sufficient strength to discourage or counter any aggressive acts by either side. Fortunately, a show of strength can help defuse tense situations and contribute to a more peaceful and stable environment.

Should the operation re-emerge into conflict, U.S. military forces have a joint arsenal of weapons that can be engaged to re-establish security and stabilize the environment quickly. Ground troops have not only their own weaponry that can influence the situation at close range but also air support and naval gunfire support that can be used as a stick to bring the belligerent parties back into a more peaceful tone. Overwhelming force—or, more important, the threat of using overwhelming force—can have a stabilizing effect to diffuse a hostile situation.

Planning. A key ingredient in conducting a peace mission is solid joint operations planning—a process that promotes the development of the best possible plans for potential crises across the full range of military contingencies. Joint operations planning is an integrated process that entails similar policies and procedures during war and peace operations, providing for orderly and coordinated problem solving and decision making. In its peacetime application, the process is highly structured to support the thorough and fully coordinated development of deliberate plans. In crisis situations, the process is shortened as necessary to support the dynamic requirements of changing events. In wartime, joint operations planning adapts to accommodate greater decentralization of planning. In all its applications, the basic process remains fundamentally unchanged, providing a consistent and logical approach for integrating the activities of the National Command Authority (the president and the secretary of defense), the chairman and members of the Joint Chiefs of Staff, and combatant commanders into a coherent planning and execution process focused on the mission's strategic objectives.

The advantage of this approach is that it provides an orderly and systematic method for using existing capabilities to achieve objectives defined in foreign policy goals. The resulting plans are accurate measurements of the nation's ability to execute military strategy successfully within the constraints of available forces and resources. This measurement provides a means of assessing the balance between strategy and capabilities, determining risks, and focusing the acquisition of additional resources and capabilities. Plans developed during this process provide a foundation for crisis management. Work performed during the planning process allows the development of routines, procedures, and expertise that are critically needed during crisis action planning.

The end product is a detailed operations plan containing a full description of the concept of operations. It identifies the specific forces, functional support, deployment sequence, and resources required to execute the plan. Should there be no other communication between a theater commander and subordinate commanders, the operation plan has sufficient detail subordinate commanders can use to carry out the theater commander's intent. The benefits of this type of planning are readily apparent in peace operations, when distances between units can be excessive and communications minimal. In light of these physical limitations, prior detailed planning allows peacekeepers to maintain a stable situation despite the absence of close supervision.

Training. U.S. military forces train for peace operations as they would for any other mission that they may be assigned. As the number of peace operations involving U.S. forces has increased, so has the complexity of those operations. Today's peace missions are apt to involve such tasks as supervising elections, protecting specified "safe areas," interacting with local people, guarding surrendered weapons, ensuring the safe delivery of food supplies, and helping rebuild government agencies or police forces. Many of those tasks are far removed from the ones U.S. forces normally expect to perform during conventional warfare. Fortunately, units usually have a substantial amount of time (two to three months) to prepare intensively for peacekeeping and peacebuilding missions as most of those missions are long-standing operations with deployments planned far in

advance. Units assigned to peace enforcement missions, by contrast, typically get far less advance notice. They may have only
enough time to prepare for deployment, with very little time for
specialized training; however, most peace enforcement missions
mirror tasks executed during conventional war.

The U.S. Army does not have a standardized training program
that all units follow to prepare for peace operations. Instead, commanders choose the training for their units on the basis of its
stated purpose and expected missions. As a result, the amount of
routine training that a unit receives in the skills needed for peace
operations varies according to the commander's guidance.[45] A
growing number of military and nonmilitary officials suggest that
some training in skills particular to peace missions be incorporated
into standard unit training for the forces likely to perform those
missions. Two conferences that the Army's Peacekeeping Institute
held to review participation in the Bosnia peace operation recommended that peace operation tasks in general—and planning and
coordinating with civilian organizations in particular—be included
in unit training. The Center for Army Lessons Learned concurred,
recommending that units assigned to peace operations train in a
variety of specific tasks before deployment.[46]

In light of these suggestions, the Army developed a comprehensive peace operations model that includes certification of
individual tasks at home station and unit certification at one
of the Army's Combat Training Centers. Units execute a three-
week Maneuver Rehearsal Exercise (MRE) in which they are
trained in peace operation tasks and are then tested on these
tasks with actors simulating local nationals and scenarios
simulating those missions found in a peace operation. Upon
completion of the MRE, the unit is certified for deployment. In
addition, unit commanders who foresee a possible deployment
to a peace operation can add "peace and stability operations"
to their Mission Essential Task List (METL) for year-round
training. The METL is a list of tasks that the commander
considers essential for a unit to succeed in its assigned mission and is reviewed annually in light of changed or altered

mission projection. Experience has shown that Army units do train for some tasks essential for peace operations in the course of their regular training. As a consequence, some Army commanders are comfortable about their basic preparation for the tasks required for peace operations. In a survey of fifty-seven active-duty Army officers at the Army War College, 64 percent reported that most or all of the tasks required by peace operations were in their unit's METL.[47] Thirty-seven percent of those surveyed believed at least one task that was "critical" for peace operations was outside the scope of the METL. Those "critical" tasks included crowd control, route clearing, negotiating skills, riot control, use of graduated force, civil affairs, law enforcement, coordination with NGOs, humanitarian assistance, and movement of small units.[48] These are the tasks that are emphasized during the training conducted at the MRE. According to General Reimer:

> Commanders in Bosnia are blazing new trails. They are dealing with the challenges of how you separate warring factions and build trust in an environment previously devoid of it. The soldiers have been well trained. I talked to a number of them and they all told me that they had not experienced any surprises. Pre-deployment training had been tough but realistic. This is the proof of the pudding and Bosnia validates the need for tough, realistic training.[49]

The U.S. Marine Corps takes a different approach. Because the Corps wants its deployed forces to be ready for almost any contingency, each MEU trains for a standard set of twenty-nine missions before deployment. Those missions include many tasks that might well be required during peace operations, such as evacuation of noncombatants; show-of-force, reinforcement, and security operations; and humanitarian assistance and disaster relief. The training program culminates in a certification exercise designed to evaluate the MEU's war-fighting and general-purpose expeditionary skills, as well as its maritime special operations capabilities. A Congressional Budget Office survey of Marine Corps units indicates that most units did not alter their training programs to prepare specifically for peace operations. Because many of the tasks performed in peace operations are part of the twenty-nine missions that MEUs train for, those tasks are seen as being a regular part of the Marines' area of expertise.[50]

Funding for Peace Operations. Funds to deploy U.S. military forces to a peace operation are immediately available should the need arise, although funding for continued operations may require budgetary reprogramming or congressional supplemental appropriation. Unlike civilian agencies that fund their activities primarily through donors, the military can draw on budgetary accounts already in existence in order to enter a theater of operations rapidly. The costs that the Department of Defense (DOD) incurs to provide troops for peace operations have increased dramatically in the past decade, from about $200 million in 1990 to more than $3.6 billion in 1998. Those costs soared in 1993 because of operations in Somalia and because of higher costs for operations in Iraq and Kuwait. Costs jumped again in 1996 because the DOD spent more than $2.6 billion that year to implement the Dayton Accords in Bosnia.[51]

Although the total costs of peace operations are not relatively large compared with DOD's overall budget, paying them can cause some difficulties in specific parts of the budget. Most of the additional costs associated with peace operations fall into areas funded by the Operation and Maintenance (O&M) account, which pays primarily for training, fuel, and supplies for troops overseas. Between 1994 and 1998, O&M costs made up at least 80 percent of the annual incremental costs of peace operations.[52] Most of the other incremental costs were paid from DOD's personnel accounts for such things as imminent danger pay and pay for reservists called to active duty. Funds to cover those costs come from supplemental appropriations by Congress, while transferring or reprogramming funds with the DOD budget pays some costs. Operations that DOD can anticipate before it submits its annual budget can be paid from the Overseas Contingency Operations Transfer Fund. Should circumstances change (for example, if an unanticipated operation occurs or if costs exceed estimates), then DOD may require supplemental appropriations.

The Defense Department's annual appropriation contains funds to pay for planned activities but not for unanticipated peace operations. If the additional O&M and personnel costs associated with such operations are small, DOD may cover them by transferring funds between accounts in its budget or by reprogramming funds within an account.[53] If the costs are high, however, the DOD generally seeks additional funding through supplemental appropriations. Since 1993, DOD has submitted several sizable requests for supplemental appropriations to cover peace operations, ranging from about $1 billion in 1993 to $1.8 billion in 1998.[54] Although Congress has routinely approved those requests, the execution of that approval has taken several months in some instances. In fiscal year 1993, for example, supplemental funding to cover the costs of peace operations was not approved until July, the beginning of the fourth quarter of the fiscal year. To circumvent this delay, the Clinton administration proposed creating a Readiness Preservation Authority in its 1996 budget request. That authority would have allowed DOD to obligate funds (up to a certain limit) for essential readiness activities during the last half of the fiscal year without prior appropriation approval.[55] Yet many members of Congress objected to the proposal because it would have diminished what leverage Congress has over peace operations through the appropriation process.

Instead, Congress established the Overseas Contingency Operations Transfer Fund in the 1997 defense appropriation bill. By transferring assets to the services on the basis of actual events during the year in question, the fund was designed to meet the requirements of contingency operations without disrupting approved defense programs. The fund has fallen short of that goal, however. Although Congress appropriated $1.1 billion for the fund in 1997, primarily to pay for ongoing operations in Bosnia and the Middle East, the costs of those operations exceeded the budget amount by $2 billion. Similarly, in 1998 the costs of peace operations were $1.7 billion higher than the $1.9 billion in the fund.[56]

To further illustrate funding contingencies, the incremental costs of peace operations to the Army in 1994 through 1998 represented a very small portion (from 1 percent to 3 percent) of the Army's total budget, but more than 80 percent of those costs were paid for out of the O&M account. Between 1994 and 1998, the share of total O&M spending accounted for by peace operations grew from 4 percent to 8 percent. Because the Army must pay for peace operations out of appropriated O&M funds until it receives supplemental funding or approval for transfers or reprogramming actions from Congress, it often has to draw on funds earmarked to pay the operating costs of the Army's forces for the fourth quarter. Measured against such fourth-quarter funds, peace operations accounted for a significant and rising share of spending—from roughly 30 percent in 1994 to 80 percent in 1998.[57] As money is moved to those units actively involved in ongoing operations, training and resources for units not involved in peace operations are curtailed and in some cases stopped toward the end of the fiscal year.

Funding is not an initial deterrent prohibiting the rapid deployment of military forces into a hostile operation. Money does not have to be secured from donors prior to deployment, and cost overruns can be handled in a variety of ways in accordance with the wishes of Congress. Although the military as a governmental entity has advantages over its civilian counterparts, the question of how best to fund the military to pay for unbudgeted contingency operations is unresolved. Regardless of the outcome of this debate, lack of funding will not stop a military deployment to a peace operation should the government decide upon that course of action, but it may alter the course of the ongoing operation once deployment into the theater is complete.

The Civilian Agency Arm

Following the end of the Cold War, much confusion concerning the roles and responsibilities between civilian and military agencies plagued the conduct of peace operations in the 1990s. Institutions that had fairly distinct roles, identities, and behaviors in the international realm found that all expectations had changed. Representatives of governments struggled with changes in the meaning and practice of sovereignty, as both global and subnational forces challenged the status quo of the international system. The U.S. State Department and foreign ministries around the world continued to play a central part in diplomacy and statecraft, but new developments, such as the increasing visibility of NGOs and IOs—particularly the appointment of special representatives by the UN secretary-general—in managing the proliferation of post–Cold War conflicts somehow heralded the arrival of a series of new actors in the official diplomatic process.[58]

International organizations in particular have assumed a growing role not only in responding to crises but also in orchestrating efforts by other international actors—namely, the military and NGOs. These roles have taken on new importance, and more is expected from them to influence state actors engaged in conflict, as readily evident by the great increase in UN-sanctioned peace operations in the 1990s. By acting as a sounding board and a discussion forum for states, IOs have immediate legitimacy should they determine crisis intervention is required. Inevitably, though, their higher profile and the greater responsibilities entrusted to them have made IOs the targets of substantial criticism. Furthermore, the peacemaking roles for nonofficial actors (such as NGOs) also opened up in the past decade, bringing many more individuals and institutions into the process, allowing private individuals and groups to intervene as third parties in troubled countries and regions.[59]

Let us examine, then, how these civilian actors stack up against the military in terms of the complementary criteria for actors that regularly participate in international interventions.

Organization. There are a variety of IOs whose charters and memberships are as diverse as the specific functions they perform. The definitive characteristic of all IOs is simply an institution that operates in more than one country, but the basic

division of IOs separates NGOs from intergovernmental organizations, such as the UN and its functional agencies. (For the
purposes of this study, IOs will refer specifically to intergovernmental organizations.)

An IO exists when two or more governments sign a multilateral treaty to form an institution that operates in more than one
country, agreeing to finance its operations. Most IOs have more
than two member states, although relatively few aspire to global
membership in such institutions as the United Nations. Most
IOs tend to make decisions by consensus rather than by majority
or plurality votes, their rationale being that substantial dissent
prevents effective action. Consensus is a double-edged sword,
however: decisions by consensus are more legitimate because
they are backed by many countries, but at the same time, they
may be watered down because they reflect lowest common
denominators. Not all decisions are binding, and member states
of IOs can and do selectively ignore even those that are.

IOs have bureaucratic structures with fixed headquarters,
but most maintain liaison offices in the member states; member
states, in turn, maintain a diplomatic presence in the city where
the IO is headquartered.[60] Most IOs have annual sessions at
which relevant issues are debated and decisions are made, with
provisions for emergency sessions if required. Once decisions
are made, IOs depend on member states for implementation. In
peace operations, for example, member states of the UN Security
Council must provide the soldiers who will be deployed in the field
once the decision to start peace enforcement operations is made.

Most NGOs, on the other hand, are quite decentralized and
relatively flat in their authority structures, discarding the
chain of command used by the military; they, too, arrive at decisions through consensus. NGOs are heavily dependent on the
individual commitment and initiative of their staff; employees
work independently for the most part. The managerial style is
informal and works through personal engagement.[61] In a sense,
the decentralized, independent approach to management can
be a great asset in a tumultuous situation. According to Pamela

Aall: "The willingness of NGOs to act when speed is essential and detailed planning is impossible makes these organizations among the best equipped to respond to sudden humanitarian challenges. But this ability to turn on a dime—to change strategies, shift resources, quickly expand or shut down operations—can appear chaotic to organizations that have detailed planning and preparation."[62]

Deployability and Logistics. Limited deployability and the lack of in-place logistics structures are obvious liabilities for international organizations that have the clout and resources to influence long-term peace processes. Simply put, the United Nations and regional organizations are poorly equipped to deal quickly with emerging crises. The problem is a technical one: it takes time to assemble an IO staff and prepare it for deployment. Most civilian organizations are loosely organized and generally lack sufficient, on-hand resources to respond quickly to complex and often dangerous situations. In addition, few IOs can coordinate large multiorganizational operations capable of providing long-term solutions to a conflict situation. The task of coordinating civilian organizations is far more complex than that of orchestrating military involvement because the range of potential civilian participants in conflict management is so much broader and the particular directions pursued by the civilian organizations are varied. Thus IOs need a sufficient period of time to get organized, gather resources, and deploy before they can become effective at spearheading a peace operation. Unlike the military, they do not have on-hand logistical assets that would allow them to deploy to a conflict situation rapidly; they require about a year to eighteen months to become firmly established in the theater of operations.

NGOs, on the other hand, are often already deployed in the theater before a crisis turns intensely violent, but their focus is primarily on humanitarian relief. Few NGOs are of sufficient size and strength to coordinate the entire peace operation effort, and most are working on only a small segment of the overall problem, consistent with their donors' interests. NGO field staff face numerous logistical frustrations and challenges. NGOs lack aircraft, ground transportation, and communications equipment that peacekeeping troops and larger UN agencies possess. Also, access throughout the theater can be delayed by damage to roads, as well as by mines, snipers, and numerous checkpoints staffed by paramilitary groups or undisciplined armies.[63] NGOs do not have the inherent capacity to overcome these problems. Their greatest impact lies at the grassroots level.

Security. Security is an enormous concern of IOs and NGOs, especially those engaged in relief, refugee, and human rights work in hostile situations. The increase in the total number of NGO workers—and, more important, in the number of local employees more likely than foreign workers to be caught up in the local conflict—has compounded the problems raised by limited security and a lack of basic security training in these organizations. In addition, international NGOs that utilize local nationals for service delivery can become liable to charges of impartiality in a conflict because of the political affiliations or activities of locals on their staffs.

NGOs rely on military forces for protection during a peace operation, but the latter cannot possibly be everywhere in a hostile theater; therefore, NGO staff working in a conflict zone are vulnerable and at times experience real danger. In the 1990s, the changed nature of international conflict meant that relief workers increasingly found their lives at risk. In many countries, NGO workers were victims of land mines, armed hijackings of vehicles, banditry, kidnapping, and bombings. As a result of these events and the deterioration of field situations, aid workers concluded that they needed sidearms in order to fulfill their mandates. In Somalia, "[t]he ICRC [International Committee of the Red Cross] suspended its normally irrevocable principle of avoiding cooperation with military forces in its relief operation in order to protect its relief convoys. The chaos in Somalia became so bad and the negotiating position of humanitarian agencies so tenuous that military force became the only viable alternative."[64]

Security concerns have prompted international NGOs to consider a variety of approaches to ensure the safety of their field staffs. InterAction, the American NGO association, has developed a training module to promote security for staff operating in high-risk zones. The training emphasizes personal conflict-management techniques rather than deterrence and physical protection. Because NGO staffs are vulnerable to assaults and other violence, the training aims to heighten their sensitivity to potentially threatening situations and gives them tools to defuse or avoid confrontations. A study undertaken by the University of Toronto and CARE Canada suggests another approach to the security problem, recommending the establishment of a private security force, a "foreign legion" composed of trained professionals who would be paid by an NGO to provide protection for its staff, just as private security firms provide protection for businesses and other institutions in many parts of the world. This idea, repugnant to NGOs a few years ago but now attracting some consideration, is a significant measure of the changed circumstances of the international community's response to intrastate conflict.[65]

Planning. One of the glaring weaknesses of the civilian aid community involves planning for peace operations. In a workshop held at the National Defense University (NDU) in 1996, NGO workshop representatives complained that U.S. government or UN objectives are often unclear, which greatly hampers planning efforts. The UN Security Council does not always spell out its objectives, leading to confused responses by both governments and NGOs. Because of unique domestic political considerations, member states sometimes prefer that the United Nations not be too definitive when identifying its objectives, allowing each country to tailor its response to a situation. This lack of clarity, however, complicates the planning process for all involved, including NGOs.[66]

Generally, the U.S. ambassador in the host country of a peace operation is the focal point to start the civilian planning process. Either the government of the country where conflict occurs will request assistance from the United States or a resolution from the United Nations will call for external action. For the United States, the ambassador declares the situation a disaster and the embassy sends a cable to Washington requesting help. The lead agency in disaster response is the United States Agency for International Development's (USAID) Office of U.S. Foreign Disaster Assistance (OFDA). OFDA will assess the situation and determine the most appropriate response from the U.S. government, which may include relief commodities, regional advisers, and NGO funding to conduct humanitarian relief. OFDA also works with the military in determining how forces can best support the effort, if required. Nevertheless, concrete, effective planning among civilian and military agencies remains weak.

Many participants at the NDU workshop raised questions about the process by which the U.S. government gets involved in peace operations. Many stated that the decision-making process was often muddled and did not always function smoothly. Communication between the military and the NGOs is stilted, and the latter are not consulted about an operation until the decisions have already been made by the military. The government planning process remains closed, and relevant NGOs cannot find effective entry points to participate; they are asked too late and too infrequently to participate in the planning process, leaving greater ad hoc responsibility to field workers once all actors in the operation are deployed. As one NGO workshop participant acknowledged, the "commander's intent" is critical to any military planning; in the NGO realm, however, it's another story: "If you can't identify the commander—and you can't on the NGO side—this will be a problem."[67]

Training. Those who work in the civilian agencies involved in peace operations need two distinct sets of skills. Facilitating meetings, developing leadership, teaching entrepreneurial skills, and building businesses might be thought of as "organizational" skills, which are relatively easy to apply in peaceful communities, where trust and confidence are the rule. In war-torn and divided societies, however, these skills must be accompanied by those of a "therapeutic" nature if they are to be effective. Therapeutic skills include re-establishing relationships across territorial or ethnic boundaries, managing the social-service needs of residual conflict, and lending support to individuals and communities lacking basic confidence in their future. Both skill sets are essential for long-term peacebuilding.[68]

Major international agencies tend to embody the organizational skills required for peacebuilding, whereas therapeutic and social-service skills often reside in smaller NGOs that may have the added difficulty of deploying and sustaining themselves in mission areas.[69] NGOs and IOs tend to have more familiarity with the culture of the host nation than do the military forces that are chosen to intervene and may have close contacts with key leaders resulting from years of providing humanitarian relief in the region. It is common for NGO staff to remain within the NGO world throughout their careers. Many who have worked in the fields of relief, development, or human rights may translate their skills to UN agencies with similar missions, such as the United Nations Children's Fund (UNICEF), the United Nations High Commissioner for Refugees (UNHCR), and the World Food Program (WFP). Those engaged in conflict management and resolution may become teachers; a number of former NGO employees can be found on the staffs of funding agencies, such as the World Bank.

In addition, the formal education level is high among NGO staff. Medical doctors work in the administration of health-related organizations and engineers give their expertise to agencies that specialize in reconstruction. Among those active in conflict resolution are university professors of political science, sociology, and psychology. Lawyers are indispensable to human rights organizations and refugee organizations. Other degrees commonly found among NGO staff include business administration, public health administration, public affairs, and international affairs.[70]

The type and mandate of the NGO itself will determine the skills required. Everything from funding sources to personnel policies will shape an NGO into the picture that its donors desire. During a crisis, an international NGO will typically deploy to the scene only a small number of its managing staff from its headquarters, requiring locals to fill other essential positions. Particular skills, local knowledge, command of the predominant languages, and the ability to provide coordination between the NGO staff and host country nationals are all criteria used during the hiring process. At times, even the ability to obtain controlled access will play a large role in the hiring of local nationals, although this requirement considerably minimizes the available talent pool. During IFOR, local nationals who were hired primarily as translators often had advanced degrees in engineering that were useful in rebuilding infrastructure and negotiating construction contracts. Some technical terms that average native speakers would not understand in their own language, much less be able to translate, proved easier for those with a technical background; local nationals with advanced degrees also had a better command of English, the lingua franca of most peace operations. Notably, the professional caliber of such workers is usually high, because in a crisis zone there is a large pool of highly trained but unemployed professionals from which the NGO can select its staff.

Funding for Peace Operations. The single biggest challenge facing civilian agencies is money. The funding community is accustomed to looking for a tangible product as an outcome, but conflict resolution is a long-term process. Foundations want projects with clear objectives and measurable outcomes within specified time constraints, but conflict resolution is an open-ended process with results that are difficult to measure. Compounding these difficulties are the financial realities of the work itself, including travel expenses and a long-term (though perhaps sporadic) time commitment.[71] Sometimes the call to work is immediate, necessitating immediate funding possibly pledged against a loosely defined deployment plan. Raising money within these parameters is extraordinarily difficult and requires an entirely different set of skills than that used in conflict resolution.

For IOs, lack of financing can have two possible effects. First, of course, it can limit the organization's peace operation activities, forcing it to select certain tasks or concentrate on specific regions rather than pursue a comprehensive approach. The consequent delay in the peace process triggers a vicious circle, ultimately requiring more funds than originally anticipated. Second, a shortage of money can lead to the complete abandonment of an operation when sources of funding expire.[72] In actual practice, the lack of funding is far less dramatic for UN peacekeeping operations, regardless of budget deficits. Countries such as the United States tend to find the money to deploy military forces under the regional organization banner in order to stop hostilities and provide a safe and secure environment. In contrast, the work of some of the UN specialized agencies, such as the UNHCR, the United Nations Development Program, or the WFP, has been severely impaired when appeals have not been met by contributions. Similarly, regional and subregional organizations have been hampered in their ability to initiate effective peace operations because of a lack of funds. Among all the restraining and conditioning factors for peace support operations, cash flow remains the key issue. Given finite funds and resources, and too many conflicts to manage, prioritization will be the watchword in the international community's response to complex humanitarian crises.[73]

On the other hand, boards of directors that reflect the particular mandates, culture, and history of the organization govern NGOs. As most NGOs raise money among members of a particular segment of the public, their constituencies' interests dominate their mission performance and direction; otherwise, their financial survival will be tenuous. Furthermore, if the institutional constituency or fundraising base of an NGO has an ideological predisposition for or against one or another party in a conflict, the organization's usefulness as a neutral mediator may be compromised. Some NGOs have political, religious, and ideological agendas that limit the type of conflict resolution work they undertake.[74] The medical professionals who founded the

International Medical Corps (an American NGO that specializes in providing emergency medical care during conflicts) dominate its board of directors. Catholic bishops, as another example, serve as the board of directors for Catholic Relief Services, giving specific ideological direction to this NGO's relief efforts, a direction that may be different if managed by a board of a different makeup.

During the 1990s, the international donor community pledged more than $100 billion in aid to three dozen countries recovering from violent conflict.[75] From Cambodia to Bosnia, El Salvador to Rwanda, and Tajikistan to Lebanon, multilateral and bilateral donors have supported postconflict peacebuilding with generous packages of grants, concessional loans, debt forgiveness, and technical assistance. Providing a bridge between emergency humanitarian relief and long-term development, these financial and material resources are designed to persuade formerly warring parties to resolve conflicts peacefully and are intended to lay the foundations for a sustainable transition to economic growth and participatory governance.

Yet in many situations, a significant proportion of the pledged resources has never materialized or has done so very slowly. Despite ostensible good intentions, too often aid promised has not been committed, aid committed has not been delivered, and aid delivered has arrived too late. In the words of the World Bank, "Pledges are made, but commitment takes longer, and there is a considerable lag before actual disbursement takes place. Sustainable transitions out of conflict take several years, yet there is a tendency for donors to disengage once the conflict has receded from public attention."[76]

ROADBLOCKS TO POSTCONFLICT RECONSTRUCTION

Despite all of the advantages that the military brings to peace operations, it, too, encounters formidable roadblocks that greatly limit its effectiveness in postconflict reconstruction. Most of these limitations derive from having no initial, explicit mandate that allows any military involvement in postconflict reconstruction in the civilian sector. This limitation becomes a downward spiral leading to limited reconstruction funds, inappropriate troop strength, and the absence of an organization for combined civil-military reconstruction planning. The result is a lack of military focus on the long-term benefits of immediate reconstruction in favor of a short-term focus on security and stability operations. This negative domino effect, however, can be prevented by an extension of the postconflict reconstruction mandate to the military.

Postconflict Reconstruction Funding

An advantage of the U.S. military is that it has available funding to deploy forces to a peace operation to stop hostilities and provide security; yet that same funding stream is not immediately available for infrastructure reconstruction—for military or civilian uses. UN funding is severely limited by the sheer number of peace operations being conducted simultaneously and also by the number of countries that are in arrears in their peacekeeping dues. Most of the available UN funding is targeted to humanitarian assistance—food distribution and public health concerns—and is the responsibility of the UN mission's director of humanitarian affairs.[77] Infrastructure reconstruction receives such little attention in the United Nations that no staff officer in the expanded Department of Peacekeeping Operations is assigned the task to develop approaches to such a vital dimension of a postconflict environment.[78]

NATO infrastructure funding is regulated through the NATO Infrastructure Committee and its subcommittee, the Supreme Headquarters Allied Powers Europe (SHAPE) Resources Committee. Infrastructure expenditures are authorized through a process of individual project approval that limits military construction to the "minimum military requirement" (MMR), requiring a consensus vote of approval by the military representatives to NATO. As the organization has acquired more experience in conducting peace operations, the bureaucratic structure to gain approval has been streamlined through intramilitary cooperation and standard operating procedures; however, the "minimum military requirement" mandate has not been relaxed. Thus no funding for civilian-only infrastructure repair during postconflict operations currently comes from NATO resources.

The only other immediate source of government humanitarian funds that the military can use for basic infrastructure repair lies in the hands of the regional U.S. combatant commander in whose area of responsibility the peace operation takes place. Regional combatant commanders are given a limited amount of funds annually to be used for humanitarian purposes throughout their area of responsibility. However, the overall amount of this funding source is small and has to be spread over continent-sized jurisdictions. In addition, these funds are to be used for emergency humanitarian needs and are not intended to be used for long-term infrastructure reconstruction. Although combatant commanders do have discretion in how they target the use of these accounts, the tendency is to use these funds to ward off impending humanitarian crises.

Forces Tailored for Postconflict Reconstruction

Without a postconflict reconstruction mandate, military forces that deploy to peace operations do not have enough of the right kinds of units in the necessary quantities to carry out reconstruction tasks. The ground units needed for peace operations under current mandates are not necessarily the same types or quantities needed for major theater wars, but neither are they adequately configured to provide postconflict reconstruction. Military forces configure themselves in specific ways to perform particular missions. Certain kinds of combat-support and combat-service-support specialties—such as transportation, civil affairs, water purification, and construction engineering—are critical for peacekeeping and peacebuilding operations, whereas combat units—infantry and armor—are key for peace-enforcing duties. Thus, some specialties may be in much heavier demand during peace operations than are other specialties.

Postconflict reconstruction requires additional military engineers and contributions by civilians who work, for example, in the U.S. Army Corps of Engineers; yet without a requirement and the authority to conduct postconflict reconstruction tasks, these forces are not readily available in the theater of operations. Moreover, a large percentage of the high-demand capabilities in the Army's combat-support and combat-service-support areas are in the reserve component. The active-duty Army may contain very few of the necessary types of units, requiring a presidential call-up. So the peacekeeping dilemma continues for the United States—now, after Operation Iraqi Freedom, the largest troop-contributing nation in peace operations around the world: U.S. forces must have reconstruction authority to fill the gap between the cessation of hostilities to civilian agency deployment, and they must have the authority early enough to configure the executing forces properly at the outset of the peace operation.

NATO forces are configured for peace operations through the use of a Contingency Establishment (CE), a document that details the generic force required for a pending mission. Upon receipt of the mission, planning staffs determine the type and amount of forces that are required to execute the various aspects of the assigned mission. Subsequently, national representatives "bid" on the various slots to fill the CE. Often, key slots are left unfilled because of national guidelines or lack of specialties. For the United States, executing such a postconflict reconstruction mandate would require official acknowledgment of the long-term peace benefits of early reconstruction by military forces, massive troop concentrations early in the operation (primarily of combat-support units), and the national political will to support a presidential call-up of required reserve forces to complete the necessary CE.

Military Engineers

To reconstruct a region's infrastructure, the United States can tap its considerable expertise in its military engineer organizations. Because the number and types of engineer units in each military service is wide ranging, a comprehensive review of the specific units found in the U.S. military is beyond the scope of this study; however, figure 1 outlines the engineer battlefield functions, indicating the scope of work that engineers can accomplish in postconflict operations.

Military engineers can perform their vital roles throughout the theater of operations, from the forward edge of the battle area back to the sea or airports of entry. The engineer force structure is packaged differently to accomplish the various missions from front to rear, with more survivable and mobile forces in the forward combat zone; however, mission requirements determine the size and composition of deployed engineer units, with a mix of different units required to achieve the proper balance. The wide variety of engineer units provides particular technical capabilities that are required to accomplish essential, diversified tasks throughout the depth of the theater of operations. Army units are primarily structured into combat units, focusing on mobility, countermobility, and survivability tasks, and construction units that provide the bulk of engineer construction capability. There are also smaller, specified units that accomplish particular engineer missions, including port construction, topographic analysis, and pipeline construction.

The Air Force has a base civil engineer structure to do routine maintenance and repair, emergency war damage repair, and minor construction; it has highly deployable units that concentrate on rapid runway repair in support of combat air forces deployed around the world. Navy engineer requirements include constructing, operating, and maintaining shore, in-shore, and deep ocean facilities in support of the Navy, Marine Corps, and, when directed, other agencies of the U.S. government.

The Navy's engineer force for postconflict operations is divided into two components: Amphibious Construction Battalions support the naval beach party during initial assault and early phases of amphibious landings. Their major capabilities are assembly, rigging, and operation of pontoon barges, barge ferries, tender boats, and pontoon causeways for off-loading operations; development of beach facilities, beach salvage, and limited underwater construction; assembly and operation of pontoon floating dry docks; and installation and operation of amphibi-

Figure 1. Engineer Battlefield Functions

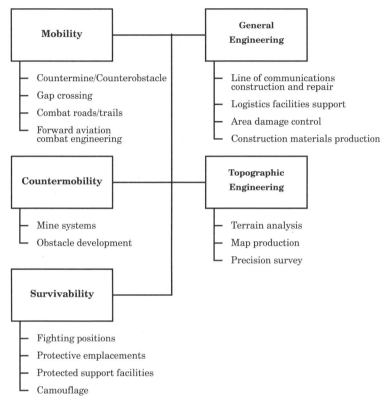

Source: Department of the Army, *Engineer Combat Operations.* Field Manual 5-100 (Washington, D.C.: Department of the Army, February 27, 1996).

ous assault bulk fuel systems. Mobile Construction Battalions provide shore and in-shore facilities construction. Their main functions include the construction and maintenance of personnel camps, waterfront structures, airfields, roadways, tank farms, communications systems, buildings, and electrical, water, and bathing utilities.

The Marine Corps has three basic engineer components. The Combat Engineer Battalion provides close combat support to the Marine division, including engineer reconnaissance and surveying; obstacle breaching; bridging; obstacle and field fortification emplacement; temporary vertical construction; and water, bath, and electrical utilities support. The Marine Wing Support Squadron supports the service's aircraft wing with engineer reconnaissance and surveying of landing force zones; construction, repair, and maintenance of helicopter and light aircraft landing sites; construction of temporary camps with electrical power, water purification and distribution, and bath facilities; construction, repair, and maintenance of road networks; and construction of drainage systems. The Engineer Support Battalion provides all of the capabilities of the Marine Wing Support Squadron but also handles the provision of airfield repair and maintenance beyond the Marine wing's capabilities and the installation and operation of bulk fuel systems.

Joint Planning Cell for Postconflict Reconstruction

Military and civilian operations undoubtedly affect each other at the strategic, operational, and tactical levels of a peace operation. Without any overriding coordination there is a risk that they may counteract each other, resulting in less than optimal performance—which, in an immediate postconflict environment, can have tragic consequences. At the strategic level, a decision about military intervention will have a large impact on the civilian humanitarian operations already in the area. The aim of civilian operations concerning refugee return, for instance, may affect the status of the military operation. Similar examples can be found at the operational and tactical levels. Successful civilian operations of various kinds are a basic precondition for long-term stability and consequently a precondition for the military operation to reach a successful conclusion. Similarly, the civil operation may need protection and support from the military authorities. Also, civil-military coordination is necessary to prevent local factions from playing different parts of the peace operation against each other. A party must not be able to block activities in one area and simultaneously be rewarded with aid in another.

Postconflict reconstruction is a prime area that requires close civil-military cooperation to ensure that there is a seamless transition from the beginning to the end of the deployment. Currently, however, there is no permanent coordination cell that brings together civilian agencies and military forces to ensure that planning for reconstruction is an inclusive and coherent action. General Joulwan argues for the creation of an overarching organization—a civilian-military implementation staff—at both the strategic and operational levels to utilize effectively the diverse organizations and resources devoted to a peace operation, as well as to successfully conduct the day-to-day management of conflict prevention at all levels.[79] So far, however, this has been used only in an ad hoc manner during the first year following the cessation of hostilities, as the cases in the next few chapters amply show.

Should the mandate for postconflict reconstruction extend to the military, a civil-military working group must be created during the planning of the peace operation to ensure that plans for reconstruction are coordinated and adequate resources are provided to allow a smooth transition from military to civilian execution without degradation or delay in the progress of reconstruction. The final chapter of this study provides a decision-making template for military and foreign policy officials to use in such planning.

BOSNIA: IFOR/SFOR

Krizevci
Sesvete
Bjelovar
Barcs
Szigetvar
Pecs
HUNGARY
Virovitica
Ivanic Grad
Velika
Gorica
Podravska
Slatina
Siklos
Sombor
Karlovac
Sisak
Daruvar
Donji
Miholjac
Valpovo
Osijek
SERBIA
(Yugoslavia)
Petrinja
Kutina
CROATIA
Borovo
Novska
Slovonska
Pozega
Nasice
Djakovo
Vukovar
Velika
Kladusa
Bosanska
Dubica
Nova Gradiska
Slavonski Brod
Vinkovci
Backa
Palanka
Bihac
Otoka
Bosanski
Novi
Bosanska
Gradiska
Bosanski
Brod
Odzak
Sid
Srem.
Mitrovica
Bosanska
Krupa
Ivanska
Derventa
Modrica
Gradacac
Brcko
Sanski
Most
Prnjavor
Doboj
Gracanica
Bijelina
Janja
Sabac
Bosanski
Petrovac
Banja Luka
Teslic
Maglaj
Lukavac
Kljuc
Kotar
Varos
Tuzla
Drvar
BRITISH SECTOR
Jajce
U.S. SECTOR
Zepce
Zivinice
Zvornik
BOSNIA AND
HERZEGOVINA
Travnik
Zenica
Kakanj
Vares
Vlasenica
Bratunac
CROATIA
Bugojno
Visoko
Breza
Sokolac
Srebrenica
Sibenik
Gornji Vakuf
Kiseljak
Sarajevo
Zepa
Livne
Jablanica
Rogatica
Visegrad Banja
Visegrad
Tomislavgrad
Konjic
Gorazde
Posusje
FRENCH SECTOR
Foca
Listica
Mostar
Nevesinje
Gnojnice
Ljubuski
Stolac
Bileca
MONTENEGRO
(Yugoslavia)
Trebinje
Dubrovnik
Adriatic
Sea
Titograd

25 miles
25 km

GERMANY
AUSTRIA
HUNGARY
ITALY
DETAIL
AREA
GREECE

Approximate territory lines agreed upon in the Dayton peace talks:

Federation of Bosnia and Herzegovina
(Muslim-Croatian territory)

Serb Republic
(Rebel Serb territory)

2

BOSNIA

THE NATO-LED OPERATION in Bosnia's Operation Joint Endeavor was NATO's first-ever ground force operation, its first-ever deployment "out of area," and its first-ever joint operation with NATO's Partnership for Peace and other non-NATO countries. It was a demonstration that the Atlantic Alliance had changed and adapted its forces and policies to the requirements of the post–Cold War world, while continuing to provide collective security and defense for its allies. But this "first" operation also brought some inconsistency and some "muddling through." NATO did not have policies and procedures that covered every aspect of the planned operation, nor did it have policies that could be used when unforeseen contingencies arose. Peacekeeping on such a grand scale was not a commonplace occurrence, and the roadmap for postconflict reconstruction was not fully developed.

Perhaps lulled into complacency by three years of threats followed by inaction, the Bosnian Serbs crossed the line, compelling NATO to act. On August 28, 1995, a shell landed in the Sarajevo marketplace, killing thirty-seven people. The Serbs attempted to blame the Muslims, as they had in past incidents, but detailed crater analysis revealed that the round had, in all probability, come from Bosnian Serb army positions in the hills surrounding Sarajevo.[1] The fact that the Bosnian government had press releases ready within minutes of the incident suggests that the attack may have been staged.[2] Despite the uncertainty, this was the pretext for which the international community had been waiting. U.S. envoy Richard Holbrooke wrote, "The brutal stupidity of the Bosnian Serbs had given us an unexpected last chance to do what should have been done earlier."[3] On August 29, U.S. ambassador to the United Nations Madeleine Albright met with UN permanent secretary for peacekeeping Kofi Annan and received the latter's assurance that UN civilian and military personnel would relinquish all veto power over air strikes. NATO aircraft commenced bombing in the early hours of August 30, 1995, in a mission termed Operation Deliberate Force.

The air campaign ran with few pauses until September 17. The operation to enforce UN Security Council Resolution 836 inflicted great damage on the Serb military infrastructure, creating an opportunity for the Croat and Bosnian governments to capture territory. Alliance planners were determined to avoid targets where there might be a chance of collateral damage to nearby civilians; that goal was achieved. So were the larger objectives of the air campaign: the Bosnian Serbs agreed to pull back their heavy weapons. More important, they agreed to take part with the Bosnian Muslims and Croats in peace talks that, from the outset, were premised upon the condition that they would emerge with only 49 percent of Bosnian territory, not the 70 percent that only weeks before had been within their grasp.[4] By using massive force but without granting any side victory, Operation Deliberate Force helped create the conditions in which the foreign ministers of Serbia, Croatia, and Bosnia reached agreement on basic constitutional principles for Bosnia, signed in Geneva on September 8 and in New York on September 26. This agreement in turn led to the General Framework Agreement for Peace (GFAP) in Bosnia and Herzegovina, known as the Dayton Peace Accords, initialed by the presidents of Bosnia, Serbia, and Croatia in Ohio on November 21, 1995, and signed in Paris on December 14, 1995.[5]

THE DAYTON AGREEMENT
AND BOSNIA'S RECONSTRUCTION

The Dayton Agreement had two goals: to end the fighting and to rebuild a viable Bosnian state. To accomplish the first goal, the agreement detailed an elaborate calendar of commitments to separate and draw down the armed forces of the Bosnian Serbs on one side and the Bosniac-Croat alliance on the other. In a separate understanding, the United States committed itself to reinforcing Bosniac forces in order to create an internal balance of power to deter any future attacks by Bosnian Serbs.[6] To accomplish the second goal, the agreement outlined a wide range of provisions, from a postwar constitution through elections to preservation of national monuments.

As a text, the Dayton Agreement consisted of a short GFAP in which the parties pledged to "welcome and endorse" the concrete provisions outlined in eleven substantive annexes.[7] The first annex covered the "military aspects" of the settlement; the rest covered what are usually referred to as the "civilian" provisions, though this military-civilian dichotomy reflects less the inherently military or civilian content of each particular provision than it does the authorized roles of the third-party implementers.

Military Responsibilities

Dayton's military annexes principally secured the cease-fire line between Serb forces and the Bosniac-Croat alliance, stabilizing the territorial allocation of the country between them. The details of the agreement brokered by U.S. envoy Richard Holbrooke divided Bosnia into two roughly equal parts: the Bosnian Federation, occupying 51 percent of Bosnian territory, and the Republika Srpska, receiving the remaining 49 percent of Bosnia. It transferred some territory between the Federation and the Serbs, allowing Sarajevo to be reunited under Bosniac Muslim control. The two parts of Bosnia technically remain part of a single state of Bosnia-Herzegovina, but only as a de jure stipulation. The parties agreed that forces were to be separated along either side of an Inter-Entity Boundary Line (IEBL) dividing the Republika Srpska from the Bosniac-Croat Federation and, furthermore, they accepted a detailed calendar of obligations governing the cessation of hostilities. The parties agreed to a modest package of regional arms control and confidence-building measures, pledging to cooperate completely with all international personnel, explicitly those working with the International Criminal Tribunal for Yugoslavia.[8] No provisions were made for the possibility of renewed hostilities between Bosniacs and Croats within the Federation.

The Dayton Accords outlined an extensive role for various international actors to help implement the peace (see table 2), and compliance with the accords' military provisions was to be supervised by a multinational IFOR led by NATO.[9] Authorized under Chapter VII of the UN Charter, IFOR was commanded by the North Atlantic Council (or NAC, NATO's standing political body), was 60,000 strong at first deployment, and was expected to complete its mission by December 1996, or one year after Dayton's signing. Although its mandate encompassed all military provisions, IFOR's widely perceived primary role was that of a classic, if particularly well-armed, peacekeeping force to separate armed forces, oversee the cantonment of troops and heavy weapons to agreed-upon areas, and stabilize the cease-fire.

Importantly, IFOR's secondary support responsibilities ran the gamut of implementation activities. Furthermore, IFOR's tasks were linked to the parties' promise to ensure the safety of all civilians under their respective jurisdictions, to provide humane and nondiscriminatory law enforcement, and to cooperate with the international criminal proceedings at The Hague. IFOR was also asked to support other components of international implementation, with specific reference to responsibilities of the UNHCR regarding refugee returns. IFOR was expressly directed "to observe and prevent interference with the movement of civilian populations, refugees, and displaced persons, and to respond appropriately to deliberate violence to life and person."[10] Related only minimally to IFOR's overtly military tasks were Dayton's provisions for arms control and confidence building, which were to be undertaken by the Organization for Security and Cooperation in Europe (OSCE), and for settling the fate of Brcko, which was to be decided by international arbitration.[11]

Civilian Responsibilities

In contrast to the agreement's military responsibilities, the tasks for civilian implementation were parceled out annex by annex to lead agencies, although some tasks—such as human rights—had no one formal steward, and some agencies—such as OSCE—had multiple responsibilities. To illustrate the reality, OSCE and the Provisional Election Commission monitored the preparation and conduct of elections. The UNHCR handled the return of refugees and internally displaced persons. UNPROFOR, which had been in Bosnia since 1992, transformed into the backbone of the International Police Task Force to monitor and help reform Bosnia's police. Oversight of human rights provisions was collectively executed by the OSCE, the Council of Europe, the UN High Commission on Human Rights, and the European Court of Human Rights, and provisions for missing persons were delegated to the ICRC. Although not articulated in the text of the agreement, the World Bank took the lead on postwar reconstruction. Finally, the EU worked within the Federation to reconnect the divided city of Mostar, a responsibility that it had assumed before Dayton.[12]

With so many international bodies responsible for implementing the various components of the Dayton Accords, some means of coordinating their efforts was sorely needed. The model adopted at Dayton, however, was loose, particularly on the civilian side, and did not provide any actor with a serious mandate to coordinate civilian efforts. Instead, to coordinate the panoply of civilian organizations, Dayton authorized an international Office of the High Representative (OHR) to oversee civilian implementation.[13] The High Representative was to enjoy final interpretive "authority in theatre" of Dayton's civilian provisions, similar to the commander of IFOR's (COMIFOR) authority to interpret military provisions. Although the representative's role was initially designed to be coequal to that of COMIFOR, it was widely recognized that the High Representative would have far less effective authority, particularly over other implementing agencies that reported separately

Table 2. The Dayton Agreement and Its Implementers

	Annexes	Key International Implementers
1A	Military Aspects	IFOR
1B	Regional Stabilization	OSCE
2	Inter-Entity Boundary Line (IEBL) and Related Issues	International Arbitrator
3	Elections	OSCE
4	Constitution	European Court for Human Rights, International Monetary Fund
5	Arbitration	N/A
6	Human Rights	OSCE, Council of Europe, UNHCR, European Court of Human Rights
7	Refugees and Displaced Persons	UNHCR
8	Commission to Preserve National Monuments	UN Educational, Scientific, and Cultural Organization (UNESCO)
9	Bosnia Public Corporations	European Bank for Reconstruction and Development (EBRD)
10	Civil Implementation	OHR
11	International Police Task Force	UN

Source: General Framework Agreement for Peace

to their respective governing bodies and had neither the habit nor the incentive to put their operational resources under the direction of a central authority. With respect to fellow implementers, the High Representative had, at best, the leverage of the bully pulpit: "to consult, inform, cajole, liaise, even hector, but not to direct, allocate, or spend, let alone hold accountable."[14]

IFOR/SFOR

While adamantly refusing to contribute ground forces to UNPRO-FOR, the Clinton administration maintained a commitment to provide forces to oversee implementation of an overall peace settlement. With the 1995 peace negotiations at Wright-Patterson Air Force Base in Dayton, Ohio, administration officials laid out their rationale and initial planning for U.S. participation in a NATO-led peace implementation force for Bosnia. Administration officials argued that U.S. participation with ground forces was necessary for two main reasons: (1) the Bosnian, Croatian, and Serb negotiators all made U.S. ground force participation a condition for their acceptance of any peace settlement, and (2) U.S. participation was necessary to ensure participation by other NATO members who took the position that they would participate only with U.S. leadership.

On the basis of the Dayton Peace Agreement, UN Security Council Resolution 1031 authorized a one-year multilateral NATO-led IFOR under the UN Charter's Chapter VII. To enforce the military provisions of the Dayton Accords, NATO sent approximately 54,000 ground troops into Bosnia proper. The UN Security Council endorsed the creation and emplacement of IFOR with a greater degree of delegation to NATO than had occurred in Bosnia before, but little different from the earlier delegations to member states to undertake potentially offensive military operations in Rwanda, Haiti, and Somalia.[15] The resolution directed IFOR "to take all necessary measures to effect the implementation of and to ensure compliance with" the agreement and "stresses that the parties shall be held equally responsible for compliance . . . and shall be equally subject to such enforcement action by IFOR as may be necessary to ensure implementation . . . and takes note that the parties have consented to IFOR's taking of such measures."[16] Although IFOR was consented to by the parties, it was not a traditional form of peacekeeping. IFOR performed a traditional peacekeeping role while the accords were being complied with, but would become an offensive operation should a faction violate the accord. Even while IFOR was performing a basic peacekeeping function, the threat of enforcement action should the peace be broken, combined with the much greater military capacity of IFOR, made it a much more capable military operation than UNPROFOR, a traditional peacekeeping force, despite the Security Council's attempts at tinkering with its mandate.

In late 1996, the lack of progress in civilian reconstruction and continued friction between the ethnic factions, including within the Muslim-Croat Federation itself, led to the widespread belief that some NATO military force would be required beyond IFOR's December 20, 1996, mandated exit. These concerns led NATO's political leaders to authorize the follow-on SFOR in December 1996, to last until June 1998. However, by the end of 1997, there was little optimism that Bosnia would have a viable national state or economy by June. Fragile government institutions and continued ethnic antagonisms led most observers to believe that an international military force of substantial size was necessary to remain in Bosnia for perhaps years if further interethnic war was to be averted. Because he believed the region's conflict to be the single greatest threat to contemporary European security and hence a long-term NATO concern, former High Representative Carl Bildt suggested the permanent stationing of NATO troops in Bosnia. Although not accepting this position, NATO foreign ministers reauthorized SFOR in March 1998 and tied the duration of its deployment to the achievement of specified benchmarks of success in implementing the Dayton Accords.[17]

THE STATE OF BOSNIA
AT THE CESSATION OF HOSTILITIES

It is important to fully understand Bosnia's state of disrepair to demonstrate the necessity of achieving postconflict reconstruction progress immediately upon the cessation of hostilities. Using six broad sectors for measure—the economy, transportation, water and waste systems, energy, telecommunications, and the residual mine threat—one can realize the impact of having no viable infrastructure on the long-term security and stability of the region. When IFOR entered the theater, it found that the war in Bosnia had wrought extensive human and physical devastation. The direct toll of the war was enormous: 250,000 killed, more than 200,000 wounded, and 13,000 permanently disabled, with the young bearing a large share of the burden. In terms of human losses, Bosnia's prewar total population in the 1991 census was 4.29 million people. Since then, about one million left the country, while 200,000–300,000 immigrated into the state as refugees from other countries. This left a net population in Bosnia of about 3.4 million, 23 percent less than in 1991. The International Crisis Group summarized the situation of the displaced people and refugees from Bosnia: "836,500 people are still internally displaced within Bosnia-Herzegovina. . . . 223,000 Bosnian Serbs are still refugees in FRY [Federal Republic of Yugoslavia]. . . . 30,000 Croats, mainly from Bosnia, are still registered as refugees in Croatia. . . . 128,000 people from Bosnia-Herzegovina are still living as refugees in Western Europe."[18]

The war made 90 percent of the population in the Federation at least partly dependent on humanitarian foreign aid and extensively damaged the country's water supply, power generation, roads, and central telecommunications facilities. All parts of the transportation system were damaged, either directly by heavy military and commercial traffic, or indirectly by a lack of adequate maintenance. Bridges throughout the sometimes

Alpine-like region were damaged, creating small population pockets without easy access to markets and urban centers. A government survey in July 1995 estimated that 63 percent of the country's housing units sustained at least some damage, and 18 percent of the units were destroyed (defined as more than 60 percent damaged).[19] Health hazards existed from deteriorating water and sewage systems; water supplies in many urban centers were grossly insufficient for the growing number of people requiring services, sewage collection systems and treatment plants did not operate, and solid waste collection and disposal practically collapsed. The number of hospital beds decreased by 35 percent, and infant mortality doubled in just five years. Education also suffered as a result of the war, with school enrollments falling by more than 50 percent and many schools damaged or destroyed. All sectors of the economy suffered from major losses in human resources as a result of migration, mobilization into the military, and war casualties.

The Economy

In the former Yugoslavia, the economy grew by an average of 5.5 percent a year from 1960 to 1990. Though this rising prosperity was broadly shared in the 1980s, Bosnia, next to Macedonia, was the poorest republic in the old Yugoslav federation. Its Gross Domestic Product (GDP) reached $8.3 billion, or around $1,900 per capita, in 1990—considerably below the $6,500 of Slovenia but more than Macedonia's $1,400. The economy was much more open and market-oriented than other socialist economies; it had a highly educated labor force, and more than half of its export products were sold to Western markets for hard currency.[20] On the other hand, agriculture was in private hands, farms were small and inefficient, and food was traditionally a net import for the republic. The centrally planned economy created some legacies: Industry was greatly overstaffed, reflecting the rigidity of the planned economy. Under Tito, military industries were pushed in the republic; thus Bosnia hosted a large share of Yugoslavia's defense plants.[21]

The economy was fairly well diversified, with a large industrial base and a highly capable entrepreneurial class that produced complex goods such as aircraft and machine tools. More than half of its output and employment was generated by the industrial sector, which was concentrated in the energy and raw material–producing sectors (especially electricity generation, wood production, coal and bauxite mining, and coke production), as well as textiles, leather, footwear, and machinery and electrical equipment. In the service sector, Bosnia developed a strong capacity in civil engineering. About 500 engineering and construction companies operated out of Bosnia before the war, generating roughly 7 percent of GDP—an important statistic defining local capacity available for postconflict reconstruction.[22]

No macro estimates of the country's physical damage can capture the human suffering, the loss of irreplaceable works of art, and the destruction of cultural landmarks caused by the war. Nonetheless, these estimates illustrate the magnitude of the reconstruction and reconciliation task that was ahead. Simply put, Bosnia's economy must increase more than threefold just to regain the level of output that it once attained. No other country in central and eastern Europe experienced such a massive economic collapse since World War II. The most severely afflicted transition economies exhibited cumulative GDP declines on the order of 30 percent (Bulgaria, Romania, Slovakia) to 40 percent (Albania, Macedonia), up to 50 percent (the Soviet Union). Bosnia, on the other hand, experienced a 75 percent drop in GDP. Annual per capita income fell to about $500, and industrial output in 1994 was 5 percent of the 1990 output.[23]

Some progress has been made, however. Because of Bosnia's strict currency board regime, inflation has remained low in the Federation and in the Republika Srpska; however, growth has been uneven, with the Federation outpacing the Republika Srpska. Bosnia's most immediate task remains economic revitalization. To do this fully, the environment must be conducive to a private-sector, market-led economy. In addition, Bosnia faces a dual challenge: Not only must the nation recover from the war, but it also must complete the transition from socialism to capitalism. A Central Bank was established in 1997, successful debt nego-tiations were held with the London Club in December 1997 and with the Paris Club in October 1998, and a new currency linked to the deutsche mark was introduced in mid-1998 and has remained relatively stable.[24] With a strong human capital base and an appropriate set of forward-looking policies, Bosnia could re-emerge from the ruins of war and become a successful economy, provided international assistance mobilizes for the initial reconstruction.

The Transportation Sector

In terms of physical losses, the government estimates the overall damages from the war at $50–$70 billion. The economic replacement cost of the destroyed assets is huge; according to initial World Bank staff estimates, it lies in the range of $15–$20 billion.[25] All parts of the transportation system were heavily damaged by excessive military and civilian traffic or by lack of maintenance for more than three years. Damage blocked access to several important transportation corridors; transport organizations were divided along territorial lines, limiting freedom of movement throughout the country; and companies were further weakened by the loss of personnel, funds, and equipment. In addition, the displacement of two million people, which is taking considerable time to resolve, greatly altered transport demand.

Prior to the war, Bosnia had a 123,000-kilometer road system, including 3,700 kilometers of main roads. After the war, about 2,500 kilometers of roads required urgent attention to avoid catastrophic failure, and an estimated fifty-eight damaged bridges were considered a high priority to repair or replace.[26] It was not uncommon to spend hours on the road traversing the countryside weaving through potholes created by shelling or simple road failure and negotiating makeshift detours because of multiple bridge outages. Tunnel ceilings and walls quickly reached failure before their normal life expectancy, accelerated by the effects of freeze and thaw. During the winter, large icicles formed inside the tunnels, endangering motorists when the huge dagger-like icicles fell from the ceiling. During the summer, it was not unusual to encounter livestock in the tunnels as the tunnels provided the only source of shade from the heat. Motorists had to enter the tunnels with care as there were no working lights to illuminate either the animals seeking relief from the heat or the horse-drawn carts transporting agricultural products. Safety equipment on the roads and bridges was nonexistent after the war.

Before the war there was a 1,030-kilometer rail network, 75 percent of which was electrified, which was generally adequate in extent and condition to support Bosnia's economic and transportation needs. As no significant river system exists in Bosnia that is capable of commercial traffic, rail facilitated the country's exports and imports. However, the war caused extensive damage to the railways. When IFOR entered the theater, only about 300 kilometers were operational—the main line south of Mostar and the lines east and west of Mostar.[27] Bridges and track were systematically destroyed during the confrontation, electrical and signaling equipment was removed by opposing forces, and switching equipment was beyond repair. In addition, the local public transport systems in Sarajevo and other urban areas ceased to function. Buses and trams were overturned and burned, track was uprooted and removed, and mines were placed in an attempt to prevent any personnel movement. These efforts greatly aided the Serbs during their siege of Sarajevo.

For air travel, Bosnia had two civil airports before the war, one in Sarajevo and one in Mostar, and three military airports in Tuzla, Bihac, and Banja Luka. As the Sarajevo Airport was located on one of the major confrontation lines of the war, the facility was badly damaged and unusable. Large craters were found in the runway from Serb shelling, all lighting and landing-assist systems were removed, and the terminal was heavily shelled.[28] A Russian IL-76 airplane remained on the western edge of the tarmac, the result of an inebriated pilot's attempted landing during the early phases of the war. This plane was recovered only after the war because of the danger of heavy shelling from Serb positions in the hills around the airport. Compounding the problem, the Bosnians built three tunnels underneath the tarmac in order to transport emergency supplies into the city. These tunnels, two of which were concrete lined and one a simple dirt tunnel, were thought to compromise the integrity of the runway. The airport in Mostar, although not located on a confrontation line, was in similar condition. Neither airport supported civilian airline traffic at the cessation of hostilities.

Finally, because Bosnia is virtually landlocked, with the exception of a small spit of land near Metkovic, the primary port in Ploce, in southern Croatia, was the only port available to the Bosnians to export goods by sea. However, Serb forces damaged the overhead lift capacity and sunk several ships in the port, blocking the entrance to the facility. Without lift capacity, the port was limited in its ability to handle container traffic. Therefore, the Bosnians were unable to transport their goods over land because of the poor roads and bridges; were unable to transport their goods by sea because the port was virtually closed to large, commercial traffic; and were unable to transport their goods by air because the civilian airports had ceased to function. The economy at the cessation of hostilities was at a standstill because of its devastated transportation sector, without a great prognosis for internal repair and improvement.

Water Supply, Sewage, and Solid Waste

In the urban areas other, more basic human needs problems were exacerbated by the poor state of the infrastructure. The massive movements of population and the heavy concentration of people in parts of the country that were considered safe resulted in major problems in the delivery of basic water and sanitation services to the people of Bosnia. Although damage from the war was part of the reason for this state of affairs, a major contributing cause was the complete lack of maintenance over the previous few years, resulting in crumbling infrastructure. Losses from water leakage, already at 30 percent before the war, increased to 50 percent by war's end. Before the war, piped municipal water supply coverage in urban areas was 90 percent, and twenty-four-hour service was the norm. Throughout the country, 56 percent of the population was supplied with piped water; the remainder in the agrarian areas was supplied with clean water by individually constructed wells. Bosnia's unique geological makeup of limestone provided an extremely pure source of drinking water, unequalled throughout Europe. Sewage collection systems covered 70 percent of the population in urban areas, and about 35 percent of the overall population was connected to a municipal sewage system. Most municipalities had well-organized waste collection services that ensured periodic delivery to landfill sites or temporary disposal areas. Few sewage systems, however, had treatment plants; Sarajevo was the lone exception. In 1976, the World Bank helped finance a project to rehabilitate and expand Sarajevo's water supply networks and install sewage treatment equipment.[29]

Immediately at the cessation of hostilities, massive population shifts caused water supplies in many urban centers to be grossly insufficient for the number of people requiring services. Waterborne diseases were common; people had to queue for extended periods of time in the cold of winter to obtain humanitarian relief, and water contamination from inadequately handled wastewater was a constant hazard. Sewage collection systems clogged, and pumping stations and treatment plants failed. In addition, arrangements for the disposal of solid waste, which was highly efficient before the war, broke down, bringing new health hazards to citizens. Because many garbage trucks were destroyed or inoperable because of lack of maintenance and spare parts, solid waste collection and disposal collapsed. As a result, riverbanks and forests became dumping sites; it was common throughout the country to see rusted cars, abandoned appliances, and garbage in the same streams that supplied drinking water. In addition, in divided communities such as Mostar, opposing sides compounded the problem by restricting each other's access to water sources and solid waste disposal sites.

As IFOR entered the theater, it was obvious that the long-term reconstruction program for water supply, sewage, and solid waste had to quickly restore services to prewar levels or there would be a massive outbreak of disease. As a force protection measure, IFOR headquarters itself daily trucked in its drinking water from a local brewery that still had an operational well free from contamination. In addition to its social, environmental, and political benefits, a water system reconstruction program would enhance the operation of industries requiring an assured water supply and allow people to turn to productive activities rather than haul water for domestic chores. Critical on-site repairs of water distribution and treatment plants, unblocking and replacement of sewer lines, and developing landfills for solid waste are the key elements of any postconflict reconstruction program.

Energy

Before the war, Bosnia operated its own electricity system and met the local demand. In 1990, generating plants located in its territory produced 13,090 gigawatt hours (GWh), while electricity consumption was 11,181 GWh. Prior to 1992, the coal mines in Bosnia produced about fifteen million tons of brown coal and lignite per year, of which 70 percent was used for electric power generation and the remaining 30 percent for industrial and household uses. Standards in most mines were high and maintenance conditions were good. Natural gas was imported under a contract between Russia's Gazprom and Energopetrol, a state-owned oil and gas company. Consumption peaked in 1990 with 610 million cubic meters, constituting 8 percent of the total energy consumption in Bosnia. Within Bosnia, distribution and maintenance of the gas networks was the responsibility of Sarajevogas. In 1976, the World Bank made a $38 million loan to help build a 265-kilometer pipeline connecting Sarajevo to the country's natural gas network. In 1990, district heating systems served 120,000 customers, equivalent to 450,000 inhabitants or 10 percent of the total population. The Sarajevo system was the country's largest, serving 45 percent of the city's population.[30]

At the cessation of hostilities, about 70 percent of electrical generating capacity was damaged or out of operation because of destroyed transmission lines. About 60 percent of the transmission network was seriously damaged, including transmission facilities and interconnection lines as well as transformer stations and maintenance equipment. The distribution network was largely destroyed. People to operate these facilities were scarce, as many of the staff were required for the war effort, while others were refugees. Residential electricity, if operational, was limited to two hours per day in urban areas; house fires were common from overturned candles used in lieu of electric lights. Coal production dropped to 1.5 million tons in 1994, less than 10 percent of the prewar level. The number of people employed by the mines decreased from 26,000 to about 7,000; most of the skilled personnel left the country.[31]

During the war, Sarajevo's district heating system was badly damaged by direct shelling and through the corrosion and cracking of boilers, substations, network pipes, and internal heating installations in buildings. Lack of maintenance resulting from war shortages compounded the problems. By early 1996, the number of flats served by district heating dropped from 45,000 to 16,000, while the number of household gas connections had increased from 15,000 to an estimated 89,000.[32] Most of the wood available in Sarajevo—trees, old furniture, and even wooden grave markers—was consumed during the war to provide heat. Many improvised and illegal gas connections were made, often leading to explosions and death. During 1996, gas made up 70 percent of all energy consumption in Sarajevo, constituting the basic heating and cooking fuel for the city's remaining 300,000 inhabitants. On a positive note, the coal-fired systems in Tuzla and Zenica were almost fully operational, as were those of smaller cities and towns in central and northern Bosnia. In all cities, lack of maintenance resulting from concentration on the war effort caused its share of damage, but generally, the damage to district heating systems in Bosnia was not overly severe.

Telecommunications

Bosnia's well-developed prewar telecommunications system suffered severe direct war damage. Before the war, Bosnia had about 696,000 lines in operation, or about 15.3 lines per 100 people, comparing favorably with other republics. The war-damaged switching and transmission equipment reduced the installed phone lines by more than 30 percent, to 472,000 lines, and international lines by 90 percent (down to 400 international lines).[33] Some lines that were not in service did not suffer direct physical damage but were either disconnected or only locally connected. Destroyed facilities included transmission and switching equipment, buildings, microwave towers, and overhead cables; many underground cables were also damaged. Daytime call completion rates from abroad dropped from 35–38 percent to 1–2 percent and no commercial calls were being directly connected from Bosnia to Croatia, one of its nearest neighbors.[34] To communicate between Bosnia and Croatia, one had to use military communications or use a cumbersome process and route messages through a third country that had restored communications to Bosnia. The telecommunications company (which also handled postal service) was split into three separate and largely disconnected networks based in Sarajevo, Mostar, and Banja Luka. The telex and data networks no longer operated. Again, human resources were scarce, because many service-sector staff had left or become refugees. Furthermore, most of the equipment documentation was destroyed in the war.

This sector, in particular, required massive technical assistance. Not only did the country require a reconnection in terms of landline service, but also no mobile phone service was available in the country. In an area where the rugged geography prohibits most routine forms of communication, mobile service becomes vital to serve the needs of business and facilitate the reconstruction effort, including areas not previously served by the fixed network.

Mine Threat

Finally, a massive problem that continues to impact all sectors of Bosnian life is the residual mine threat. During the war, half a million mines were placed in more than 17,000 minefields, largely around the lines of confrontation. Because the lines of confrontation constantly moved during the four-year war, the exact locations of all of the minefields were never known. Standardized minefield records were either improperly used, unavailable, missing, or never filed at a responsible secure headquarters. Mine locations, for example, were recorded on the walls of houses, bunkers, pavements, or other structures and were subsequently damaged or forgotten. According to Colonel Steve Hawkins, Engineer Brigade Commander, 1st Armored Division (U.S.) (the first American unit to enter Bosnia):

> The Serb Army did the best job of minefield recording. The Croatians were second, the Bosnian Muslims were hit and miss on their minefields. They didn't have a lot of mines. They used to go over and steal mines from the Serbs, take them out of the ground and put them over in different places for their minefields. And their reporting wasn't all that great. In addition, you could tell soldiers were rather intoxicated when they filled out some of the forms and put their minefields in, and sometimes they used dubious markers—like the strawberry bush was the marker with which to find the minefields in the area.[35]

Mine pollution in Bosnia was a significant obstacle to the re-establishment of normal development activities. Landmine hazard was a factor affecting decisions on refugee return and the pace of reconciliation. Dr. Pramod K. Sethi, the inventor of the Jaipur Foot (prosthetic device), succinctly captures the true danger of the mines:

> A much more devastating cause for disabilities has now appeared on the global scene: the widespread and continuing use of landmines in countries where civil wars have become endemic. Even if a ban on the use of landmines could be imposed and implemented, we shall still be saddled for years to come by the "silent war" waged by these weapons that are meant to maim rather than kill, the victims often being the poor in the countryside where such mines are laid. Not surprisingly, they include many innocent women and children.[36]

At the point of IFOR's entry into Bosnia, minefield locations were virtually unknown. The British, who were in theater as part of UNPROFOR, had a comprehensive mine database for only the British sector, not the entire country. Entering Bosnia in December 1995, Colonel Hawkins attempted to get minefield data. During an oral history, he stated:

> I said [to the British] I'm getting ready to bring about 20,000 soldiers down here. I'm the engineer; I'm supposed to know where the minefields are. I need your database. They had a database, and all it had was the British sector minefields that they knew about already, and they had big swatches that said be careful, that's the ZOS [Zone of Separation], because you might find a minefield in here. Under the Dayton Peace Accords, the three formal factions were to identify and clear all mine-fields within the first 30 days of implementation. Having been out into the country and having talked to the UN, even though they didn't have records, they gave you a picture that was pretty scary on what the threat was. It's winter. There is snow on the ground. Clearing mines is a tough business in good weather. It's not what you want to do if you don't have to in winter.[37]

THE MILITARY RESPONSE
TO POSTCONFLICT RECONSTRUCTION

Minimum military requirement: that is the phrase that governed the military's commitment of resources to Bosnia's postconflict infrastructure reconstruction. If the project did not directly aid the military mission, monetary resources could not be used for the project. For small humanitarian projects funded from other sources, troop labor and military equipment could be used when not otherwise engaged in projects contributing to the military mission. Any project outside of these guidelines was considered "mission creep" and was not authorized for execution.

In addition, the engineering structure in Bosnia was not the cleanest organization. Because there were two large military engineer staffs executing countrywide engineer operations without any engineer forces directly assigned to either of them for tasking, it was decided that the strategic level of operations would be assigned to the IFOR staff, made up

Figure 2. Implementation Force Engineer Structure

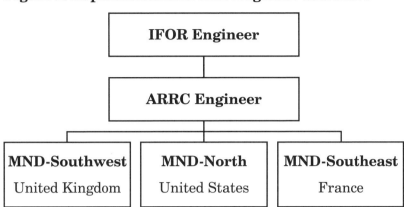

mostly of officers and military members from the staff of Allied Forces Southern Europe (AFSOUTH). The operational level was assigned to the Allied Command Europe Rapid Reaction Corps (ARRC), a multinational staff designed for quick deployment to conduct NATO operations. Another anomaly of the Bosnian peace operation, Operation Joint Endeavor, was that it was NATO's first "out-of-area" operation. Very little doctrine existed to govern this type of operation; therefore, most of the standard operating procedures were written as the operation progressed. Figure 2 depicts the command and control relationships that existed in the engineer structure in the first year of the peace operation.

There was much redundancy and overlap of missions between the IFOR engineer staff and the ARRC engineer staff. Furthermore, the Multinational Divisions (MNDs) received loose guidance and instruction from the ARRC but also had to be responsive to national concerns. In NATO, where most decisions are decided by a consensus vote, military "orders" in NATO's first deployment were usually issued only after first asking the nation if it had any objection to the *potential* draft order. Only after the MND agreed would the final "order" be published concerning a mission. This procedure greatly slowed decisions and operations. During the IFOR period there was constant concern over the command and control structure and the division of labor between staffs. The initial structure caused so many problems that when SFOR was created to replace IFOR, the IFOR and the ARRC staff functions were melded into one SFOR staff, thus eliminating the redundancy and creating a more streamlined staff capable of both strategic and operational levels of operations.

NATO Engineering Effort

When IFOR and the ARRC deployed into Bosnia, the engineering staffs could not agree on who was to take the lead in developing the Theater Engineer Program for Operation Joint Endeavor. The French provided the IFOR engineer (IFOR-ENG)—Brigadier General Claude De Wilde—who was militarily competent but did not have a full appreciation of the NATO process. The British provided the ARRC engineer (ARRC-ENG)—Brigadier General John Moore-Bick—a forward-thinking individual who could easily explain engineer grand strategy and promote the Theater Engineer Program; the difficulty was that he advocated policies that were not promulgated by IFOR, which was his senior headquarters. It was the responsibility of IFOR-ENG to initially develop an engineer vision that would provide guidance and control to the subordinate units of IFOR; however, the first IFOR engineer vision statement was not written until May 1996, about four months after the ARRC-ENG had already published his Theater Engineer Program. The two visions did not mesh. The ARRC vision should have been a subset of the IFOR document; however, competing priorities prevented the two headquarters from fully meshing their capabilities.

The IFOR engineer staff in Sarajevo that supported De Wilde was thin. The most it could hope to accomplish with its eight officers was broken down into five broad areas: the creation of theater engineer policy for the reconstruction of roads, bridges, ports, and airfields; construction/rehabilitation management of IFOR headquarters buildings; the procurement and subsequent management of NATO Infrastructure Committee funds; professional engineer advice to Civil Affairs personnel on humanitarian projects funded externally; and the coordination of the mine awareness training in theater. There was little hands-on construction management, except for the creation of IFOR headquarters, as the staff was mostly preoccupied with the development of policy and NATO procedures. Outside of Sarajevo, IFOR-ENG created three Regional Engineering Offices (REOs) in each MND sector. The REOs' task was to provide construction management and contract maintenance for civilian-contracted road and bridge rehabilitation throughout the three MND sectors.

The ARRC staff, on the other hand, was much more robust. Moore-Bick was supported by a large staff of professional engineers whose expertise ranged from bridge and road design to airfield construction and port rehabilitation. The ARRC's capabilities included a terrain team able to make local maps when existing maps were terribly outdated; an intelligence section able to create minefield overlays to enhance force protection; and a project planning section able to make detailed project assessments that could be handed over to civilian firms for civilian infrastructure reconstruction. Moore-Bick's staff developed detailed plans on how to open up Bosnia's infrastructure to fully support the military's freedom of movement, including rapid deployment and redeployment of military forces. In addition, his designers completed a comprehensive assessment of the Sarajevo airport, enabling an outside contractor with World Bank funding to complete enough rehabilitation to allow civilian air traffic by August 1996. Rehabilitating the airport required comprehensive demining of the site to humanitarian standards with mechanical demining machines. But, again, all of the IFOR projects had to meet military missions. None of them were solely for civilian support, and many projects that should have been completed in the first year to promote civilian freedom of movement were not accomplished because of the limitations imposed by NATO and the troop-contributing nations.

A project summary produced by the ARRC in December 1996, titled "1996—Year of the Sapper" (using military parlance for combat engineers), best sums up the efforts of the IFOR engineers, as shown in table 3.

In December 1996, the IFOR engineer staff produced an update of the Coalition Joint–ENGR Strategic Vision in an

Table 3. IFOR Engineer Project Summary

Project	Description	Cost
Roads	2,500 kilometers under stable maintenance; snow and ice removal through the winter; IFOR repaired/maintained only 3 percent to meet the minimum military requirement.	$22 million
Bridges	62 bridges of varying types; military equipment, timber, and masonry reconstruction; 10 equipment bridges emplaced.	$20 million
Bosnia-Herzegovina Access	8 routes from Croatia and Serbia into Bosnia.	——
Rail	480 kilometers of network rehabilitated; IFOR replaced/maintained only 5 percent to meet the minimum military requirement. None of the rehabilitation was electrified track. Additional signaling and safety equipment is required for civilian use.	$10 million
Gorazde Access Road	75 kilometers of single-track built in advance of the road to be completed by the Bosnians.	$3 million

Table 3 (continued)

Project	Description	Cost
Headquarters Facilities	Renovations of existing buildings heavily damaged by shelling during the war.	$13 million
Airports	Opened airports at Sarajevo and Mostar to military and civilian traffic.	$8 million
Other	Numerous hydrological, utilities, and construction projects in support of CIMIC and military operations.	Unknown
Total: More than $76 million, about $22 million completed with troop labor; incalculable contribution to nation building.		

Source: Allied Rapid Reaction Corps, "ARRC Bridge Replacement Plan: Phases 1-3" (briefing slides with scripted commentary), Sarajevo, ARRC Engineer Branch, December 30, 1996, 3.

effort to determine the future direction for engineer operations during 1997. The staff anticipated a noticeable reduction in troop strength at the theater and divisional levels, requiring a greater reliance upon contractor support and minimizing SFOR's ability to support civil agencies.

SFOR continued to maintain the designated corps and theater route networks and the corps redeployment routes; however, the total kilometers under SFOR contract were reduced, expanding the number of kilometers of road not scheduled for routine maintenance and exacerbating the already poor road network. SFOR bridging repairs were couched in terms to support military freedom of movement; however, the International Management Group's Emergency Transport and Reconstruction Project (ETRP) subsequently proposed a bridge replacement program into which SFOR planned to integrate its limited efforts. The ETRP proposal was for the future; no permanent civilian bridge reconstruction had occurred in the

Table 4. U.S. Foreign Policy Goals for Bosnia

1. Sustaining a political settlement in Bosnia that preserves the country's territorial integrity and provides a viable future for all its people.

2. Preventing the spread of the conflict into a broader Balkan war, threatening the stability of Europe's new democratic states in Europe.

3. Stemming the destabilizing flow of refugees from the conflict.

4. Halting the slaughter of innocents.

5. Helping to support NATO's central role in Europe while maintaining its role in shaping Europe's security architecture.

Source: The White House, *A National Security Strategy of Engagement and Enlargement* (Washington, D.C.: The White House, February 1996), 35.

critical first year. Rail reconstruction was projected to be even more dismal. The theatre minimum military requirement was achieved in 1996. Activities in 1997 were above and beyond the MMR and were to be executed based on funds and troops available.[38] The emphasis here is on *civilian* funds available. The Italian Railway Company (military unit) had rehabilitated 480 kilometers of rail during the first year of IFOR using NATO Infrastructure Committee funds, but that constituted only 5 percent of the total network and was targeted at lines that would support IFOR's deployment and redeployment needs.

United States Engineering Effort

Whereas IFOR's overall mission was constrained by minimum military requirements, the U.S. engineering effort in Bosnia was even more focused by President Clinton's National Security Strategy published in February 1996, as shown in table 4.

Nowhere in this strategy does it discuss the aftermath to peace enforcement. Attaining these objectives was largely dependent on the effective use of the other economic, diplomatic, political, and informational instruments of power by the international community. This lack of postconflict direction to the military implied that once the military provisions were in place, the area stabilized, and the threat reduced, IFOR would have completed the required prerequisites to allow the civilian provisions to be implemented. Unfortunately, the civilian agencies that were mandated to do the remaining parts of the Dayton Agreement were not yet deployed.

The U.S. postconflict engineering effort can be categorized into five tasks: maintain the mobility corridors for military freedom of movement; construct and maintain military base camps, observation points, and checkpoints; establish, clear, and destroy the Zone of Separation between the former warring factions; collect and distribute minefield data and monitor demining operations; and resolve critical infrastructure shortfalls. The first four tasks directly stem from the military mandate as outlined in Article I of the GFAP. The last task was an attempt at "mission creep"—an effort by engineer leaders, recognizing the need to help the locals repair their infrastructure, yet having insufficient funding to make a significant long-term impact.

Freedom of Movement. The initial engineer task to facilitate military freedom of movement was to construct a float bridge over the Sava River to enable the initial peacekeepers to enter Bosnia in December 1995. This major undertaking completed in the most treacherous of weather circumstances was the signal of U.S. resolve to solve the Bosnian crisis. However, once the force was in Bosnia, the engineer mission to support freedom of movement became a constantly evolving dictum. To clarify the mission somewhat, Major General William Nash, the U.S. commander of Task Force Eagle (MND-North), articulated his views of civilian freedom of movement in his initial commander's intent: "Civilian freedom of movement is not within IFOR's mandate, but the responsibility of the parties. IFOR, in conjunction with the international police, will facilitate civilian freedom of movement by dismantling illegal checkpoints and assisting repatriation efforts."[39]

This guidance in a sense promoted negative construction, the dismantling of artificial barriers to movement, and did not enable the military engineer to construct positive infrastructure that would in addition facilitate civilian freedom of movement or repatriation. Consequently, the initial work pursued by IFOR rebuilt routes only to rough-terrain, four-wheel-drive standards—the standards minimally required of the vehicles deployed by the military. Throughout the year, many roads were upgraded with IFOR graders and gravel to allow civilian cars, trucks, and buses to easily transport both workers and commercial goods throughout the sector; however, this was not the justification for the upgrade, nor was it a permanent upgrade, requiring almost continual, daily maintenance. Instead, the justification for these upgrades on MND-North routes was to help stabilize the routes for military traffic, and the gravel was added to save on maintenance costs for military vehicles. The benefit to civilian traffic was officially deemed to be a collateral benefit.

Likewise, military engineers applied their professional expertise to several civilian routes to assess the causes of route failure and used their methods of persuasion to link local governments, factional engineers, civilian deminers, civilian construction assets, and flood control agencies to a common goal of repairing the route. Lacking a direct funding link to the military to resource these projects, U.S. soldiers were forced to solicit the aid of U.S. governmental relief agencies to pay for the reconstruction.

The result was that many of these road projects were finished long after the first year in theater, although the initial plans for construction, mine clearance, and execution timelines were adopted and completed within the initial critical year.[40] The ultimate endstate proved to be well worth the effort: renewed flow of refugees, economic goods, and freedom of movement between sectors of the ZOS. These results would have been too hard for the former warring factions to accomplish independently. But the time lost because of complicated funding schemes caused delays in the projects' completion, delays to the great benefits the former warring factions ultimately enjoyed because of these projects, and delays to the economic revitalization that these projects helped to facilitate.

Base Camps, Observation Posts, and Checkpoints. Entering Bosnia, the military engineers did not have the mission to create base camps for the deployed 20,000 U.S. soldiers. According to Hawkins: "I actually started most of all this [base camps] with combat engineer labor, and with Seabees and RED HORSE [Air Force engineer unit]. We had to get the initial force in there and be able to provide security for Brown & Root [a U.S. civilian contractor hired to construct base camps in Bosnia], and then Brown & Root had to have time to mobilize its operation in country."[41]

The initial base camp concept envisioned three large base camps for a brigade combat team, which was the most efficient concept for an extended mission. However, applying this template to the existing ground conditions demonstrated that it was not feasible, in terms of both actual physical location and the commander's scheme and intent for peace enforcement operations. The agrarian infrastructure and poor soil conditions, combined with the existing harsh winter conditions, prevented the construction of massive base camps for 1,200 to 1,800 soldiers on Bosnian farmlands. Camp designs were created on vehicle hoods and construction was managed in portable notebooks. Engineers created common bed-down standards, and construction phases were separated in three tiers of escalating force protection and comfort. The creation of efficient construction management systems, the assignment of 400 extra construction engineers, and the equitable distribution of more than $10 million in initial contracts across all factions' economies allowed for the completion of the peace enforcement construction mandate. After the first ninety days, fifteen major camps and six remote facilities had tier 1 (tents with wooden floors) and tier 2 (tents with wooden floors and walls) essential base camp and force protection construction completed.[42]

In addition, engineers constructed IFOR checkpoints throughout the sector to randomly monitor and control the movement of the former warring factions. During the initial opening of the ZOS, the guaranteed presence of IFOR checkpoints was used as a diplomatic tool to encourage factions to remove their defensive positions. Although $10 million in local contracts helped to jump-start the construction economy and the construction of the base camps necessary to protect the peacekeeping soldiers, the final product did not contribute to a revitalization of the local infrastructure. The checkpoints helped to enhance the security of the country, but, again, that was in direct support of Article I of the GFAP—not as part of a well-conceived postconflict reconstruction plan encouraging civilian normalization.

The Zone of Separation. Since the conflict started in the spring of 1992, the confrontation lines grew into major defensive networks composed of integrated fires, obstacles, and defensive structures. The creation of the ZOS became a permanent scar on the face of Bosnia, marking hundreds of kilometers on the now-famous demarcation between Bosnian Serb and Federation forces. Aerial overflights clearly showed the exact position of the warring factions' front lines and the complexity and depth of the fortifications. Nothing was permitted to cross the ZOS—all communication and infrastructure was permanently cut; roads were cratered by demolitions preventing even four-wheel-drive traffic; high-tension power lines, phone lines, and water systems were destroyed; rail lines were severely damaged with railroad ties uprooted and subsequently used for bunkers; and bridges ranging from two-lane international to local farm routes were destroyed beyond repair. Even the bobsled run that was prominently featured in the 1984 Winter Olympics was destroyed as the Serbs used the concrete track as a secondary fighting position and mined all approaches to the track. It appeared as if someone took a hammer and chisel and carefully separated the country along the IEBL.

The factions' defenses were built in depth with connecting trenches spaced 500 to 800 meters apart and large earthen bunkers built every 200 meters. The bunkers could house two men for a three-day rotation and included a wood stove, bed, and small kitchen. Enhancing the defenses were the minefields. Nothing was emplaced to standard; there were no set doctrines, techniques, records, or types of mines. Minefields were placed between the factions' front lines to prevent offensive actions. Roads, trails, rail lines, and all avenues of approach were heavily laced with antitank mines, supported by antipersonnel mines to deter manual clearance by the opposing faction. Perpendicular access trenches were booby-trapped with trip wires curtailing the attacking force's ability to pursue the retreating force.

The mission to remove the ZOS fell to the military engineer—again, a military mission to support the GFAP. In the U.S. sector alone, there were sixty-nine miles of ZOS to control, containing more than 2,400 bunkers, 1,850 minefields, and 120 miles of trench line.[43] At coordination meetings, engineer company commanders met with the factional engineer to determine the weekly work schedule. To ensure IFOR safety from mines and booby traps, factional engineers would enter and proof the bunker to ensure that there was no threat to IFOR soldiers, who would then rig the bunker for demolition. After six months, all bunkers in the U.S. sector had been destroyed. A subsequent decision allowed the connecting trench lines to naturally collapse from the rains in the spring and summer. Finally, IFOR engineer vehicles brought in gravel, filled trenches, and compacted the road subgrades, restoring the traveled road surface to an acceptable 15-MPH travel speed. Trees and shrubs that had grown over the road were cut back at the minefield edge and any berms, bunker debris, or barriers (old buses, vehicles, and armored vehicles) were cleared to allow unimpeded movement of two-lane IFOR convoys. Again, this was a mission designed to promote military implementation of the GFAP, but one that also contributed greatly to the political objective to break down the barriers between factions.

Minefield Data. Upon entering Bosnia, the United States had to develop a database on mines. Under the Dayton Peace Accords, the three former warring factions were to identify and clear all minefields within the first thirty days of implementation. Without the luxury of an established database or even an established system for gathering the data, Hawkins used his brigade intelligence section to collect and disseminate the minefield data. As the maneuver commanders deployed and started to implement the accords, volumes of minefield recording forms were submitted by the former warring factions. Six interpreters and six soldiers worked twenty-four hours a day, first translating the available forms into English and then translating the locations determined from the different local map systems onto the WGS-84 map system, the system used by NATO. According to Hawkins:

> They were on a different scale, and so if you look at the grid coordinates they had on their forms, it didn't quite match their overlays. We took the grid coordinates and overlays, and by terrain association off of their maps, not necessarily the records, we translated the location of the minefields one-by-one onto a WGS-84, 1:50,000-scale map. Over the course of the year, we recorded 4,439 mine belts, had about 12,000 records—minefield records that we had to deal with. We had minefields reported that didn't have records, but we knew about where they were. And we had about 5,000 minefields that we hadn't had recorded anywhere.[44]

There was unexploded ordnance (UXO) all over the sector, mostly a result of the NATO air campaign, which was just as deadly as the recorded minefields. Dual-purpose improved conventional artillery rounds and mortars that failed to detonate littered the countryside as well. To add more confusion, the Serb army gave every soldier twenty antipersonnel mines to use. As infantry soldiers, the Serbs used these mines as point minefields, emplacing the mines in front of the defensive position, but never properly recording the minefield as an engineer soldier is trained to do.

The brigade attempted to centralize the minefield data reporting and recording in order to standardize the effort across all the maneuver brigades in the U.S. sector. They started by producing see-through minefield overlay maps that soldiers could lay on top of their map and determine where the minefields were located, but the overlays tended to shift and move, causing an inaccuracy that the soldiers could ill afford to have. Therefore, the engineer brigade negotiated with a British topographic unit to produce "tacky" prints, tactical prints that depicted the geographic map along with the individual minefields by minefield number. This enabled the soldiers to look anywhere in the area, cross-reference the geographic location with the minefield number on the tacky print, and further cross-reference the minefield number with the paper copy of the minefield data sheet to obtain the details of the minefield. Should soldiers depart on a mission, they would determine their route by a map reconnaissance, pull the minefield data sheets out of the paper copy database for those minefields that they would possibly encounter, and have a translated copy in English of the minefield record on the ground should it be needed.

Toward the end of the first year, the brigade was able to computerize the effort so that one could enter the computer database, bring up the map, bring up the data of the minefield, and then bring up the actual minefield record on disk. The final result was that there were twenty-four mine strikes in the first year in the U.S. sector alone—most were by multinational units from other countries crossing the sector, although the United States did suffer one death and one casualty from mines.

Resolve Critical Infrastructure Shortfalls. The most important postconflict reconstruction role that was performed by U.S. engineers was the identification of damaged facilities and the assessment of potential repair costs, funding alternatives, and the interrelationship of the required project with the larger geopolitical and economic context of Bosnian peace and stability. Individual requests came from all directions: local mayors, NGO deminers, other multinational engineers, well-meaning maneuver brigade and battalion Civil Affairs officers, and tactical

Table 5. Operational Engineer Assessment Priorities

Priority 1:
INTERNATIONAL PROJECTS
The completion of these projects supports economic, resettlement, political, or diplomatic initiatives in Bosnia and adjacent countries.

Priority 2:
NATIONAL PROJECTS
These projects involve at least two factions and create favorable political, economic, or diplomatic ramifications outside
the Posavina Corridor region.

Priority 3:
REGIONAL PROJECTS (MULTIFACTIONAL)
These projects are within the corridors but are designed to
generate relationships and agreements among factions, as well
as an economic or humanitarian improvement for both sides.

Priority 4:
REGIONAL PROJECTS (ONE FACTION ONLY)
These projects create economic or humanitarian improvements for only one faction. Used by IFOR to balance an
unequal distribution of aid by external agencies to the opposing side. No significant multifactional interaction; limited
political potential.

Source: Lieutenant Colonel Todd T. Semonite, *The Military Engineer as a Critical Peace
Operations Multiplier.* Strategy Research Project (Carlisle Barracks, Pa. United States
Army War College, April 7, 1999), 88.

commanders. Requests included removing building rubble for the
mayor of Brcko (a strategic center of gravity because of the town's
evenly divided ethnicity), clearing mines from cemeteries for
cross-ZOS religious groups, and moving a Serb Catholic church
bell located in Muslim-controlled land. Without an engineer-
designed, brigade-approved concept to focus engineer capabilities
to achieve a regional objective, it was apparent that the entire

first year would be spent on localized, unilateral support. This would do little to unite the factions into one interdependent country postured for long-term peaceful coexistence.

According to Lieutenant Colonel Todd Semonite, 23rd Engineer Battalion Commander: "Working within the general maneuver concept for the 'peacekeeping' phase, engineers concentrated on orchestrating the infrastructure repair plan. NGO and IO assistance was welcome but at this time, they were not prepared to assume the lead in any functional sector. Bottom line—during 'peacekeeping' operations, IFOR would take the lead on using limited IFOR engineer assets and funds to rebuild critical, politically important projects to carefully shape and set the conditions for the civil element to assume this mission when capable."[45]

The engineer staff designed an operational set of reconstruction and humanitarian assessment priorities that could create second- and third-order ramifications on strategic-level peace initiatives. All efforts focused on projects, programs, and initiatives that brought the factions together, creating a dialogue and interdependence between the sides. Projects that supported only one faction were avoided as these seldom created any strategic potential to substantially bring the sides closer together. However, only limited humanitarian funds were available through the Civil Affairs chain; all other funding had to be solicited from NGOs, IOs, or other donors. The scope of the proposed reconstruction projects was usually the rebuilding of an existing structure (limiting factional disagreement) to improve the quality of life for all sides. Most projects that were completed were localized and considered humanitarian rather than infrastructure reconstruction.

The few large infrastructure projects that were funded by IFOR, which also provided great physical relief to the factions, continued to meet the guidelines of the minimum military requirement. For example, the priority-one project to conduct the Brcko Transportation Study and reconstruct the Brcko highway bridge between Bosnia and Croatia not only opened the Brcko hub to civilian transportation, but also enhanced the resupply route of U.S. troops in Bosnia. The priority-two project to rebuild the Tuzla corridor rail line re-established the rail traffic between Bosnia, Croatia, and the European central region, but also allowed IFOR to save $650,000 by bringing more than 70 percent of the U.S. division's fuel by rail.[46] The priority-three project to create the Arizona Market allowed the civilians to meet at a critical point in the IEBL in order to create an open market for trade, but also allowed IFOR to staff a secure checkpoint so soldiers could inspect vehicles for contraband. Finally, the priority-four project to remove rubble from Brcko helped the locals regain access to critical sections of their town, but also allowed IFOR to better patrol the area to enhance security. None of the projects that were funded by IFOR was strictly for civilian use. All postconflict infrastructure projects that U.S. engineers completed were funded either by IFOR to support the military mission or by third parties as part of their humanitarian mission.

Mine Awareness and Demining Efforts

In addition to creating a minefield database, IFOR forces had to work at forming a demining program. There are two types of mine clearance processes: military and humanitarian. Military mine clearance is the process undertaken by soldiers to clear a safe path so they can advance during conflict. The military process of mine clearance specifically clears only those mines that block strategic pathways required in the advance or retreat of soldiers at war. The military term used for mine clearance is breaching, and it is accepted that limited casualties may occur. Humanitarian mine clearance aims to clear land so that civilians can return to their homes and their everyday routines without the threat of land mines and UXO. This requires that all mines affecting the places where ordinary people live must be cleared, and their safety in areas that have been demined is guaranteed. All mines are cleared and the areas are thoroughly verified by clearance teams so that they can say without a doubt that the land is now safe and that people can use it without worrying about possible injuries. The aim of humanitarian demining is to restore peace and security at the community level. Military organizations involved in mine action do not carry out mine clearance directly. In most countries they advise and assist the national authorities or a UN peacekeeping mission to carry out mine clearance. The United Nations typically establishes a Mine Action Authority or Coordination Center responsible for overseeing clearance activities. The actual clearance operations are then carried out by national civilian agencies, military units that agree to take part in humanitarian operations, national or international NGOs, or commercial contractors. Bosnia was no different, placing the military into a monitoring role and a mine awareness role.

According to the Coalition Joint–ENGR Strategic Vision:

> Demining is the responsibility of the former warring factions. Our engineers are charged with monitoring the lifting and clearing of minefields by the former warring factions with a priority to lifting known minefields. SFOR engineers will only lift mines in the interest of our own freedom of movement. . . . A key element of our strategy is the recognition that the UN Mine Action Center (UNMAC) is the lead agency for the long-term demining strategy for the country. We will support the UNMAC with the transfer of information and will collocate our Mine Clearance Center (MCC) with the UNMAC. The UNMAC will hold the definitive database for mine information.[47]

Very little was done in the first year. Multiple training bans were imposed on the Entity Armed Forces for failure to cooperate and little more was accomplished than stretching thousands of kilometers of mine tape across the country at places deemed likely to contain a minefield. The initial UN efforts to train and employ local deminers faltered in the first year as the Bosnian government imposed a 100 percent tax on the deminers' income, thus discouraging the United Nations from pursuing this approach. Only when this tax was repealed did training commence a year later. IFOR engineers, however, scored success by developing a comprehensive mine awareness training plan. Targeting the local communities and schools, IFOR engineers produced training packets (using such training aids as Superman comic books specifically produced for mine awareness) that would educate the local nationals on what the mines and UXO looked like, where potential minefields were located, and what to do should a person stumble across a mine. These efforts led to a steady decrease in mine incidents, reaching a monthly total of zero by August 1996.

With SFOR encouragement, the entities produced a detailed plan for demining operations in 1997, and more than 20,000 mines and 1,100 other unexploded objects were removed.[48] Since then, Bosnian demining teams have carried out demining operations as part of the National Demining Plan. The Bosnians had forty-three nine-person demining teams operating in Bosnia, in accordance with SFOR's requirements. Three permanent demining schools were opened in Banja Luka, Mostar, and Travnik to train the Bosnian armed forces in demining and handling UXO. The Federation and the Republika Srpska Mine Action Coordination Centers carried out quality assurance and general survey activity in the field. They identified remaining mine clearance tasks and certified and registered areas as being cleared. In addition to the Bosnian forces, a number of organizations including commercial demining companies contracted by the International Trust Fund for Mine Clearance and Victims Assistance, international and national NGOs, and Entity Departments for Civil Protection are carrying out mine clearance. Future strategies by the Bosnian government will aim to make the country free from the impact of mines by 2010. As many as 18,000 known mined areas still infest the country and the total area requiring clearance is estimated to be in the order of 400 square kilometers. A rapid clearance of affected areas will increase the pace at which displaced persons can return and will also provide a foundation for future growth.[49]

Combined Joint Civil-Military Cooperation

Although all provisions of the GFAP were broad in nature, the third provision—the promotion of a permanent reconciliation and the facilitation of political arrangements—presented the greatest amount of ambiguity. Successful accomplishment of IFOR military responsibilities would constitute only one leg of a three-legged stool that included political and civil responsibilities—all of which were required to create a stable, solid structure. Recognizing this fact, the GFAP provided supporting tasks that IFOR could undertake within the limits of the identified principal tasks and available resources. These supporting tasks included the following:

- Create secure conditions for the conduct by others of other tasks associated with the peace settlement.

- Assist the movement of organizations in the accomplishment of humanitarian missions.

- Assist the UN agencies and other international organizations in their humanitarian missions.[50]

For the most part, the responsibility for coordinating the vast array of implied supporting tasks fell to a small, often unnoticed staff section—CIMIC/Civil Affairs. CIMIC (the NATO acronym for civil-military cooperation) played an unprecedented role in achieving the objectives of the GFAP. The implementation of the civil aspects of the GFAP was essential to IFOR's exit strategy and the return to normalcy for the people of Bosnia, and CIMIC became the vital link between the military and the civilian organizations operating in theater. According to Admiral Leighton Smith, commander of IFOR, "In November [1995], we had never heard of CIMIC, we had no idea what you did . . . now we can't live without you."[51]

The primary and supporting military objectives outlined in the GFAP that had civil or political implications were translated into a comprehensive CIMIC Campaign Plan, which was to eventually guide civil-military activities during the IFOR deployment. This CIMIC Campaign Plan had five major portions, outlined in table 6. Translated into a comprehensive set of tasks, CIMIC operations facilitated a wide variety of activities in support of the OHR and other organizations such as the OSCE, UNHCR, World Bank, European Union, Red Cross, and others who were responsible for implementing the majority of civil actions outlined in the GFAP. CIMIC personnel participated in Joint Civil Commissions set up by the OHR at the regional level to facilitate

Table 6. CIMIC Campaign Plan

1	Conduct civil military operations in support of the military implementation of the GFAP.
2	Promote cooperation with the civilian populace, various agencies, and national governments.
3	Leverage capabilities of NGOs, IOs, and national governments.
4	Create a parallel, unified civilian effort in support of the GFAP implementation.
5	Prepare to assist governmental, international, and nongovernmental humanitarian, public safety, and health contingencies.

Source: James J. Landon, "CIMIC: Civil-Military Cooperation," in *Lessons From Bosnia: The IFOR Experience,* ed. Larry Wentz (Washington, D.C.: National Defense University, 1998), 121.

civil actions throughout Bosnia. It also set up CIMIC centers at the cantonal (local) level to implement civil reconstruction and improvement plans.

Early on in the IFOR deployment, however, it became clear that there was a lack of coordination and purpose between the Combined Joint Civil-Military Cooperation (CJCIMIC) at IFOR headquarters and the ARRC CIMIC. To illustrate the point, the CJCIMIC became heavily involved in infrastructure projects relating to Sarajevo, while the ARRC CIMIC assumed responsibility for political/military interface and the resolution of constitution development issues—a seeming reversal of roles. Because Sarajevo occupied a key strategic position, specifically with regard to the world media, the IFOR chief of staff decided to create a special CIMIC center just to deal with the implementation of civil projects in the city. CJCIMIC assumed this responsibility, but when it commenced operations in Sarajevo, it did so in the backyard of the ARRC CIMIC, causing jurisdictional friction. One hundred CIMIC personnel, or almost 30 percent of the total CIMIC personnel in Bosnia, ended up supporting those two headquarters alone.

The problems inherent in having two headquarters responsible for the same area of operations are obvious. While addressing the needs of the immediate situation, the two headquarters deviated from the Operations Plan, which resulted in the loss of the traditional command functions of the higher IFOR headquarters over the subordinate ARRC headquarters. To solve this situation, the chiefs of staff of IFOR and the ARRC published terms of reference for CIMIC operations and responsibilities in the IFOR theater to help define and clarify the overall CIMIC command structure. Closely related to the IFOR-ARRC "turf battle" was an overall failure to put in place a command structure capable of synchronizing the efforts of both the military and civilian components in what should be a tightly integrated operation. For example, CJCIMIC had approximately seventy people, half of which were active with project management, and the other half were involved in liaison. Despite the human resources, CJCIMIC did not coordinate or cooperate with CIMIC activities in the French-led division sector—the sector that included Sarajevo.[52] From the civil-military perspective, the CIMIC mission was to help create a parallel, unified civilian effort in support of NATO peace plan implementation. However, the formidable civil-military obstacles standing in the way of this objective were many and varied.

Shortfalls

The civil-military mission of the IFOR deployment had among its goals to promote cooperation with the civilian populace, various agencies, and national governments; leverage the capabilities of NGOs, IOs, and national governments; and create a parallel, unified civilian effort in support of the Dayton Accords. Quick implementation of the military aspects of the agreement provided the essential secure environment and freedom of movement for the commencement of the civil aspects of the agreement. What had not been fully anticipated, however, was the amount of lag time that the civil coordination structures required before they could become operational. In the absence of functioning civil implementation institutions, IFOR received intense public pressure to take a larger role in the implementation of the GFAP's civilian tasks.

The Dayton Agreement divided the overall responsibility for the implementation of civil and military tasks; however, no formal mechanism existed to develop the unified political direction necessary to synchronize civil and military policy between these two bodies. Under the Dayton Accords, the OHR was to coordinate the activities of the civilian organization in Bosnia to ensure the efficient implementation of the civilian aspects of the peace settlement and to remain in close contact with the IFOR commander to facilitate the discharge of their respective responsibilities. But the civilian implementation institutions mandated at Dayton began the operation under considerable disadvantages. These organizations had to be created, funded, and staffed on the ground after the military deployment. This delay resulted in public pressure for IFOR to take on a larger role in implementing civilian tasks. Once the OHR established itself in theater, the impression created was that where the OHR should have been taking the lead on projects such as providing gas, electricity, and water, it was expected that IFOR would take the lead. As a result, mission creep was a natural occurrence because of the competence and ability of the CIMIC organization and a lack of visible activity in these areas by civil agencies.

This method of mission extension had problems, however. With no visible OHR staff to tackle civilian infrastructure problems, and because CIMIC did not immediately assume this mission, there was considerable delay in assessing what exactly required reconstruction. It took until August 1996, a full eight months after the standup of IFOR, before CJCIMIC completed a comprehensive assessment by *obstina* (county) and even longer to mobilize funding and resources to begin solving many of these problems. The locals continued to experience life without drinkable water, reliable electricity, or safe heat. The High Representative was not a UN Special Representative—that is, a representative with UN authority. The High Representative's political guidance originated from the steering board of the Peace Implementation Council, which was not a standing, internationally recognized political organization. As such, the absence of an organization with which the North Atlantic Council could coordinate policy hampered synchronization of civil-military implementation of the GFAP. Given the UN's reluctance to play a lead role, there was effectively no internationally recognized political organization providing overall direction. As a consequence, actors operated autonomously within a loose framework of cooperation, but without a formal structure for developing unified policy.

INTERNATIONAL CIVILIAN RESPONSE

The civil cooperation situation in Bosnia was unique in that members of many NGOs and some humanitarian relief IOs were already actively engaged when the IFOR deployment commenced. In fact, there were an estimated 530 NGOs in theater at D+1. But this situation created its own set of problems. When IFOR entered the theater, the CIMIC deployment was modestly delayed. As UNPROFOR forces withdrew or transferred into IFOR, valuable CIMIC turnover opportunities were lost. Without advanced information, the NGOs assumed that IFOR would continue, if not increase, the same type of support that UNPROFOR had provided to them. The philosophy advanced by IFOR, however, was quite different than UNPROFOR's vision. IFOR refused to provide what it thought the NGO community could provide for themselves because of a fear of causing a dependency on IFOR for essential aspects of support. The root of this philosophy was the promotion of self-sustaining activities in preparation for IFOR's eventual withdrawal. The ARRC sent personnel in early to educate the NGOs on what IFOR troops would be doing, but the briefing was given only in Sarajevo and not in the field, where a majority of the NGOs were located. There was much confusion.

Authority to rebuild the Bosnian infrastructure and restore public services was derived from the GFAP. Specifically,

Annex 9, Article 1: Bearing in mind that reconstruction of the infrastructure and the functioning of transportation and other facilities are
important for the economic reconstruction of Bosnia and Herzegovina . . .
[t]he Parties hereby establish a Commission on Public Corporations (the
"Commission") to examine establishing Bosnia and Herzegovina Public
Corporations to operate joint public facilities, such as for the operation
of utility, energy, postal, and communication facilities, for the benefit of
both Entities. . . .[53]

Annex 10, Article 1: The Parties agree that the implementation of the
civilian aspects of the peace agreement will entail a wide range of activities including continuation of the humanitarian aid effort for as long as
necessary [and] reconstruction of infrastructure and economic reconstruction. . . .[54]

Restoration of public services occurred in three stages. As
IFOR deployed, either military components or various NGOs
and IOs provided emergency public services and humanitarian
aid on an ad hoc basis as they followed the military into Bosnia.
Simultaneously, the major international donors, led by the European Commission (EC), the World Bank, USAID, and the European Bank for Reconstruction and Development, met to assess
the damage to the Bosnian economy and infrastructure and to
develop a three-year plan to rebuild the vital elements of Bosnia.
The second phase focused on the construction of power plants,
roads, telephone lines, water services, and sewage, initially near
the major population centers and then spread throughout the
region. Finally, the international community would transfer the
operation and maintenance of public services to local officials,
seeking methods to improve efficiency so that they better serve
the needs of local communities and the international investors
they hope to attract. The following sections examine each of
these phases in more detail.

Phase One (1995–early 1996)

The collapse of the Bosnian economy left the civilian population
highly dependent on outside aid. In support of the IFOR mission, IFOR military engineers breached and cleared obstacles to
enable ground troops to move into position. Although the engineer effort was in support of the security tasks, the local civilian

population took advantage of the newly constructed roads and bridges, thereby increasing their freedom of movement. Moreover, numerous NGOs tended to closely follow the IFOR forces; after temporary bridges were established and mines cleared, the NGOs would re-enter the newly reconnected local communities and provide immediate relief (such as emergency health services and fuel). In some rare cases, the minimum military requirement governing construction equaled the civilian requirement, therefore serving as the initial reconstruction of the civilian infrastructure.

The vast share of multilateral assistance to support post-conflict reconstruction and economic transition in Bosnia was organized by the World Bank through a series of periodic pledging conferences. Recognizing the need, World Bank architects held their first planning meeting with Bosnian officials in Warsaw in January 1995, ten months before the Dayton negotiations. Meeting again in Warsaw in the spring of 1995 with the representatives of the government of Sarajevo, the architects of this project began to generate support and provided official recommendations for Bosnian reconstruction at an informal donor meeting in October 1995.

The pledging conferences started well, with the first two conferences exceeding pledging expectations; however, the momentum quickly slowed. The first formal pledging conference occurred in Brussels on December 21–22, 1995, when donors were asked to support a four-year, $5.1 billion Priority Reconstruction and Recovery Program (PRRP), prepared by the government of Bosnia with the aid of the World Bank, the EC, and the EBRD.[55] Fifty countries and twenty-seven IOs pledged $615 million, exceeding the conference's target by $97 million. Its key objectives were to initiate a broad-based rehabilitation process that would jump-start economic recovery and growth, strengthen government institutions, and support the transition to a market economy. The framework divided reconstruction efforts into thirteen sectors, each of which was to be "chaired" by one of the four major donors.[56] The International Management Group, an IO falling under the umbrella of the UNHCR, provided technological advice and information on high-priority needs and was to loosely coordinate activities among the sectors. But little actual long-term reconstruction occurred. Basic needs in the form of humanitarian relief were being met; however, major reconstruction was conspicuously absent during this phase.

The Brussels meeting was succeeded by a sectoral technical meeting in Paris in January 1996 and a donor information conference in Sarajevo in March 1996. A second pledging conference took place in Brussels on April 12–13, 1996. Fifty-two countries and twenty IOs pledged another $1.23 billion, exceeding the conference's target by $30 million.[57] Of the approximately $5 billion pledged in humanitarian, peace implementation, and postconflict reconstruction assistance to Bosnia, the overwhelming preponderance, an estimated $4.2 billion, was pledged at the four Brussels pledging conferences to support the PRRP. The United States alone had pledged some $30 million, but $15 million of this was blocked by congressional prohibitions on aid to the Republika Srpska.[58] In addition, neither the $10 million pledged by the European Union (EU) nor the $17 million for the UN Trust Fund were delivered. These shortfalls in aid significantly delayed reconstruction. According to Hertic, Sapcanin, and Woodward:

> Much of the pledge gap in Bosnia reflected delays in delivery and implementation, not nonfeasance or default. Causes of these delays could be found on both the donor side, where inexperience created heavy start-up costs, and the recipient side, where host-government procedures were woefully underdeveloped. Delay was exacerbated by the decision-making procedures of the peace agreement itself, by the dominant role of political conditionality in the use of aid, and by the complex coordination problems of so large an operation as the "Dayton" mission.[59]

Given the size and complexity of the PRRP and the large number of donors helping to implement it, success required close aid coordination among the donors and with the government. Deliberations among the World Bank, the EC, the Group of Seven (G-7) countries,[60] and the Netherlands produced an elaborate and evolving structure to coordinate assistance to Bosnia, but little actual construction to improve the physical infrastructure was completed on the ground.

Phase Two (1996–1999)

By mid-1996 a combination of NGOs and IFOR forces provided most emergency public services (although at different levels of efficiency) and major international donors mobilized plans to begin reconstructing the critical infrastructure. Although each of the major donors adopted different strategies to coordinate efforts in their assigned sectors, all of the donors attempted to coordinate the particular needs of each locality with the overall development plans,[61] contracted work to private corporations (either local or international corporations),[62] and coordinated their efforts with the local IFOR/SFOR commanders.[63] According to High Representative Carl Bildt:

> It was certainly important that so much money was pledged, but it is even more important that it should be spent wisely, in fairness both to the people of Bosnia and to the taxpayers in the donor countries. My office holds meetings at the strategic level both in Brussels and in Sarajevo, where we aim to prevent the agencies stepping on each other's toes and running competing programs. We express our concerns where funding is inadequate in the key infrastructural areas like power, water supply, transport, and communications. But it is important to understand that we are not an executive agency with programs and budget of our own. My job is to coordinate and advise, to monitor and persuade—often to cajole and to be the catalyst.[64]

A sample of various infrastructure challenges in coal production, the natural gas sector, and the rehabilitation of district heating illustrates the immediate problems that Bosnian post-conflict reconstruction faced. The coal-sector reconstruction efforts identified the lowest cost and most competitive mines in order to restore output to minimum acceptable levels to provide sufficient fuel for coal-dependent combined heat and power plants. Extensive war damage made rehabilitation of some mines prohibitively expensive; others were clearly not economical; and long-term demand was likely to decline as the country modernized from its command-economy past to more efficient methods in the country's heat and power plants. In addition, efforts were made to transfer low-cost mines to private-sector ownership. The immediate priority in the natural gas sector was to restore safe service to acceptable levels, to help fund consumption, and to manage excess demand by introducing tariffs that cover basic costs. Reconstruction programs helped to reconfigure the gas network and helped to train staff in modern gas utility management.[65]

To rehabilitate district heating throughout Bosnia, the highest priority was given to the restoration of urban heating services to adequate levels as soon as possible. Repair made sense because there was no readily available and efficient alter-native supply of heat, and these services were essential to the health of the population. Destroyed, cracked, and rusted heat exchangers, pipes, radiators, and valves within buildings had to be reconditioned or replaced. A major network planning effort was launched to determine the optimal configuration of each city's future heating system. Sectoral institutions were strengthened through staff training in modern district heating management and operating techniques.

Initially, NGOs delivered supplies and constructed new components of the infrastructure under a high degree of threat from either mines or locals. Further, political instability between the two entities of the Bosnian state (the Bosnian-Croat Federation and the Republika Srpska) and inside the Federation (between the Croat and Muslim governments) persisted throughout much of the second phase. Conflicts among various ministries over development priorities were symptomatic of the political instability. The military role in the reconstruction process tended to evolve with security conditions. Early in the phase, IFOR focused on providing protection (including demining and providing escorts) for the delivery of supplies, providing security at construction sites, transporting construction crews through dangerous points in the region, and providing assets to deliver supplies. However, as security concerns eased, various IFOR and SFOR components devoted more human and equipment resources to the actual construction of infrastructure. For instance, in 1998 SFOR helped repair a waste management plant near Sarajevo, and the SFOR Engineering Branch assisted with snow removal in primarily civilian areas during the February 2000 blizzard. But, again, these military efforts were either equipment or personnel related—no funds were expended to promote civilian-only endeavors.

Phase Three (1999–present)

By 1999, the major international donors shifted their efforts from construction to the transfer of ownership and maintenance of the various public services to the Bosnian government and private companies. The remaining challenge was to train locals to properly run and maintain the facilities and transfer the management in such a manner to move Bosnia toward a successful private-sector, market-led economy. Since the end of hostilities, the condition of the transport infrastructure has significantly improved, mainly through the implementation of the World Bank's ETRP and SFOR activities to restore strategic infrastructure. Major transportation bottlenecks remain, however. More than half of the main road network still needs to be rehabilitated. Road maintenance needs to be urgently undertaken to avoid further deterioration of infrastructure, and maintenance organizations need to be organized and equipped. In the railway sector, the economically important part of the network was restored to minimum military standards, but implementation of the operating agreements and further rehabilitation are needed before commercial trains can run regularly. Extensive work is still required on the Sarajevo Airport to accommodate regular civilian traffic. The bottom line is that the public transport systems will continue to require a considerable level of assistance in the years to come.

ASSESSMENT

Soon after the beginning and toward the end of the twentieth century, Sarajevo found itself at war. At the end of the century,

Sarajevo enjoys peace, at least a short-term peace. The guns have remained silent in Bosnia for more than eight years, but the precarious truce concluded at Dayton has not yet made the transition into a permanent state of stability. Large parts of the country were destroyed and depopulated, and the incomplete transition from communism to democracy and a free-market economy has compounded the task of postconflict reconstruction. But the way to long-term peace lies through reconstruction. Breaking the cycle of destitution and hopelessness is the only way to break the continuing cycle of violence.

In their final chapter, the authors of the first Carnegie Report on the Balkans, writing in 1913–1914, observed that the future seemed "well-nigh hopeless." Such pessimism was well warranted. Shortly after the publication of the report, Europe was engulfed by World War I. As of now, no comparable catastrophe looms on the European horizon, although Bosnia is now at a crossroads. IFOR was able to stabilize the security situation in Bosnia with impressive efficiency. IFOR deployed rapidly along the cease-fire lines, separated the three armies, and created a weapons-exclusion zone at the IEBL. In accordance with precise requirements and timetables set out in the Dayton Agreement, heavy weapons were destroyed or moved into cantonment sites and were subjected to regular inspection by international forces. The three armies were demobilized to peacetime levels, and their deployment and movement in the field were controlled by IFOR to reduce tensions.

Through these measures, the military mission successfully contained the risk of renewed armed conflict. It did little, however, to promote the creation of an effective state. In the Dayton Agreement, IFOR was given the authority, but not the obligation or the funding, to assist with the broader civilian goals of the peace process. In the first year of the peace process, it was resistant to deploy its forces to prevent interethnic violence, apprehend indicted war criminals, or support the return of refugees and displaced persons through a comprehensive infrastructure reconstruction program. In addition, the military objective to physically separate the armies tended to undermine the long-term prospects of unifying the territory. With no progress to date in merging the three armies, the division of territory into separate military zones continues to support illegal parallel military structures.

On the civilian side of the mission, the greater part of available resources was directed into physical reconstruction, driven by urgent humanitarian considerations and the need to stimulate the economy. Jointly coordinated by the World Bank and the EC, the priority reconstruction program attracted more than $5 billion in international aid; however, much of it was delayed in its arrival or was tied strictly to humanitarian uses. At the time of the Dayton Agreement, more than 2,000 kilometers of roads, seventy bridges, half of the electricity network, and more than a third of the housing stock was destroyed. Despite the logistical difficulties, by 1999 the reconstruction program had repaired a third of the housing, and most urban infrastructure had been restored to prewar levels, from telephone lines to electric power generation, from water services to the number of primary schools.[66]

Disbursing this volume of international aid in such a short period of time was an enormous operational challenge for the international agencies involved—a challenge that was not met with success in the critical first year. It required that the responsible organizations make the rapid disbursement of funds their principal objective; however, much of the funding was not available, nor was the organization established to accomplish disbursement. In the first two years, aid was withheld from the Republika Srpska because of the influence of indicted war criminals on the government; the aid was made available in large quantities only in 1998, following the election of a new government. In the federation, however, political and institutional considerations played little part in the reconstruction program. The World Bank entered Bosnia on the basis of a post–natural disaster operational policy, which explicitly excludes institution-building objectives; this policy would serve to have long-term negative effects.

In order to carry out urgent reconstruction in the postconflict environment, the international agencies tended to bypass the new constitutional structures and deal directly with the local authorities that had direct control over the physical infrastructure. Aid was disbursed at local levels by implementing agencies or through municipal, cantonal, or entity authorities. This enabled local warlords and separate ethnic power structures to greatly benefit from the reconstruction program—both materially, through the control of construction companies and the provision of goods and services to international reconstruction agencies, and politically, by being able to nominate the beneficiaries of international aid.

As long as the distribution of financial or material assistance was involved, the ethnic power structures were willing to cooperate with the international community. However, to reach certain political objectives such as minority return or implementation of the new constitutional structures, international efforts met with strong resistance. As a result, international agencies focused on physical reconstruction, where results were achievable, at the expense of institution building or other political objectives. The lack of attention to long-term civilian institutions ultimately became an important limiting factor for the reconstruction program. For example, the failure to establish local authorities responsible for ongoing maintenance means that roads repaired with international funds now require a second round of repairs, but nobody in the local government was capable of managing the required ongoing maintenance program. Although most of the rail track was repaired by 1999, the lack of central authorities to operate inter-entity transport means that the volume of rail traffic remains low.

Over the next two to three years Bosnia must begin to generate a sustainable-growth momentum in order to survive. Postwar growth of the past four years has been strong—brought about by a slow but successful reconstruction effort and sound macro performance—but it is not yet sustainable. Though recovery has brought a generalized increase in incomes, many Bosnians remain worse off than before the war, and unemployment is painfully high. Consensus is difficult because of a fragmented postwar governance and has been at the root of a slower-than-hoped-for reform effort. Two external factors will also affect the development outlook in the next two to three years: with completion of the postwar PRRP (1996–1999), donors will now begin to phase down their programs of support. Therefore, fiscal and external adjustment as well as other less tangible adjustments will be required over this critical two-to-three-year period. Finally, the Stability Pact for Southeastern Europe presents an opportunity for closer integration with European institutions; however, accelerated structural and institutional reforms to bring the country closer to European standards will be required to take the most advantage of this opportunity.

Bosnia was NATO's first deployment and served as a crucial test case for policies grounded in theory but little practice. There are better ways to conduct postconflict reconstruction—methods that can eradicate the delays in funding that can jump-start the economy and kick off its formation of the required institutions to promote long-term peace. The international community must perfect these methods for peacekeeping and peacebuilding or the cost, not only in money but also in human lives, will continue to escalate.

Bridge repair in Bosnia. German army engineers in NATO's Implementation Force undertake repairs to two Mabey-Johnson bridges in Bosnia: one across the Drina River going into Gorazde (right) and a span in the vicinity of Sarajevo (below). Gorazde was one of the UN's original "safe havens" and later connected to the Bosniak ethnic enclave by the Gorazde Road; the bridge was purchased with NATO/IFOR funds.

Demining activity in Bosnia. IFOR's marking of a culvert over a river bed where a cache of mines had been stored off a road south of Sarajevo (above), and Croatian army troops checking for mines on railroad tracks near Sisak, Croatia (left). The Croatian troops had no personal protection or demining equipment; usually, they probed, looked for trip wires, and removed the mines, resulting in higher casualty rates in demining actions than those experienced by IFOR UXO units.

Bunkers south of Sarajevo before destruction by NATO forces. These bunkers, on the confrontation line that Serb forces used to shell the Bosnian capital in 1993, were poorly constructed and often failed during heavy snowstorms or sporadic Bosnian artillery fire. As part of IFOR engineers' mission to clear the Zone of Separation to promote freedom of movement, the removal of these and many other bunkers in the ZOS posed a challenge to the engineering units; the unsteady bunkers typically had stores of ammunition and were mined.

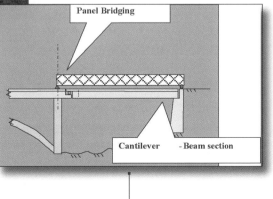

Bridge repair along the Main Supply Route in KFOR's U.S. sector. The American contingent of KFOR contracted with a Macedonian firm to repair the fifty-year-old bridge, south of Urosevac headed toward the Macedonian border, which was beginning to fail because of increased heavy traffic. The schematic diagram depicts the engineering techniques the Macedonian firm used—techniques that engineers in the U.S. and western Europe would probably find antiquated but were successful nevertheless.

Panel Bridging

Cantilever   - Beam section

KOSOVO: KFOR

3

KOSOVO

IN 1998, NATO'S ATTENTION TURNED to the Kosovo region of Serbia because of the increasing flow of refugees into western Europe and Albania and concerns about the conflict spilling over into the Former Yugoslav Republic of Macedonia (FYROM). Open conflict between Serbian military and police forces and Kosovar Albanian forces resulted in the deaths of more than 1,500 Kosovar Albanians and forced 400,000 people from their homes. Of large concern was Yugoslav president Slobodan Milosevic's disregard for diplomatic efforts aimed at peacefully resolving the crisis and the destabilizing role of militant Kosovar Albanian forces.

The military intervention into Kosovo proved to be unlike any other experience. Unlike Bosnia, where NATO entered the country supported by a UN mandate and on the heels of a UN Protection Force, an international security organization conducted the Kosovo intervention without the benefit of an initial legitimizing UN mandate. Whereas Bosnia was a separate, autonomous republic of Yugoslavia and later a state in its own right, Kosovo was a province of a larger state—a state that did not want NATO intervention within its borders but that was coerced by aerial bombing to accept NATO forces. Whereas Bosnia was heavily industrialized with a relatively developed baseline infrastructure throughout the country with peaks of modernity in Sarajevo, Kosovo was agrarian, with minimal infrastructure. Even the largest town, Pristina, was somewhat backward.

The difference in governmental structures also plays a role in determining the infrastructure starting point for each mission. Although the Dayton Agreement established a Bosnian government consisting of three ethnicities, the subgovernment, primarily the ministries that ran many of the day-to-day activities, existed before the war and could be rebuilt after the war. There was a lack of infrastructure maintenance through four years of war, and many skilled workers and managers fled the country; however, the entire ministerial structure did not have to be reinvented and could be revitalized with external help. Kosovo, in contrast, did not have that advantage. Extensive Serbian oppression caused the Albanian majority to establish a parallel government, concentrating on things such as basic and higher education. The infrastructure, however, was untouched, by either the higher Serbian government or the ethnic Albanian parallel structure, for more than a decade. Lack of funds, the absence of a viable governmental structure, and lack of interest by the Serbian government in building Kosovo resulted in a province lacking many of the most basic infrastructure needs required for self-sustainment.

After numerous rounds of sanctions, the six-nation Contact Group (United States, Britain, France, Germany, Italy, and Russia) met on January 29, 1999, and agreed to convene urgent negotiations between the parties to the conflict under international mediation. They invited the two sides to Rambouillet, near Paris, to start peace talks on February 6.[1] To stop the interethnic violence and to induce the parties to comply, the NAC authorized Secretary-General Javier Solana to launch NATO air strikes against targets in Serbia if the warring Serb and Albanian factions failed to reach a peace agreement by February 20. The draft peace plan taken to Rambouillet called for a three-year interim settlement that would provide greater autonomy for Kosovo within Yugoslavia and the deployment of a NATO-led international military force to help implement the agreement.[2] The parties' goal was an Interim Agreement for Peace and Self-Governance in Kosovo, known as the Rambouillet Accords, affirming the territorial integrity of the FRY and providing that an international meeting would be convened in three years to determine a mechanism for final settlement of the Kosovo problem. The FRY would withdraw its army forces from Kosovo, withdraw Ministry of Interior units from Kosovo not assigned there prior to February 1, 1998, and withdraw air defense forces beyond a twenty-five-kilometer Mutual Safety Zone. NATO would lead a military force to ensure compliance.[3]

A second round of talks was held in Paris, from March 15 to 18. At the end of this round, the Kosovar Albanian delegation signed the proposed peace agreement, but the Serbian delegation refused to sign. Immediately, FRY Army and paramilitary troops deployed from their garrisons in Kosovo in violation of the October agreement and, with 20,000 additional Serb troops massed at the northern Kosovo border,[4] compelled tens of thousands of people to flee their homes in the face of a systematic offensive. In response, NATO's Operation Allied Force began on March 24 with air strikes directed against targets in Serbia and Kosovo, signaling the first military offensive action undertaken by NATO without specific UN endorsement. Russia and China, each with veto power on the UN Security Council, continued to oppose the use of force to resolve the Kosovo crisis; therefore, UN Security Council approval was not pursued. However, the September 23, 1998, UN Security Council resolution, which called for the immediate withdrawal of Serbian security forces from Kosovo, did reference the UN Charter's Article VII and permitted military force to maintain international security.

At the start of the operation, only a small number of targets were approved for strike, but after protracted discussions about the Serb acceleration of ethnic cleansing of Kosovar Albanians, the NAC authorized attacks against a broader range of fixed targets throughout Serbia proper and to escalate attacks on Yugoslav forces in Kosovo.[5] General Naumann argued that NATO should start "attacking both ends of the snake by hitting the head and cutting off the tail"[6] to hit targets most closely associated with the regime's sources of authority throughout Serbia. On April 1, NATO began to strike infrastructure in Serbia, including a major bridge over the Danube River at Novi Sad, but restricted targets in the immediate Belgrade area. On

April 12, NATO struck the oil refinery and oil storage facilities at Pancevo. As Belgrade continued its killing of Kosovars, NATO faced mounting pressure to halt the ethnic violence, to end the conflict on terms acceptable to NATO, and to put greater pressure on the Yugoslav leadership while preserving NATO's unity.

NATO started to attack electric power transformers and official radio and television stations. The United States advocated extensive attacks on electrical power generation, but other NATO members, especially France, counseled restraint. To address the French concerns, the United States offered to use CBU-94, a then-secret cluster bomb that ejects large numbers of fine carbon-graphite threads, short-circuiting electrical lines and causing power outages until the threads can be removed. Although these attacks were ostensibly aimed against the military use of electrical power, they actually had greater effect on the civilian economy. Military users had backup generators, especially to support the vital communication function.

THE MILITARY TECHNICAL AGREEMENT

Beginning in late May 1999, U.S. deputy secretary of state Strobe Talbott (representing NATO), former Russian premier Viktor Chernomyrdin, and Finnish president Martti Ahtisaari (representing the European Union) discussed the conditions required to end the conflict. Chernomyrdin subsequently met with Milosevic; the Yugoslav leader insisted that all countries that had participated in the air campaign should not deploy peacekeeping forces to Kosovo, excluding all of NATO's prominent members, and wanted Russia to occupy a northern sector where the Serb population was concentrated. The United States rejected this idea because it could have led to partition. During a dramatic final negotiating session in Bonn on June 1, the United States and Russia finally reached agreement on terms for ending the air operation. Ahtisaari and Chernomyrdin delivered these non-negotiable terms to Milosevic in Belgrade on June 2.

Faced with a solid front, which included the only major power that might have sided with Yugoslavia, Milosevic capitulated.[7] After seventy-eight days of increasingly intense air strikes that inflicted damage on Yugoslavia's infrastructure and its armed forces, Milosevic agreed on June 3 to a peace plan based on NATO's demands. On June 9, military officials signed the Military Technical Agreement (MTA) affirming the terms of the peace plan, providing specific details on its implementation. The agreement was signed by Lieutenant General Sir Michael Jackson, on behalf of NATO; Colonel General Svetozar Marjanovic of the Yugoslav Army; and Lieutenant General Obrad Stevanovic of the Ministry of Internal Affairs.[8]

On June 10, Secretary-General Solana announced a temporary suspension of NATO's air operations against Yugoslavia, stating that NATO was ready to undertake its new mission to bring the people back to their homes and to build a lasting and just peace in Kosovo.[9] Later that same day, the United Nations approved Security Council Resolution 1244. The resolution announced the Security Council's decision to deploy an international civil and security presence in Kosovo under UN auspices.[10] In part, UN Security Council Resolution 1244 demanded a political solution based on the general principles set forth by the Group of Eight foreign ministers on May 6, 1999, and further contained in the Ahtisaari-Chernomyrdin Agreement of June 2, 1999: the full cooperation of Yugoslavia in the rapid implementation of the principles of the MTA; an immediate end to violence and repression in Kosovo; and a complete phased withdrawal of all military, police, and paramilitary forces in Kosovo. The United Nations was also designated to lead the interim civil authority, later termed the UN Interim Administration in Kosovo (UNMIK).[11]

KFOR—Operation Joint Guardian

Following the adoption of UN Security Council Resolution 1244, Lieutenant General Jackson, serving as the Kosovo Force (KFOR) commander and acting on the instructions of the NAC, prepared for the rapid deployment of the security force (Operation Joint

Table 7. KFOR Responsibilities

- Deter renewed hostilities, enforce the cease fire, and both ensure the withdrawal and prevent the return of Yugoslav military, police, and paramilitary forces.

- Demilitarize the KLA and other armed Kosovar Albanian groups.

- Establish a secure environment in which refugees and displaced persons can return home in safety, the international civil presence can operate, a transitional administration can be established, and humanitarian aid can be delivered.

- Ensure public safety and order and supervise the removal of mines until the international civil presence can take over.

- Support the work of the international civil presence and coordinate closely with it.

- Conduct border monitoring duties.

- Ensure the protection of movement itself, the international civil presence, and other international organizations.

Source: United Nations, UN Security Council Resolution 1244, S/RES/1244 (1999), June 10, 1999.

Guardian) mandated by the UN Security Council. The resolution set forth very specific guidelines for KFOR, and Lieutenant General Jackson tailored his forces to reflect that guidance (outlined in table 7).

On June 12, 1999 (D-Day), NATO entered the province with a force of 20,000 troops divided into six brigades (France, Germany, Italy, the United States, and two from the United Kingdom). Within six days, all lead elements had entered Kosovo, facing serious challenges immediately upon arrival. Yugoslav military forces were still present in large numbers, the Kosovo Liberation Army (KLA) was armed and highly visible, fighting had not subsided, and nearly a million people were refugees. There was little electricity or water, homes were destroyed, roads were mined, bridges were down, and schools and hospitals were out of action. Radio and television were off the air—ordinary life in Kosovo was suspended.

The immediate priority was to fill the security vacuum that developed between the outgoing and incoming forces, one that could have been filled by the KLA or any other armed group. In eleven days, the operation achieved the stated aim: the withdrawal of Yugoslav forces from Kosovo and their replacement by KFOR as the only legitimate military force under UN Security Council Resolution 1244.[12] On June 20 at 5:25 P.M., the full withdrawal of Yugoslav forces from Kosovo was confirmed, more than six hours ahead of schedule.[13] At confirmation, Secretary-General Solana announced the formal termination of the air campaign.

NATO forces were at the forefront of the humanitarian efforts to relieve the suffering of many thousands of refugees forced to flee Kosovo by the Serbian ethnic cleansing campaign. In FYROM and in Albania, NATO troops built refugee camps, refugee reception centers, and emergency feeding stations, as well as moved many hundreds of tons of humanitarian aid to those in need. NATO assisted the UNHCR with coordination of humanitarian aid flights and supplemented these flights by using aircraft from member countries. The Euro-Atlantic Disaster Response Coordination Center established at NATO in May 1998 also played an important role in the coordination of support to UNHCR relief operations.[14]

The Multinational Brigades (MNBs) established order, provided human-itarian assistance, and supported UNMIK and the other agencies. Each brigade adopted schools and facilitated spring planting through the delivery of seed, fertilizer, and fuel. The MNBs ran countless patrols to increase freedom of movement, enabling the citizens of Kosovo to return to their farms and businesses. The brigades and the UNMIK police jointly investigated numerous reports of criminal and suspicious activities.

KFOR was actively involved in the demilitarization of Kosovo. With the arrival of KFOR, military and police forces from Yugoslavia completed their withdrawal and met the final timelines of the MTA. KLA forces complied with the terms of the "Undertaking of Demilitarization and Transformation by the KLA," signed on June 20. This agreement provided for a "cease-fire by the KLA, their disengagement from the zones of conflict, [and] subsequent demilitarization and reintegration into civil society."[15] Scheduled to occur within ninety days, KFOR units established weapons storage sites throughout the province to collect all weapons in accordance with the agreed turn-in procedures. Although the KLA was initially slow in turning in its weapons, the numbers increased significantly as the deadline approached. By September 20, Lieutenant General Jackson certified that the KLA force had completed its process of demilitarization and had ceased to display the KLA insignia.[16]

Tons of weapons and ammunition were seized or handed to KFOR: thousands of pistols and rifles, hand grenades, antipersonnel mines, rocket launchers, artillery pieces, mortar bombs, rifle bombs, antitank mines, fuses, explosives, and even antitank rockets and missiles. The transformation of the KLA occurred through resettlement programs, the creation of the Kosovo Police Service, and the establishment of the Kosovo Protection Corps (KPC), an unarmed civil relief organization dedicated to the rebuilding of Kosovo's infrastructure. Under the direction of KFOR and UNMIK, the KPC was established on September 21, 1999, to provide disaster response, conduct search and rescue, provide humanitarian assistance, assist in demining, and contribute to rebuilding the infrastructure and communities. It had no role, however, in defense, law enforcement, riot control, internal security, or any other task involving the maintenance of law and order, and the maximum strength of the KPC was established at 5,000 (3,000 active and 2,000 reserve).[17] The result was a country safer than it was before, with less illegal activity, a decrease in violent interethnic crimes, and the opportunity to rebuild its infrastructure and economy. Although KFOR's main responsibility is to create a secure environment, the multinational force provides human and other resources, and skills, to various organizations and agencies working under the UNMIK umbrella.

THE CONDITION OF KOSOVO
AT THE END OF HOSTILITIES

The war in Kosovo in 1998 and 1999 and the NATO air campaign in 1999 caused immense physical destruction—of housing and electricity, water, sewage, transport, and other infrastructure—and eliminated social, public safety, and other government services. In mid-1999, UNMIK assumed the administration of the province and found a daunting challenge. In the first six months following the war, emergency humanitarian assistance facilitated the return of refugees and provided food and other immediate assistance to help people survive the winter. Reconstruction and development efforts, however, may take many years, cost billions of dollars, and require support from multiple donors.

Although a number of estimates of postconflict reconstruction needs were developed while the war was still raging, all were conjecture; none was based on a comprehensive on-the-ground survey. NATO forces attempted to gain insight into the extent of damage using satellite imagery and refugee accounts; however, neither provided much credible information. Infrastructure conditions up to Kosovo's borders were well documented in the AFSOUTH Contingency Engineer section archives, but there was a significant void as to the postconflict condition of Kosovo itself. Therefore, little quality intelligence existed on which to base a reconstruction plan. The first major assessment conducted by a European Commission Task Force in July 1999 focused on housing and local village infrastructure. It estimated that 58 percent of the houses in 1,300 villages had been damaged, most of them severely. The estimated cost to repair this housing was

$1.2 billion, and for other village facilities—including schools, clinics, local electricity, and clean water—$43.9 million.

The EC and the World Bank conducted a second, more far-reaching round of assessments, covering energy, telecommunications, transport, and commercial and social infrastructure prior to the second donor conference held in mid-November 1999. Laying out reconstruction and development objectives in Kosovo over the next four to five years, the EC–World Bank report estimated the cost of reaching those objectives at $2.3 billion in external financing, on highly concessional terms. According to the task force, nearly half the funds were needed before early 2001. In addition, government operations during this period, taking into account local revenues, were expected to suffer a deficit that would have to be made up by external financing—estimated at $107 million in 2000. At the November 1999 donor conference, donors were asked to contribute to the operational budget, as well as to undertake programs outlined in the reconstruction strategy. A brief look at the starting point for reconstruction will help in the understanding of the huge reconstruction challenge that faced KFOR and the international community.

The Economy

Kosovo was traditionally the poorest and least developed part of Yugoslavia. Throughout the 1990s, the region suffered a severe economic crisis, with GDP contracting by 50 percent between 1990 and 1995, falling to less than $400 per capita by 1995, and unemployment rising as high as 70 percent. According to the International Monetary Fund, the underlying causes of crisis (lack of competitiveness in a changing international environment and economic sanctions on Yugoslavia) were further compounded by the so-called "enforced measures." Facing hardship, Kosovars adjusted to the situation in three main ways: (1) emigration, mainly to western Europe, building up a diaspora that may play an important role in the region's economic recovery; (2) return to rural areas, which resulted in more than a doubling of the active population in the agriculture sector between 1990 and

1997; and (3) development of a large "gray" economy (informal activities of a legal nature) and of some "black" activities (of an illegal nature).[18]

Before 1989, Kosovo was transforming from a predominately rural society to a more urban one, and the portion of the active population engaged in agriculture had fallen to about 26 percent. But, throughout the 1990s, after a number of industrial workers and employees lost their jobs, the rural population increased substantially. In 1998, agricultural activities, together with forestry and agro-business, accounted for about 60 percent of employment and played a key role in food security at the household level. Agriculture was largely based on small family farms, and productivity was low. Typically, farming provided about half of the family income, the other half coming from both remittances and off-farm incomes.

At the cessation of hostilities, agricultural production and related processing industries came to a standstill. In the view of the World Bank, the 1999 spring cropping season was largely forgone, 50 percent of the cattle and 85 percent of the poultry were lost or killed, 55 percent of the farm equipment was damaged, many farm buildings were destroyed, agro-processing equipment was looted or made unusable (particularly privately owned small and medium enterprises), and housing and rural infrastructure suffered severe damage.[19] Kosovo relied heavily on commercial imports and large-scale donor assistance to meet its immediate food demand. Throughout the past decade, formal services (veterinary or advisory services) were not available for privately owned farms, access to farm fertilizers was severely limited, investments were curtailed, and major irrigation schemes that were developed in the 1970s collapsed. On the other hand, Kosovars developed informal parallel structures covering a wide range of agriculture services—fertilizer, equipment, and processing facilities. These structures, which were marked by an impressive capacity for private initiatives, may be able to be replicated and could be key factors in driving rural recovery. In the long run, growth and employment will be driven both by the development of nonagricultural activities and by the reorientation of agriculture toward activities in which Kosovo farmers may have a decided comparative advantage, possibly competing internationally (for example, labor-intensive cultivation of fruits and vegetables, and some livestock production, rather than grain and industrial crops).

The Transportation Sector

The transportation sector in 1999 was in poor condition, and substantial donor assistance, estimated to be $165 million by the EC, was needed for its rehabilitation. The 3,800-kilometer road network, including 623 kilometers of main roads and 1,300 kilometers of regional roads, was generally poor, with a fairly low network density at 0.35 kilometers per square kilometer.[20] Conflict-related damage was relatively limited (only about a dozen bridges were destroyed on the main highways), but the lack of maintenance throughout the 1990s produced deplorable effects. Damage was most severe on roads that were the responsibility of municipalities, including parts of the main and regional roads going through the municipality. In a number of cities, some sections of the main network deteriorated to the point that vehicles actually drove on the sub-base. Much urgent work was done by KFOR, putting temporary bridges or bypasses into place wherever needed for military purposes. But large parts of the road network were unstable, with a long backlog of maintenance. Services to clear roads during the winter were suspended, causing stoppage along many of Kosovo's secondary roads. KFOR contracted with local companies for snow and ice clearance for its military designated routes; however, most roads throughout the region were not included as part of this network. Reconstruction priority for the road network include:

■ Permanent reconstruction of all damaged bridges.

■ Patching, overlays, reconstruction, and drainage works on about 450 kilometers of main and regional roads.

- Rehabilitation of 450 kilometers of gravel and dirt roads, with labor-intensive methods, to help rural employment.

- Constructing bypasses in key locations (border crossing points with FYROM).

- Provision of essential equipment to local companies (trucks, earth and overlay works equipment, spare parts for asphalt plants and crushing units) as payment for their work.

The prewar railway network in Kosovo consisted of 330 kilometers of single, nonelectrified, standard-gauge track, much of which was in relatively mountainous terrain with steep slopes and sharp curves. The network consisted essentially of two lines, one north-south and one east-west, that cross at Kosovo-Polje, and one branch line between Klina and Prizren. In the 1980s, the rail traffic was about three million tons of freight.[21] Most of this consisted of bulk commodities needed for or produced by the mining, metallurgical, and chemical industry. As Kosovo was an agrarian economy, passenger traffic was limited to about four million passengers per year, mainly over short distances. Financial problems and the need for hefty subsidies were a permanent characteristic of the antiquated system.

Traffic on the lines to Peja and Prizren ceased in early 1998 because of security concerns, and the line to Podujeva was discontinued several years ago. In addition, the section between Kosovo-Polje and the airport suffered heavy damage during the conflict. In June 1999, KFOR re-established traffic between Pristina and Volkovo (at the border with FYROM) where it runs an average of four trains daily for KFOR and humanitarian supply needs. The future of the railway network, however, is closely tied to the political situation in Kosovo. The EBRD recommended that no railway investment take place until the situation in the FRY was clarified—especially the opening of the line to Belgrade—and until the future of the mining, metallurgical, and heavy chemical industries in Kosovo is determined. Until then, money spent on an underused railway network could be spent in other more deserving sectors.

There is one airport in Kosovo, about fifteen kilometers south of Pristina, and four landing strips (about 500 meters long). The Pristina airport was built in the mid-1960s as a regional airport able to handle mid-sized commercial aircraft, such as the B737. It was not designed to handle the heavier wide-body aircraft that were using the Belgrade airport. The runway has a length of 2,500 meters, and the apron and the terminal are small.[22] Despite its limited importance, the airport suffered serious damage during the conflict. The control tower and technical block were damaged beyond use, the luggage area in the passenger terminal building was destroyed, and the pavements of the runways and taxiways received some relatively minor damage. For military purposes, the British military re-established daylight operations by repairing the runways and taxiways; establishing temporary control-tower radio communications and radar coverage; installing military navigational aids and emergency approach lighting; reconditioning the instrument landing system; and establishing rescue and fire fighting services, emergency power, refueling facilities, and ground-handling operations. Civilian flight operations ceased during the conflict; however, civilian flights have recently resumed. The operations are under some restriction, mainly because of weather conditions, but otherwise are not particularly unusual. According to the EC, the financial benefits are considerable, with estimates ranging up to more than $100,000 per month.

Water Supply, Sewage, and Solid Waste

Most of Kosovo's water supply systems were relatively small and covered urban areas only. The six larger regional schemes supplied water to one or more cities and nearby villages, and served about 900,000 people. A dozen small systems served an additional 150,000 people. Rural water supply systems, however, were nonexistent. Most rural dwellings operated private wells or drew water from artesian springs. Rural wells were generally in bad condition and water quality was poor—not always from pollution of groundwater, but also from negligence of the users.

Most urban areas had combined wastewater and storm water collection systems, but the systems were old and badly maintained. Drainage channels were filled with soil and debris, and caused serious flooding during heavy rains. Sewer systems were of poor quality and frequently had broken pipes, allowing wastewater to infiltrate into the water table. In addition, wastewater treatment plants did not exist throughout the country. Apart from some very simple and hardly maintained industrial wastewater pretreatment facilities, there was no other wastewater treatment. In order to avoid immediate danger to health, wastewater outlets were often located a few kilometers downstream of the city limits. Many riverbeds did not, however, carry water during the summer, and hygienic conditions in rivers downstream of urban areas were very poor. During the 1980s, engineers designed wastewater treatment plants for the few bigger urban areas such as Pristina, but construction never started.

Physical damage to the water collection and treatment facilities as a direct result of shelling was limited to the urban supply systems. Only two pumping stations, a water treatment plant, and some civil structures at the water intake of a storage lake received direct hits. Damage to the plumbing in burned-out houses, however, caused serious problems. Because water companies were short of tools and parts to repair the leaks, water continued to run unabated at many damaged locations. The situation in rural areas was even worse. During the conflict, about half of the rural boreholes and wells were deliberately contaminated, and returning refugees found not only their homes destroyed but also their access to clean water denied. Moreover, other wells, which were not contaminated during the conflict but which had not been used for some time, were subject to pollution from dust and dirt. The EC estimated that 15,000 to 20,000 wells required cleaning or rehabilitating.[23] Overall, adequate institutional frameworks for efficient operation and maintenance of the schemes were virtually nonexistent. In the immediate aftermath of the conflict, a number of key staff left Kosovo. Among other things, service vehicles, tools, protective clothing, and remaining spare parts were lost.

Vehicles and tools left behind were often out of order and certainly beyond cost-effective repair.

Finally, the solid waste situation was critical. The first impression upon entering Kosovo was one of piles of trash along the roadways. Refuse continued to pile up without any system for removal. Most of the trucks that handled the trash containers were lost or damaged, and the trash accumulated, particularly behind apartment buildings in the urban areas. As alternatives, people threw their solid waste into natural watercourses or drains. Many drains were full of refuse along with debris, raising the potential for major flooding. In addition, people washed and swam in the streams. Children playing in the streams became ill from the pollution. A serious consequence was that medical waste was commingled with municipal waste. Hospitals were disposing waste on-site, throwing it in with other waste or attempting to burn it in pits. This waste contained sharps, syringes, bandages, blood-saturated dressings, and body parts, and all posed grave threats in exposing the public to blood-borne pathogens.

Energy

Electricity, primarily from lignite-powered thermal power plants, was Kosovo's main source of energy. Additional sources of energy were four district heating systems and coal production for use by the province's industries and households. Electricity was widely used for all household purposes, including space heating where district heating was not available. In the preconflict period, industrial consumers, mainly Feroniki and Trepca, the two large metal-mining areas, used about 30 percent of the electricity. Kosovo used to be an important net energy exporter, feeding into the high-voltage transmission system of Yugoslavia. Reliable data on electricity generated, generation costs, and consumption patterns are not available; however, the EC study revealed that Kosovo used to produce 4,912 GWh of electricity, of which 2,907 GWh was for domestic consumption and the remainder for export outside the province.[24] As there was no direct conflict-related damage, the power plants suffered mainly from lack of maintenance and mismanagement. The plants were nearing the end of their lives and required heavy maintenance. Conflict-related damage to the secondary distribution network, however, was extensive, estimated to affect 30 percent of the network. Damage was particularly extensive in the Gjakove, Gnjilane, Mitrovica, Peja, and Prizren areas. During recovery, demining operations will have to be carried out in certain areas before reconstruction can begin. As in the water sector, the distribution companies also suffered from lack of tools, vehicles, and equipment, all of which were essential for maintenance purposes.

Coal was extracted from two large mines, Mirage and Bardh. They were large surface mines, extracting low-grade lignite under favorable overburden/coal ratios. The mines were at an advanced state of development and all overburden was dumped into the pits. From 1989 onward, the production of the Kosovo mines dropped gradually to about eight million tons per year—about 50 percent of its design capacity. A further drop, to about six million tons per year, occurred in 1993 and 1994 during the Bosnian conflict.[25] There was no conflict-related physical damage to the mines; however, all mobile equipment was removed from the sites. The main mining equipment remained in operable condition, confirmed by testing of the equipment and on-site inspections, but the mines themselves were in very poor condition because of continued neglect. The amount of coal uncovered and readily available for extraction is limited to one to two months, with a high buildup of overburden material. As a result, mine operations are hampered by steep fronts ripe for dangerous landslides. Immediately at the cessation of hostilities (July 1999), the mines restarted production at a rate of about 200,000 tons per month. Despite the low level of production, there was a stock of 550,000 tons of coal available at the power plants. The high level of stocks enables the mines to meet the reduced power plant demand, despite the lack of auxiliary and mobile equipment, the frequent power outages, and the inability to restart the mining equipment because of the low voltage supplied by the power plants.[26]

Preconflict Kosovo had district heating systems in only four cities. All systems were run by municipally owned district heating enterprises, which ensured the supply and distribution of heat. In addition, district heating prices were well below production costs. Whereas consumption by public facilities such as hospitals, hotels, and administrative buildings was metered, households were invoiced based on an average charge per square meter of living space. In general, the district heating systems appear to have suffered only minor conflict damage. However, in all cities, damage caused by lack of maintenance was significant. The district heating system in Pristina, for example, was more than twenty-five years old and was recognized to be relatively inefficient.

Pollution resulting from power generation, district heating, and associated coal mining was prevalent in the area around Pristina. Estimates from the late 1980s for particulate emissions exceeded World Health Organization guidelines. For the district heating plant, pollution resulted mainly from the poor quality of heavy fuel oil—and it is likely that the only solution is to replace the plant in its entirety, as well as major sections of the distribution systems. There is no adequate institutional framework for the efficient operation of Kosovo's energy system. There is no company structure, no business culture, and no functioning billing service and collection service. Proper records and planning tools are missing and the previous higher-level managers have left, leaving a vacuum at the top. Kosovar Albanians filled most of these positions, but many have insufficient experience.

Telecommunications

With only about 130,000 phone lines in service, Kosovo's telecommunications network had the second-lowest telephone penetration rate in Europe, amounting to about six lines per 100 people (about a quarter of Yugoslavia's average of twenty-two per 100 people).[27] Because very little investment was made in the sector throughout the 1990s, the current network is little different from that of 1989. Only 34 percent of the network was digital, and the remainder was made up of obsolete technology. Party lines and tandem exchanges were common, with all international routing through the exchange in Belgrade. At the cessation of hostilities, telecommunications infrastructure had suffered heavy damage to key installations during the conflict. Communications on the fixed network were limited to local calls, and international access was not available except for limited service on a few exchanges in Pristina. There was no mobile service in the province. Many facilities were destroyed, including a local exchange in Pristina, a tandem exchange in Pristina allowing inter-city service, and two secondary transmission stations in other parts of the country. Although the local exchanges remained mostly in service, there were no spare parts and there were no test equipment, tools, or vehicles for rehabilitation and maintenance. Most exchanges were likely to fail if power outages exceeded their battery capacity. There are no firm estimates of the number of subscribers' lines that were destroyed during the conflict, but it is thought that some 110,000 lines remain in service.[28]

A rapid rehabilitation of the telecommunications network is key for successful recovery because the current situation may hamper the restart of large-scale economic activity. In principle, telecommunications is an income-generating activity, and some part of the development program could be financed from private sources. It is expected that the private sector could and should play a leading role in the development of a functioning mobile service and the modernization effort. Still, in view of the urgency of the situation, the extent of damage, and the poor development of the network in the first place, as well as the current uncertainties concerning Kosovo's political status, some donor support will be needed for repair of the fixed network and to catalyze private-sector activities. Such support should be heavily front-loaded so as to allow for a rapid resumption of telecommunications in the region.

Mine Threat

Before the recent conflict erupted in Kosovo, the province was uncontaminated by land mines, booby traps, and UXO. Unlike other areas of Europe, no explosive materials had been laid during the two World Wars. The inhabitants of Kosovo were, therefore, unaware of the dangers of land mines and UXO. In spite of the danger and in defiance of the advice of the international community, 800,000 refugees spontaneously returned to the province in June 1999 as KFOR forces moved in. At the time, there was no data available regarding land mine and UXO contamination. However, during the refugee crisis, UNHCR coordinated a massive land mine awareness campaign in asylum countries and at the borders. The toll paid for the spontaneous return was relatively limited, with 232 casualties, of which 40 were fatal (from June 12 to August 31, 1999). Most of the refugees had returned to Kosovo by the end of August and were trying to resume productive activities; however, up to 25 percent of those activities were directly affected by the presence of land mines and UXO.[29]

Generally, the danger that land mines and UXO posed can be characterized in three distinctive cases:

■ The Yugoslav forces laid minefields both to defend the provincial borders and to protect their defensive positions. They also laid mines in and around some villages in order to limit the movements of KLA forces.

■ The KLA forces laid some mines which, as part of the negotiated agreement, they were to remove. The KLA reported that they had completed this task, but did not provide records.

■ NATO aircraft dropped Cluster Bomb Units (CBUs), which was the major type of UXO contamination.

Initial data was lacking, but as NATO entered the country, some statistics showed that the army of the Federal Republic of Yugoslavia recorded 616 minefields, and NATO identified 333 CBU drop sites on which a total of 1,400 bombs were dropped. As part of the peace settlement, the KLA quickly removed the mines it used during the conflict. All in all, 1,000 suspected mined areas were reported, but 30 percent of the casualties that were reported occurred in other locations that were not identified as contaminated. This indicated not only that it was critical for the existing database to expand by gathering additional information, but also that nuisance mines placed in and around many villages were not reported and remained a hazard.[30]

MILITARY RESPONSE
TO POSTCONFLICT RECONSTRUCTION

The rules for military reconstruction in Kosovo reflected the rules that were in effect in Bosnia. The major difference between the two operations is that, unlike the situation in Bosnia, NATO did not have advance knowledge of the status of Kosovo's infrastructure before deployment. Trying to specifically determine the extent and scope of work required was an effort that went largely unfulfilled prior to NATO's entry into the province. Records of previous Central Intelligence Agency (CIA) reports from ongoing clandestine operations in Kosovo were scoured for bits of engineer information, but these reports were often dated (more than two years old), the source of the information could not be verified, or the data in the reports did not provide enough engineer-specific information to adequately determine the future infrastructure effort. U.S. intelligence officers at AFSOUTH, the NATO headquarters in Naples, Italy, employed CIA operatives in its intelligence section to help further refine the intelligence picture, but the raw data necessary to develop and paint the intelligence picture did not exist. To gather additional data, AFSOUTH, through the American Joint Intelligence Center in England, directed its satellite overflights over key portions of Kosovo, but, because of intense cloud cover, was unable to gather the type of specific engineer data required to refine the postconflict reconstruction mission that NATO was going to face. Finally, AFSOUTH was unable to predict the damage that the NATO air war would inflict in its attempt to stop Belgrade's campaign of violence.

Therefore, AFSOUTH military engineer planners assumed the worst. Having recently completed a thorough reconnaissance of Albania's infrastructure in 1998, and of FYROM's infrastructure in 1999, and having extensive knowledge of Bosnia's infrastructure as result of the ongoing IFOR/SFOR mission, engineering assumptions as to the state of Kosovo's infrastructure were made in order to complete the engineer plan. Against those assumptions, a generic engineer force structure was developed and subsequently proposed at various force-generation conferences held at SHAPE in Mons, Belgium. Once again, however, nations were reluctant to offer up their limited engineer resources in light of the insufficient data foundation on which the plan rested. A competing factor at the force-generation conference was the ongoing commitment of NATO troops in Bosnia. Peacekeeping was taking a huge toll on NATO's military forces. The results of the first two force-generation conferences were dismal at best—many engineer force requirements went unfulfilled at the point of deployment.

NATO Engineering Effort

Building on the success of the engineer reorganization during the transition to SFOR, KFOR established its engineer command structure in a similar manner. Just like IFOR and SFOR, unity of command was not achieved in the multinational KFOR operation—the NATO commander lacked the necessary leverage and control, and nations reserved the right to dictate how, where, and when their contributing forces would be employed and deployed. However, an attempt was made to at least achieve unity of effort—agreement and common understanding of the objectives and the desired endstate of the operation. Mirroring this tactic, the KFOR engineer developed a theater engineer campaign plan designed to rebuild Kosovo's roads, bridges, railroads, and airports in support of military forces and provide a comprehensive mine awareness campaign to enhance stability and security. The initial project approval process began in winter 1999, before NATO's air war. In order to secure early funding for such broad project headings as repair and maintain roads, repair and maintain bridges, repair airfields, and establish and maintain international military headquarters, ten generic projects were submitted from the AFSOUTH Contingency Engineer Section to the NATO Infrastructure Committee using the project approval process developed in Bosnia. Unable to conduct a thorough infrastructure reconnaissance, and not knowing what infrastructure the future air campaign was going to damage, NATO approved the submissions in very short time, allowing AFSOUTH flexibility to adjust the scope of work for each project once on-the-ground reconnaissance could be completed. Upon entry into the theater, MNB forces were funded to execute designated reconstruction on NATO main supply routes, or else civilian contractors were hired to perform the work.

Unlike Bosnia, local construction capacity in Kosovo was lacking; therefore, many projects were contracted to sources external to the country or were executed by military engineers with NATO funding. In the first year, KFOR built or repaired 260 kilometers of road and reconstructed or repaired six major bridges. A major Italian construction company was hired to completely repave NATO Route "HAWK" from Blace to Pristina during the summer of 2000, and other international construction organizations were brought in to execute repairs to bridges that had been in place with little maintenance for more than fifty years. The Italian Railway Company, the same military unit that executed the initial repairs to the rail network in Bosnia, repaired 300 kilometers of railroad and two bridges in the first year in order to facilitate military resupply. With Kosovo having such an immature road network, rail significantly helped KFOR meet its resupply objectives, not only in timeliness but also in required commodities. At Pristina airport, British military engineers installed a temporary control tower, and new navigation aids, including a new instrument landing system, are being brought into service to facilitate the reinstatement of round-the-clock operations. In the interim, the airport was opened for traffic under visual flight rules, primarily for military and humanitarian flights but with limited commercial services. Working with in-place NGOs, KFOR helped repair and bring back into service key infrastructure such as schools and utilities. Key to this effort was the restoration of the region's aging power plant near Pristina.

International Demining

When New Zealand Major John Flanagan arrived in Kosovo in June 1999 to open and head the UN Mine Action Coordination Center (UNMACC), about a hundred people a month were getting blown up by land mines—a legacy of yet another stage of the long-running Balkans conflict. With a mandate from the United Nations to be the focal point for mine action, Flanagan gathered information from NATO and local villagers, and, with his knowledge of former Serb-held areas, took two months to build up a picture of the massive demining task ahead. Despite his UN position—he had just spent two years in the UN's mine action service group in New York—Flanagan ran into massive institutional resistance. His plan was to clear the country in less than three years by setting an aggressive endstate and getting the resources to meet that target, rather than have the operation drag on for decades. According to Flanagan:

> People from [NGOs] and the UN scoffed at my proposal. They thought it was going to be a twenty-to-thirty-year operation. I could see the same mistakes from Bosnia being made all over again. It's seen to be job creation. Mine clearing agencies are the biggest local employer—it creates a dependency, an end in itself. Organizations were setting up ten-year leases on buildings.[31]

Flanagan said that this attitude was symptomatic of a huge growth in civilian agencies' involvement with mine clearing, starting in Afghanistan in 1989. Backed by specialist knowledge and mine-clearing experience in countries including Cambodia and Bosnia, he was determined that his team would not end up plodding its way across the country. With a budget of $70 million, his plan involved hiring 1,400 mine clearers, six mechanical clearers (which work by flailing the ground), and thirty sniffer dogs blitzing through Kosovo. He had to convince the powers of the United Nations that it did not make sense to spend months in any one area, covering every blade of grass. Speed was the key—moving deminers away from minefields if they did not find any mines in two weeks. In two and a half years, 350 square kilometers were cleared of 25,000 unexploded mines, 8,500 NATO cluster bombs, and 13,000 other types of explosives. "The number of people now getting their limbs blown off has dropped to about one a month, lower than the death rate from road accidents," Flanagan said in June 2002. "It's hugely satisfying."[32]

The UNMACC successfully completed its objectives, and the problems associated with land mines, cluster munitions, and other UXO in Kosovo have virtually been eliminated. Though it may take some years to completely eradicate all items of explosive ordnance from Kosovo, as indeed it will in most other afflicted countries in Europe, the situation is such that the level of contamination no longer impedes social and economic development within the province. The closure of the existing UNMACC in December 2001 coincided with the overarching move toward provisional self-government in Kosovo, as directed by UN Security Council Resolution 1244.

United States Engineering Effort

The U.S. Engineering Regiment concentrated its engineering operations on one main mission with five supporting tasks: base camp construction to house the American force was the central focus, with supporting tasks that included maintaining roads and bridges for military operations; clearing mines and UXO for the base camps and marking the remainder for humanitarian demining; closing routes into Serbia to prevent illegal smuggling; providing equipment and labor for small humanitarian projects; and providing a backup snow and ice clearance (SNIC) capability should there be a failure in the civilian capacity. As in Bosnia, no money was allocated to the Engineer Regiment to execute postconflict reconstruction for civilian facilities, and only a little money was provided to the Civil Affairs section to conduct limited humanitarian operations.

Base Camp Construction. Since the summer of 1999, U.S. engineer elements from across the armed services, uniformed and civilian, including the private sector, worked on one straightforward mission: house the American force and its allies in Kosovo. Knowing U.S. forces would be in Kosovo for an extended period allowed planners to build using temporary construction standards (three-to-five-year planning horizon) early during the deployment. According to LTC Jim Shumway, chief of the Military Engineering and Topography Division in Europe:

> In Bosnia, construction was more incremental because of the political implications and changing operational requirements as the mission went from peace enforcement to peacekeeping. In Kosovo, we knew we were going to be there a while, so the decision was made to build SEAhuts (South East Asia huts) in an effort to be good stewards with our resources. The decision to move directly from Tier II tents (tents with wooden floors) to SEAhuts avoided spending millions of dollars to stair-step construction of base facilities over several years. Additionally, construction materials used for Task Force Hawk in Albania were harvested and shipped for use in Kosovo.[33]

Fewer base camps were constructed in Kosovo because of geographic, economic, and operational considerations. Working with the U.S. Army Engineer School at Fort Leonard Wood, Missouri, the Engineer Regiment used lessons learned to develop contingency engineer doctrine into a long-term base operations strategy. With this framework, military engineers established base camp master plans so construction could begin on SEAhuts, force protection bunker emplacements, and other, more durable facilities. With 1,700 Army, Navy, and Air Force engineers deployed, this project became the largest base camp construction mission since Vietnam. It was also the first experience in using a civilian sustainment services contract (Brown & Root Services, Inc.) to build a military infrastructure of this magnitude.

In planning the contingency operation for Kosovo, the Army chose to establish two base camps and to commit the engineering resources needed to build adequate facilities quickly. The rationale was based on previous experience in the Balkans. In Bosnia, because of the projected short-term deployment, troops intended to stay in tents for the duration. When the mission continued through the first cold winter, living conditions deteriorated and tents were poorly heated, often needing replacement as moisture took a toll on the fabric. "The decision for Kosovo was that we would do it right the first time," said Colonel Robert McClure, commander of the 1st Infantry Division Engineer Brigade and the first Task Force Falcon engineer. "From the time we were on the ground in June, the engineers' goal was to have soldiers inside before winter—and to only move everyone once."[34]

The two base camps were named Camp Bondsteel and Camp Monteith—both named after previous Medal of Honor recipients. With an order from the corps commander to have all soldiers in SEAhuts by October 1, 1999, construction began on July 1 with the arrival of the Navy Seabee battalion overland from Albania, where they had been a part of Task Force Hawk during the NATO air war. The Seabees occupied the sector's smaller camp, Camp Monteith, located on the edge of Gnjilane in what were Yugoslav army barracks before the war. The camp was largely untouched by the conflict, except for two precision-bomb craters that destroyed the maintenance facilities. But retreating forces and the locals trashed and looted the buildings to the point that it took weeks to make them usable. The closeness of the city raised force protection concerns that led to the decision to abandon many of the buildings on the base. Instead, more than seventy-five SEAhuts and support structures were built on an adjoining field for a force of 2,000. The importance of Camp Monteith is its location—it is the locus of tactical activity in the American sector because of the mixed ethnicity of the surrounding population and its proximity to the Russian battalion, which served alongside the American peacekeepers.

The second and much larger camp, Camp Bondsteel, is the "Grande Dame" in Kosovo of what engineers do. Spread over almost 900 acres of rolling wheat fields, it was picked early to become what it is today, the major American base camp in theater. Within its fenced perimeter is a helicopter airport with more than fifty parking pads, more than 175 SEAhuts supporting 5,000 soldiers, a 30,000-square-foot headquarters building, an ammunition holding area, motor pools, and chapels, as well as recreation and dining facilities for soldiers. Water from several wells on camp is piped into each hut from huge holding bags, and there is even a wastewater treatment plant for effluent—something not found in the rest of Kosovo. The numbers involved in the effort of building both camps were staggering. At the project's height, 1,000 expatriates hired by the contractor, plus more than 7,000 ethnic Albanian locals, joined 1,750 military engineers. From early July until well into October, construction at both camps ran twenty-four hours a day, seven days a week, with perhaps a half day each week for soldiers to do personal and equipment maintenance. The final tally for this period was ten million personnel hours and 500,000 equipment hours. More than six million board feet of lumber, two million square feet of plywood, 84,000 sheets of drywall, 200 tons of nails, and 100 miles of electrical cable were consumed in the first year. More than half a million cubic yards of earth were moved on Camp Bondsteel alone. The amount of gravel used at both camps would have covered a two-lane road from St. Louis to Kansas City. In the end, the Engineer Regiment built more than 700,000 square feet of living space—equal to a subdivision with 355 houses—in less than ninety days.[35]

Maintaining Roads and Bridges. Only a few roads throughout Kosovo can handle major commercial and military traffic, and there are very few alternate routes should the major arteries be blocked. The Main Supply Routes (MSRs) that U.S. engineers were tasked by NATO to repair and maintain in the American sector were Route HAWK, which connected the border crossing point at Blace, Macedonia, to Pristina, and Route STAG, which connected Urosevac (near Camp Bondsteel) to Gnjilane (near Camp Monteith). In addition, U.S. engineers constructed the Gnjilane Ring Road bypass, a fifteen-kilometer road that moved military and civilian traffic out of downtown Gnjilane to reduce congestion in this key inter-ethnic town. Both of the MSRs were in treacherous shape, having sustained only limited damage from the conflict but considerable damage from overuse and no maintenance for a decade; the ring road was initial construction connecting several smaller existing one-lane gravel roads.

Using MMR standards, the Engineer Task Force assessed the job, giving priority to Route HAWK in the first year, allowing Route STAG to remain temporarily in its dilapidated state, and the ring road to remain on the construction list of priorities until the spring construction season. Between the Macedonian border and Camp Bondsteel, Route HAWK had six critical tunnels and bridges (designated as Targets 1-6 in the construction plan), all built at the end of World War II in the early Tito years; failure of any one would shut down the route indefinitely as no alternate roads existed to reroute traffic out of this steep, mountainous region. This route was key to the U.S. force's survival as all supplies were transported to Camp Bondsteel and Camp Monteith via this route. No airport was available to handle U.S. resupply planes, and the rail network was not functioning. To ensure the route remained open, U.S. engineers with NATO funding constructed a one-lane gravel bypass around each "target" allowing military traffic to pass while repairs were being made should a "target" fail. These bypasses were completed in June 2000.

In August 2000, the 120-meter bridge at Target 2 began to fail. The northern bearing roller, an elongated reinforced concrete roller that allows flex and movement in the bridge to naturally absorb the shock of passing truck traffic, rotated ninety degrees, turned on its side in the bearing channel, and begin to crack. The northern side of the bridge dropped eighteen inches and was in danger of total collapse. U.S. engineers, using a form of tele-engineering (a network of secure, sophisticated, high-frequency satellite communications systems), sent inspection photographs to the Engineer Research and Development Center (ERDC) in Vicksburg, Mississippi, for evaluation and engineer assessment. Immediately, ERDC recommended closing the bridge because catastrophic failure was imminent. As Route HAWK was a NATO-designated route eligible for NATO funding, the NATO engineer (a British colonel) asserted his command authority and employed a British engineer and design unit to rappel off the side of the bridge, conduct an inspection, and make a second evaluation. The NATO conclusion was that the bridge was not

approaching catastrophic failure, but that it should be constantly surveyed for further deterioration and restricted to one-lane
traffic going south, with the gravel bypass used for all northern
traffic. This lasted for two weeks until it was determined that the
structure was continuing to fall. NATO immediately closed the
bridge, hired a local contractor to asphalt the bypass (as it, too,
was beginning to show severe wear from the large amounts of
truck and military traffic), and hired a Macedonian construction
firm to fix both ends of the bridge because the southern bearing
roller was also showing signs of failure. In less than six weeks,
the civilian contractor constructed rudimentary scaffolding
under each end of the bridge (about seventy-five meters high),
hydraulically raised the bridge off its bearing roller by twenty-
four inches, removed the defective rollers, cleaned the channel,
and installed new rollers. The bridge was quickly reopened so
that the truck traffic, so vital to Kosovo's fledging economy, could
resume in full force.[36]

During the 2000 construction season, attention was given
to Route STAG, a two-lane asphalt road connecting Camp
Bondsteel to Camp Monteith. In many places, the asphalt had
failed, with cars traveling on the sub-base of the road—again,
with no available alternate routes. It would often take military
four-wheel drive vehicles up to one and a half hours to traverse
this thirty-kilometer route, and it would take civilian cars even
longer, not to mention the damage caused to the vehicle frames
and suspensions by the poor road conditions. U.S. engineers
deployed Detachment 1 of the 277th Asphalt Company to repair
the road. In addition, in an effort to speed up the repair and
employ the newly created KPC, U.S. engineers transported
twenty members of the local KPC engineer unit to the construction site each day, where they would work side-by-side with the
Asphalt Detachment fixing Kosovo's roads. This partnership
effort had several positive postconflict ramifications.

First, the road was completely repaired during the available construction season—something that could not have been
accomplished without the additional KPC personnel. This

enhanced the freedom of movement, not only for the military, as the project was designed, but also for the Kosovars. Second, the effort created a partnership between the U.S. forces and the KPC, leading to greater security and stability in the area. Although the KPC was forbidden to carry arms and engage in security efforts, they still had unofficial influence in the region from their previous status as the KLA and used that influence to significantly lower the violence level of the area. Third, by having KPC members work alongside U.S. soldiers, it gave the KPC a sense of legitimacy in Kosovo. The local Kosovars were initially leery of the KPC and its motives. By seeing the KPC working hard for the reconstruction of Kosovo's infrastructure, much of this trepidation was removed and the KPC was accepted into Kosovo society—vital for any public organization, especially one that previously was the source of great violence. Finally, as a humanitarian gesture, the twenty KPC members who worked daily with the asphalt platoon received an American-prepared hot meal—food was something that they would not often have had if they were not working with U.S. forces.

The third major road mission was the construction of the Gnjilane Ring Road. Initially started by the same Navy Seabee battalion that constructed Camp Monteith, the project also employed horizontal construction elements of the two National Guard/Reserve construction companies in the Engineer Task Force and used elements of the Swedish Excavation Platoon for some limited earthwork around embedded obstacles. The road, constructed through the countryside and suburbs of Gnjilane, was designed to move the military traffic out of town in order to eliminate the traffic delays and minimize the chances for vehicle accidents in town. As the road progressed, more and more civilian traffic used the ring road, causing major delays with the ongoing construction; however, employing a military police unit to help control traffic allowed construction to continue. Once NATO conducted an on-site project inspection and realized the benefits of this extended bypass, they further authorized the road to be upgraded to asphalt and contracted for the one bridge on the route to be rebuilt at NATO expense, hiring civilian companies to complete both of these tasks. The final product was a permanent two-lane asphalt road allowing both military and civilian traffic to escape the traffic congestion of downtown Gnjilane.

Despite the limitation and mandate to repair the MSRs to the minimum military requirement, there were several instances in which U.S. engineers employed their equipment for civilian advantage. In the Gorni Kusce sector, Lieutenant Colonel Bryan Foy, commander of 1st Battalion, 37th Armored Regiment, received repeated complaints in his local town hall meetings of injured civilians dying enroute to a hospital because their cars could not physically travel certain dirt roads. He also heard complaints of roads so bad that local Serbs were physically cut off from Serbia. A road that allowed more direct access to the ring road north of Gnjilane not only would provide a route that would bypass Kosovar Albanian enclaves, but would more than cut in half the travel time to Gate 5 (the Russian traffic control point into Serbia near Kamenica). Local Serbs preferred hospital care in Serbia instead of care at the dual-treatment hospital facility in Gnjilane.

Foy submitted a project to the 16th Engineer Battalion commander to use horizontal military equipment to grade the dirt roads so the cars could reach the hospital. In addition, he convinced a local ethnic Albanian gravel quarry owner to provide free gravel that was then used by Serbs to build a road with equipment that they had stolen from the quarry at the beginning of the war. The stipulation was that the stolen equipment would be returned to the rightful owner after the project was completed. In these cases, the work completed by the horizontal section was for civilian purposes only. No military traffic would routinely travel these routes, but the impact of this work was a great quality-of-life improvement to the local nationals and created an opportunity to integrate the ethnic Albanian and Serb workforces at the quarry, increasing Serb employment in the region and raising the standard of living in the nearby Serb enclaves.[37] Because of the funding limitations, these roads, although built to Western standards, were made of gravel and would require constant maintenance to ensure that they remained open. These roads did not qualify for NATO or U.S. funding, so only equipment and personnel could be used; artful military diplomacy with the locals secured the free material. When the beneficial aspects of these roads were realized, the routine maintenance of the civilian roads was added to the Engineer Task Force construction priority list.

The missions to maintain the task force main supply routes used "reach back technology," employing the high technology of the engineer laboratories in the United States to conduct in-depth assessments of the road network in Kosovo. ERDC's Topographic Engineering Center in Alexandria, Virginia, applied its Engineering Route Studies program, a graphic product designed to provide country-scale terrain, climate, and natural disaster data in conjunction with current route conditions. The graphic highlighted such items as areas of potential flooding, steep grades, switchbacks, potential choke points, and areas of landslides. Road information included distances in kilometers, surface type, and road classification (such as expressway or single lane). The studies allowed military planners to assess the overall impact of terrain and climate for major routes throughout the southern Balkans. This added capability allowed the U.S. Engineer Task Force to properly deploy its limited equipment and material to meet mission standards.

Mines and Unexploded Ordnance. The U.S. engineer effort for demining Kosovo was strictly limited by national policy to the execution of a mine awareness campaign, identifying and marking the minefields and UXO fields for humanitarian clearance, and the establishment of the Minefield Quick Reaction Force in the event a person required extraction from a minefield. Because young children were more likely than adults to find a mine or UXO while playing outside and exploring new places, the Mine Action Center at Camp Bondsteel established a program of instruction that targeted elementary through high school–age children. As in Bosnia, some munitions that were painted bright colors for easy identification attracted children's attention because they appeared to be toys. Therefore, engineers placed a high priority on the local schools, supplementing their mine awareness teaching with posters and mine awareness Superman comic books provided for free by various international organizations. Instructors brought disarmed examples of mines and UXO to help students learn how to recognize them. Training included mine-marking practices that flag unsafe areas, as well as how to safely exit an accidentally entered minefield. In order to capture the children's short attention spans, soldiers would devise games and activities, rather than rely on less exciting lectures that might not convey their message as well.

As the mission unfolded in Kosovo, U.S. engineers were successful in obtaining the Serbian records of minefields emplaced in the MNB-East sector and also the bomb-targeting grid references used during NATO's air campaign. Using this information, combat engineers marked each minefield and UXO field with standard NATO materials—barbed wire, pickets, and international mine signs. Because the locals would remove the marking material to use on their farms to corral their livestock, the engineers were forced to check each minefield every two weeks to ensure that the minefield marking materials were still in place and, if not, would replace them until the minefield was cleared by the UN-contracted civilian humanitarian demining firms. The effort started with a database that had more than 100 minefields in the eastern sector alone, but MNB-East was virtually cleared of mines by December 2000.[38]

Should people find themselves in a minefield, the Engineer Task Force established and maintained the Minefield Quick Reaction Force, designed to be able to clear a path through the minefield to the victim using mechanical means, extract the victim and the vehicle, provide any required medical aid on-site, and provide overall security for the operation. The engineers had two Panthers and three Mini-Flails to help them with their mechanical mine-clearing missions. The Israeli-developed Panther, a modified M60 tank, used nine-ton forward rollers to detonate mines, which typically do little or no damage to the vehicle.

The Panther works by a remote control consisting of a personal computer with video simulation software and radio devices that trigger actuators on the tank. The remote control can start and drive the Panther from as far away as 800 meters, yet the control fits in a suitcase. The Mini-Flail uses a small skip loader chassis without the operator cage. A forward-mounted drum rotates at high speed, flailing the ground with chains that strike with a force of about 300 pounds per square inch. The Mini-Flail controller is a small, hand-held device, no bigger than a field radio, with small joysticks that allow the user to maneuver the vehicle. Both systems are diesel-powered, and the Panther has controls that can be overridden to allow manual operation. During the first year, the Minefield Quick Reaction Force was employed only twice; however, the Panthers and Mini-Flails were often used at construction sites with great results. Of all the areas, minefield awareness and clearing were the biggest lessons learned from Bosnia. This highly successful mission resulted in relatively few casualties once Task Force Falcon was established in Kosovo.

Smuggling Routes. The boundary between Kosovo and Serbia was porous, with many logging trails crossing the border every one or two kilometers. As KFOR entered Kosovo, it quickly discovered that a massive ongoing smuggling operation used these small trails. Illegal drugs and arms were taken across the eastern Kosovo boundary into the Presevo Valley in Serbia to support a rogue, but persistent, insurgency of the old KLA called the Liberation Army of Presevo, Medvedya, and Bujanovac (UCPMB). The UCPMB established its headquarters in Dobrosyn, three kilometers into Serbia proper, recruiting members and conducting a type of basic training in the immediate area of the boundary. The UCPMB was a destabilizing element in the region and a source of concern for the KFOR leadership. In an effort to starve the KLA holdovers of illicit materials, the engineers developed a plan to close eighty-four trails using explosives, downed trees, and artificial obstacles, attempting to force all boundary crossings to occur at Observation Point Sapper or Observation Point Terminator, the two authorized crossing points on the boundary into the Presevo Valley.[39] Planned and managed out of the Engineer Task Force operations office, platoon-sized patrols of about twenty-five soldiers would ensure that no people were in the immediate vicinity, detonate explosives to create a truck-sized crater in the trail, and tie barbed wire and logs on the sides to prevent any bypass of the crater by local vehicles. Although the obstacles were well emplaced, there is a saying in the Army that an obstacle not covered by observation or fire is not an obstacle. Unfortunately, the boundary was too extensive and the force levels too low to monitor each trail; most of the obstacles were filled in by hand by smugglers and loggers to allow vehicle passage.

Humanitarian Projects. With the large base camp mission, the minefield marking mission, and the border-closing mission, U.S. engineers were hard pressed to find opportunities to execute humanitarian projects under the UN Security Council Resolution 1244 task to "support the SRSG and international organizations and NGOs in Kosovo in their . . . infrastructure repair tasks." Outside of the horizontal construction equipment opportunities to improve local dirt and gravel roads, funding limitations precluded the engineers from attempting many projects that would directly improve the quality of life for the locals. Replacing the entire electrical grid or water system for a village, for example, was beyond the mandate and the funding allowances for the engineers. However, as many of the deployed soldiers were also parents, the depressing state of Kosovo's education sparked an initiative to adopt local schools and rebuild them using what free material and labor the soldiers could gather. Each engineer company adopted a local school, voluntarily using their half day of downtime each week to clean and execute minor repairs to schools that had been closed for about a decade. Depending on the individual school's needs, the engineers repaired dilapidated floors and ceilings, fixed chairs and desks, and completed basic ground leveling.

The inside of a schoolhouse was very basic: several small classrooms, battered tables and chairs, and wood stoves. There were no computers in the classrooms and most did not have a blackboard. The walls in the classrooms had a mixture of decor: one had a picture of a KLA hero, others had cartoon murals painted on some walls, and still others simply had dull green, cream, or gray walls in dire need of repainting. The floors were wooden, with much of the wood in decay. Most of the facilities needed extensive cleaning and painting, whereas others needed replacement windows and electrical rewiring for lights and power. Electricians checked wiring and lights, keeping a close tally on the number of light bulbs that needed replacing. It was ironic that many of the lights were stamped "Made in USSR" in English; however, the soldiers replaced only two or three of the six lights in each fixture because the aging circuits could not handle the full electrical load. Other teams replaced broken windows with Plexiglas as a quick fix to keep out wind and snow; most classrooms were heated with a small, inefficient wood stove in the corner as central heating did not exist.

Outside, external latrines were refurbished, as most were clogged, gates and perimeter fences were repaired, and children's sports fields were cleared of saplings and scrub brush that had grown up in the decade of neglect. Horizontal construction equipment was used to regrade the sports fields, and combat engineers replaced soccer goal posts and volleyball nets. Commonly, a soccer ball would magically appear and an impromptu game would start. It was almost comical as the game would feature children of all ages, usually wearing tee-shirts donated by various humanitarian relief agencies, playing against U.S. Army soldiers wearing helmets and flak vests, with unloaded weapons strapped to their sides. According to Specialist Javier Varela, "From these kids' view, I don't know if it will matter that the school is clean and the walls are painted. I just remember growing up in Chicago that the important thing is to be in school. If we helped get them back here learning something, that's all that really matters."[40] Most soldiers wrote to their communities and churches in the United States describing the school conditions and received an amazing response. The communities sent countless boxes of school supplies, clothes, and, in one case, new computers to help the schools get back on their feet. Through these soldiers' efforts, the Kosovar children restarted their education and began to regain some of the childhood that had been taken away—something that the soldiers could point to as having made a tangible difference during their deployment.

Snow and Ice Clearance. Completing the primary SEAhut construction by early fall, Task Force Falcon engineers looked ahead to see what challenges winter storms would pose. A single winter storm may dump as much as twenty-two inches of snow in the area. For a task force that was heavily dependent on one supply route that traverses through some of the highest terrain in southern Kosovo, it was imperative to develop a capability to keep the route clear of snow and ice. During the SNIC planning, KFOR engineers tried to develop local contacts to help with snow removal; however, not much equipment was available.

To provide backup equipment for local contractors, the Army deployed civilian engineers from the United States Army Cold Regions Research and Engineering Laboratory to field a snow and ice clearance/abatement package. The package included five-ton truck snowblades, Humvee snowblades, and both towed and mounted sand/salt spreaders. The SNIC plan focused on NATO's main supply routes, ensuring that roads in the assigned regions were passable for operational and humanitarian missions. SNIC within the villages and towns remained the responsibility of the locals. In most cases, there was no local capacity, and locals could rely only on rising temperatures to help dig themselves out.

Nearly every military activity in Kosovo depended on the Army's terrain and mapping capabilities, and SNIC was no exception. The Geographic Information Systems (GIS) allowed planners to model multiple variables and create maps reflecting their relationships. For example, a 100-year storm could be superimposed with maps showing damaged roads to predict whether a particular route would be passable. During winter preparations, engineers used GIS for mapping main supply routes, alternate routes, and local roads to allocate plows and other equipment. According to the Engineer Brigade intelligence officer: "We've been modeling terrain and weather factors that could potentially contribute to a 'state of siege' when people are isolated from food, water, and power. Elevation is the primary concern. We're also looking at terrain features—how landforms on slopes, called spurs and draws, will affect people's ability to move about after a storm."[41]

This assessment used historic weather data from the Pristina Weather Observation Center along with satellite data from the National Imagery and Mapping Agency and other sources, including NATO reconnaissance. The information indicated from a tactical standpoint where snow removal equipment was needed to help quick reaction forces respond to emergencies. During the first year, one major snowstorm closed Route HAWK. More than twenty inches fell and many civilian trucks slid and jackknifed on the road, making the road impassable. U.S. engineers used their snowplows and wreckers to remove the snow and the vehicles from the road in order to reopen the route within eighteen hours. In addition, B Company of the 142nd Engineer Combat Battalion (North Dakota National Guard) used their own equipment for snow removal as the local capacity was not capable of achieving the same results.

Kosovo Protection Corps Projects

In an attempt to involve former KLA personnel in positive activities, NATO and UN officials agreed to the creation of the KPC. NATO and the United Nations intended the 3,000-strong organization to be a uniformed civilian force to deal with emergency situations; however, some of the KLA leaders saw the KPC as the nucleus of a future Kosovo army, a view rejected by NATO and UN officials. The KPC officially came into being on September 21, 1999, with the promulgation of a UNMIK Regulation and Statement of Principles providing provisional legal status for the KPC within Kosovo. According to the Statement and Principles, the KPC would:

■ Provide a disaster response capability, including major fires and industrial accidents or spills.

■ Conduct search and rescue.

■ Provide humanitarian assistance in isolated areas.

■ Assist in demining.

■ Contribute to rebuilding infrastructure and communities.[42]

The KPC had no role in defense, law enforcement, riot control, internal security, or any other task involved in the maintenance of law and order. The KPC consisted of six regional headquarters with a support detachment of sixty-eight personnel in each region responsible for engineer construction and demining. With the onset of winter, the immediate priority in the first year was housing reconstruction assistance to organizations providing basic life support. Much was accomplished with little equipment, and returning refugees had sufficient housing to survive the first winter. However, the KPC suffered from a chronic lack of international support. It was not included in the regional Kosovo budget, and financing was dependent on contributions from a few interested nations. The hand-to-mouth approach did not help maintain the independence of the KPC, some of whose members were suspected of engaging in intimidation and corruption. To help with the training, U.S. engineers developed and executed a training plan to provide the KPC with basic engineering and English-language skills. Adequate engineering equipment remained a problem as the U.S. engineers were prohibited from lending tools to the KPC. Despite these roadblocks, the KPC concentrated on refurbishing the remaining schools in the region during the second year. Receiving large amounts of international funding, the KPC completely overhauled schools in the Urosevac and Gnjilane areas, achieving high-quality results using only basic hand tools.

CJCIMIC Effort

There were many problems constraining the civil-military affairs effort in Kosovo, from the lack of overall organization in KFOR headquarters to the lack of a campaign plan in MNB-

East; however, there were also success stories that contributed to the reconstruction of Kosovo. Organizationally, civil-military missions in KFOR headquarters were split among a number of directorates beyond the civil-military operations staff. Whereas the Civil-Military Operations directorate conducted most civil-military liaison and provided all of KFOR's civil-military expertise and assessments, a separate Civil Affairs directorate run by an independent group of French CIMIC officers was dedicated largely to the support of economic development. Strategic Plans provided operational planning and project management assistance to UNMIK, whereas Current Operations conducted liaison with local police forces. Therefore, no cohesive or coherent organization that coordinated all civil-military affairs efforts existed. Along with the lack of an established clearing mechanism for projects at the KFOR level, there was a CIMIC Campaign Plan that was never implemented. Many KFOR CIMIC officers, in fact, had no knowledge that a KFOR CIMIC Campaign Plan existed. This caused action officers to work redundantly, or even at cross purposes. According to the MNB-East Civil-Military Affairs Officer in May 2000:

> KFOR has not provided a plan to coordinate and synchronize CMO [civil-military operations] activities between the MNBs. . . . KFOR provides broad CIMIC guidance and intent along several lines of operations: freedom of movement, humanitarian support, public safety, civil administration, infrastructure repair, economics and commerce, and democratization. Measures of effectiveness and endstates for the lines of operation are not specified. An overall CMO campaign for MNB(E) does not exist. This is due in part to the lack of guidance and direction from higher headquarters in Pristina. Even though our teams are engaged in CMO activities on a daily basis, there is no clear statement of what the priority/main effort actually is. This being said, many of the CMO activities are reactionary (based on the current situation) rather than deliberately planned and synchronized to attain an overall objective.[43]

In light of this lack of coordination and direction, infrastructure reconstruction was minimal. MNB-East used its nearly sixty U.S. Army Civil Affairs personnel to support programs such as the Village Employment Rehabilitation Program, which was part of the UN Development Program. In addition to conducting

more than 500 village and school assessments and maintaining a
significant database, Civil Affairs teams performed "hearts-and-
minds" projects to promote overall military mission legitimacy to
target audiences identified by the current operations staff. They
assisted UNMIK and NGO-led capacity-building projects such
as business seminars for small- and medium-enterprise owners
(the majority of Civil Affairs personnel are reservists, many of
whom have business experience of their own).[44]

More than $3.4 million of Department of Defense humanitarian
assistance funds were provided to rebuild schools, public utilities,
and health-care facilities. Task Force Falcon Civil Affairs teams
coordinated and facilitated the restoration of electrical power and
telephone services, especially to the Serbian enclaves. As a mark
of Civil Affairs persistence, when MNB-East began to experience
increased ethnic violence in its sector as well as hostilities along
its border with Serbia, particularly in the Presevo valley, Task
Force Falcon Civil Affairs continued to support UNMIK, NGOs,
and other efforts of international organizations to restore fundamental public services and lay the groundwork for the eventual
transfer of functions to the appropriate civil institutions.

THE INTERNATIONAL CIVILIAN RESPONSE

The immediate priorities of the international community after
the end of the Kosovo conflict were to establish order and security
and avert a humanitarian catastrophe. Despite the short duration
of the armed conflict between NATO and Yugoslav forces, which
lasted seventy-eight days, the Kosovo conflict caused significant
human dislocation. At the peak of the conflict, nearly one million Kosovars—mainly ethnic Albanians—representing about 45
percent of the prewar population of the province fled their homes.
Following the end of the conflict, 210,000 Serbs and other non-
Albanian minorities were displaced and remain so to this day.
After the end of the war, KFOR and UNMIK inherited a precarious domestic security situation: widespread possession of arms,
human rights abuses, violence, and the risk of generalized conflict

between armed ethnic Albanian groups. KFOR and UNMIK's first major tasks were thus to establish a secure environment and provide emergency assistance to the population. During the first four months after the conflict, relief agencies distributed food rations to about 1.5 million people in Kosovo, and 900,000 continued to receive food aid throughout the winter of 1999–2000. Construction materials were provided for home reconstruction, and emergency repairs were carried out on damaged health-care facilities. The handling of the immediate postconflict humanitarian crisis by the international community was a success: by the early summer of 2000, the humanitarian emergency was over.[45]

In parallel, UNMIK used its authority under UN Security Council Resolution 1244 to establish a civilian administration in Kosovo. UNMIK established four sections, or "pillars," each run by an international agency: humanitarian affairs (UNHCR), civil administration (UN), democracy building (OSCE), and reconstruction (EU). An international UNMIK staff managed the four pillars as well as the thirty municipalities in Kosovo. In July 2000, after the humanitarian emergency was over, the humanitarian pillar ceased to exist as a formal component of UNMIK, and the number of pillars was reduced to three.

However, the lack of funding, as in Bosnia, was a major issue and deterrent to immediate postconflict reconstruction. On July 30, 1999, donor nations met in Sarajevo to launch a Balkan Stability Pact that sought to promote political and economic reform, promote cooperation, and integrate the region into the rest of Europe. But it was not until March 29–30, 2000, that donors met in Brussels for a Regional Funding Conference to support the Balkan Stability Pact. They pledged roughly $2.3 billion to fund a package of quick-start projects that could begin within a year in the areas of economic infrastructure, anticorruption, regional security, and democracy and human rights, but it was also the first time that donors began to identify and set up the process to develop "near-term" and "medium-term" projects. At this point, KFOR and UNMIK had already been in theater for nine months, and the international community was just beginning to identify the processes to develop and complete reconstruction projects in a country ravaged by war and plagued by unemployment.

For Kosovo specifically, a number of estimates of postconflict reconstruction needs were proposed even while the war was still raging, although all were mere conjecture. In July 1999, several international task forces began making assessments that would lead to a more realistic estimate of needs and costs. The European Commission Task Force focused on housing and local village infrastructure, estimating the cost to repair damaged housing to be $1.2 billion, and for other village facilities—schools, clinics, local electricity, and clean water—$43.9 million. The EC and the World Bank organized the international economic assistance efforts through their joint chairing of a High-Level Steering Group, including the United States and other major donors. The first donor conference, the topics of which were based on the EC's assessment, was held in Brussels on July 28, 1999, and concentrated on short-term humanitarian needs arising from the return of refugees. To prepare for a second donor conference, a more far-reaching round of assessments covering energy, telecommunications, transport, commerce, and social infrastructure was conducted. Detailing the reconstruction and development objectives in Kosovo over the next four to five years, the EC–World Bank report estimated the cost of reaching those objectives to be $2.3 billion in external financing.[46]

The second donor conference, held on November 17, 1999, focused on reconstruction and development concerns and yielded slightly more than $1 billion in pledges (only $36.2 million was pledged for humanitarian programs). The total amount closely matched the $1.1 billion required through the end of 2000. However, funds pledged for the different categories of required assistance—civil administration budget, peacekeeping, and reconstruction—did not meet the specific monetary needs in each category, and actual money received amounted to only 75 percent of that pledged. The EU and its member states were the main providers of financial support; however, the lengthy approval processes of the EU apparatus severely inhibited the speedy allocation of urgently needed sums. Millions of euros were committed but not disbursed, and EU finance ministers objected to making budgetary contributions to an entity that could not in the ordinary sense be understood as a country.

To further compound the problem, EU leaders at the European Council meeting in Cologne, Germany, asked the EC on June 4, 1999, to set up an agency for the purpose of reconstructing Kosovo. On June 23, the EC proposed a draft regulation to establish the agency. However, it was not until December 15 that the EU formally established a European Agency for Reconstruction of Kosovo to administer its reconstruction program—a full six months after KFOR entered theater. Despite glowing reports from the European Court of Auditors, the established structure was exceedingly cumbersome.[47] Two administrative committees—one in Pristina and one in Brussels—created unnecessary duplication for every decision of the agency. They had to base their deliberations on eighty different EU regulations, and the various committees failed to meet more than once a month, causing additional delay. The agency was additionally controlled by an administrative committee that consisted of representatives from all of the fifteen member states. Thus, Brussels red tape impeded not only the reconstruction of Kosovo, but also the recovery of the wider Balkan region.[48] As a bright spot, despite the political limitation that excluded Kosovo from receiving money from many international aid agencies, the World Bank provided $2 million from a Community Development Fund for infrastructure and services projects and for budget support for the civil administration of the province. It also provided $60 million in grant assistance through a Trust Fund for Kosovo over an eighteen-month period.[49]

Although relief funding may have been sufficient to avert the humanitarian crisis, transitional administration startup funding was lacking. Compounding the typical planning shortfalls, limited funding contributed to staffing shortages as high as 50 percent, hampered service support operations, and delayed key infrastructure repair and public service restoration projects. Because reconstruction was key to the strategy of KFOR's second commander, General Juan Ortuno of Spain, he offered military assistance aiming to "provide a long-term economic perspective to the province" and to endow it with "a mechanism to facilitate the flow of international donor funding to regional and municipal levels."[50] KFOR conducted its own field assessment in March 2000 and determined that the international community did not have a Kosovo-wide capacity to assess specific reconstruction needs. In response, the planners at SHAPE set up the Kosovo Development Group, detached under the authority of the EU's Kosovo reconstruction department. Belgium, Denmark, Finland, France, Germany, Greece, Italy, and Spain volunteered a staff of eighteen trained officers, who worked in teams of three in the province's five sectors and in Pristina. Starting in July 2000, Kosovo Development Group teams traveled throughout the province, identifying and prioritizing reconstruction, projects in cooperation with the local authorities and the 120 NGOs operating in Kosovo. These projects covered all aspects of reconstruction, from repairing infrastructure to regenerating the economy, and were all allocated EU funding. The Kosovo Development Group remained in operation until July 2001, when the EU civilian structure was able to take over the specific tasks of project identification and management.

By most accounts, Kosovo has made much progress since the end of the war, although it has a long way to go before it is a self-sustaining, self-governing entity. Despite an almost two-year delay for the EU to fully staff its reconstruction agency, basic infrastructure—roads, airport, communications, schools, housing—was repaired. Basic services—health, education, electricity, and water—are being provided. A basic framework of government is in place—with Kosovar nationals matched with international personnel in all departments of the UN administrative structure—and a judicial system, with police and courts, has been established. Elections at the local level were successfully held in October 2000, and municipal assemblies have taken responsibility for basic government functions. Small businesses and signs of civil society, including independent media, are growing. But until the various local ministries required to maintain Kosovo's infrastructure base are fully resourced, the province's physical infrastructure will have to be maintained by international aid or it will fall quickly back into its immediate postconflict condition.

The barest elements of government are in place and they function at minimal levels. Standards need to be improved across the board. Public utility infrastructure is antiquated and needs replacement. Teachers, police, and civil servants need training, and sporadic violence between ethnic Albanians and minority Serbs continues. Whereas the United Nations estimates that donor support for the operating budget may end by 2003, it anticipates a need for donor activity in multiple sectors of Kosovar life for years to come.[51] Unfortunately, the terrorist events of September 11, 2001, and the subsequent global War on Terror, are causing donors to move their money out of the region and into other places. This does not bode well for Kosovo's future.

ASSESSMENT

Kosovo was a beautiful country that had been ravaged by war. The mountain villages were collections of tiny houses with red tiled roofs, which probably looked like they did centuries ago. Most homes had no indoor plumbing, requiring outhouses. Water was obtained from springs and wells, many of which were fouled by animal carcasses thrown into the water by departing Serbs. Villages that relied on streams suffered the pollution effects of rusting cars, dead animals, and general refuse. Compounding these basic challenges, driving in Kosovo was a nightmare. The roads were in terrible shape and people were more likely to be injured or killed on the road than by a sniper or an act of violence. Drivers would swerve to avoid potholes without worrying about oncoming traffic. KFOR made extensive road repairs for military traffic, but this had the unintended consequence of enabling drivers to travel at more dangerous speeds. There were no driving tests or licenses, most cars did not have license plates, many cars had been stolen from western Europe, and drivers ignored internationally accepted rules of the road. Many UNMIK, OSCE, KFOR, and international aid workers adopted Kosovo driving habits as well, adding more chaos to the congested highways with tanks, trucks, buses, Humvees, Jeeps, and Land Cruisers.

Despite this ongoing chaos, Kosovo is a qualified successful case study in economic institution building. The province's economy emerged from a decade of gross neglect, exacerbated by a short but destructive conflict, with its human capital and physical capital severely diminished. Economic institutions were virtually nonexistent, and the vacuum was filled by parallel structures of dubious legality. The financial system was obliterated, and the economy had reverted to cash-based transactions. Against this background, the postconflict reconstruction and institution building undertaken by the international community since the end of the conflict is impressive, although too late to mitigate some of the violence. Today, Kosovo's economy has a recognizable face: private business is thriving, financial institutions are restarting in a supervised manner, physical infrastructure is on par with its previous state in the 1980s, and a government provides public services partly financed through taxation. Almost every part of this economy suffers severe shortcomings and distortions, but the basic building blocks are there for a solid foundation.

Within these accomplishments, however, is the reminder that the international aid community, again, responded to the emergency humanitarian crisis but could not immediately respond with reconstruction aid once the fighting ceased. The simple fact is that international aid agencies must have ample time to organize, gather funding, and deploy. Recent history continues to show us—and Kosovo is just another example—that this process consumes most of a year. At the one-year mark, violence and instability increased in Kosovo. Young fighters had regained their strength, and separatist factions raised their heads once again as alternative employment opportunities still did not exist. The emergence of the UCPMB in the Presevo

Valley, followed by violence on the Macedonian border, was the unfortunate result. The international community will continue to have a key responsibility in Kosovo. Continued engagement is necessary at all levels if Kosovo is going to be a viable province, capable of self-sustainment. First and foremost, under the current arrangements the initiative to resolve Kosovo's constitutional status cannot be taken by anyone but the international community, which, through the United Nations, is collectively responsible for the administration of the province. Moreover, regardless of the shape of the final political settlement, Kosovo's political and economic institutions cannot continue to develop without significant assistance from the rest of the world. Last, considerable resources and technical expertise are required to employ the significant capital investment needed to lift Kosovo's economy from poverty and place it onto a sustainable growth path. These resources cannot materialize without donor support. The international community's "exit strategy" from Kosovo, therefore, must be a very gradual process if Kosovo is to have any chance at stable, long-term peace.

However, the presence of the international community in Kosovo, though crucial, will not by itself be enough to achieve any of these goals. The ubiquitous presence of expatriates in Kosovo today, occupying virtually every position of authority, conveys a misleading impression. The fate of Kosovo is ultimately in the hands of the Kosovars themselves, and the positions of authority must be gradually turned over to the locals. The new democratic institutions of self-government, however provisional, have already given Kosovars considerable influence in shaping events in Kosovo, and this influence is bound to increase with time. They now have to make the choice to build a peaceful, well-governed society and a strong market economy. They have a key piece—their physical reconstruction—well in hand. Now they need to develop the institutions with which to maintain, sustain, and promote all that they have accomplished in such a short time.

Recovering Kosovo—above and below the surface. *Right:* Former members of the Kosovo Liberation Army—now the Kosovo Protection Corps, devoted to rebuilding and helping to provide public security for their province—team up with the Texas National Guard's 277th Asphalt Detachment, attached to the 16th Armored Engineer Battalion, to repair Route STAG, between Urosevac and Gnjilane in KFOR's U.S. sector in August 2000.

Left: Task Force Falcon's Explosive Ordnance Disposal unit found literally tons of mines in its regular patrols of KFOR's American sector. Here, an EOD soldier places C4 explosive on top of some captured antitank mines in a controlled detonation pit in September 2000. The EOD unit would execute a controlled detonation about twice a week.

Selective destruction. As part of its ethnic cleansing campaign in the province, the Milosevic regime targeted ethnic Albanian homes and schools for destruction, while leaving adjacent Serb structures untouched. American KFOR engineers "adopted" many ethnic Albanian schools as their special projects, including these two destroyed Albanian schools near Urosevac, Kosovo, in July 2000, rebuilding the structures on their scant off hours. By September 2000, the U.S. engineering battalions had most of Kosovo's children back in the classroom.

A CJCMOTF success story. Getting Afghanistan's children back in school was a very high priority of the Afghan interim government, and by summer 2002, a U.S. Army Civil Affairs unit operating near Kabul took on the repair work for this school. Below, a Civil Affairs officer provides basic English instruction to Afghan children.

Base camp repair during Operation Enduring Freedom. Restricted from doing repair and reconstruction work outside base camps, U.S. military engineers undertook major repair to supply bases in Afghanistan during the spring of 2002. At left, troops from the 18th Airborne Corps use concrete to repair bomb damage to the camp's airfield in Kandahar.

International demining. Contractors used a variety of methods to help rid Afghanistan of a serious "mine pollution" problem. Left to right: a "sniffer" dog, mine detector wands, and mine detector probes. Many different companies using many different methods of mine detection all operated from one centralized office in the postconflict phase of Operation Enduring Freedom.

171

4

AFGHANISTAN

IMMEDIATELY AFTER THE ATTACKS on the World Trade Center and the Pentagon on September 11, 2001, it seemed that America had more questions than answers. It was apparent that these attacks were a dramatic escalation of al Qaeda actions that included the 1996 Khobar Towers bombing in Saudi Arabia, the U.S. embassy bombings in Kenya and Tanzania in 1998, and the attack on the USS *Cole* in 2000—all attacks on U.S. installations abroad and at sea. What would be the appropriate response to al Qaeda's devastating direct assault on American soil? Should the United States continue with its policy of increased security and selected limited cruise missile strikes, or was a new response warranted? What action could the nation—or the world for that matter—mount against a stateless enemy whose purpose was to end the American way of life? Where and in what direction should the United States direct its wrath, and how could it prevent such an attack from happening again?

Within hours of the tragedy, a worldwide coalition assembled to fight terrorism—literally hundreds of countries contributing in a variety of ways, some militarily, others diplomatically, economically, and financially. In Washington, D.C., the White House re-established the Command Center, and President George W. Bush cobbled together what would soon become a comprehensive response that included disruption of financial assets to terrorist organizations and the creation of a worldwide coalition for the conduct of the global War on Terror in preparation for a military option to attack the terrorists at their source in Afghanistan and surrounding areas.

Operation Enduring Freedom, the military phase, began October 7, 2001, and was directed against an unconventional enemy—not a nation or an ethnic group but, rather, a variety of terrorist networks that threaten the way of life of all peaceful people. As the War on Terror is the first war of the twenty-first century, it required a twenty-first century military strategy. In that light, Secretary of Defense Donald Rumsfeld worked with coalition allies and General Tommy Franks, commander of U.S. Central Command (CENTCOM), to craft a military strategy that minimized civilian casualties, integrated local opposition forces, and brought quick destruction to the Taliban who supported the al Qaeda terrorist network. The coalition achieved broad military success while putting fewer than 3,000 American troops on the ground in Afghanistan. In some cases, soldiers conquered terrorists by welding together twenty-first-century technology with nineteenth-century tactics. U.S. Special Operations Forces (SOF) troops chased terrorists on horseback while using mobile phones and global positioning systems (GPS) to pinpoint targets for the Air Force; bombers used twenty-first-century targeting technology: laser- and GPS-guided "smart" bombs to destroy specific targets, including centuries-old caves used as terrorist redoubts.

On October 7, the Taliban controlled more than 80 percent of Afghanistan, anti-Taliban forces were on the defensive, and al Qaeda operatives were entrenched in camps and safe houses throughout the country. Afghanistan was, in fact, a terrorist-sponsored state. By October 20, United States-led coalition forces had destroyed all Taliban air defenses and had conducted a highly successful direct action mission on the residence of Taliban leader Mullah Mohammed Omar in the middle of the regime's capital, Kandahar. Simultaneously, SOF detachments linked up with anti-Taliban leaders and coordinated operational fires and logistics support on numerous fronts. Twenty days later, the provincial capital of Mazar-e Sharif fell; Herat, Kabul, and Jalalabad followed in rapid succession. By mid-December, U.S. Marines had secured Kandahar Airport, and the Taliban capital was in the hands of opposition forces. Within weeks, the Taliban and al Qaeda were reduced to isolated pockets of fighters. On December 22, General

Franks traveled to Kabul to attend a ceremony marking the inauguration of the Afghan interim government—seventy-eight days after the beginning of combat operations.[1]

The goal of stability and security was not fully realized throughout Afghanistan during the first year, although the situation is much better than it was prior to October 2001. The major goals of the ground war—to overthrow the Taliban and to reduce the influence of al Qaeda—were accomplished. Yet enough Taliban and al Qaeda remnants remain in the country to adversely affect the long-term peace and stability of the region.

PARALLELS WITH OTHER RECONSTRUCTION EFFORTS

It is difficult to draw exact parallels between the military interventions that NATO conducted in Bosnia and Kosovo with the intervention that the United States led in Afghanistan. The only major similarity is that postconflict reconstruction of the physical infrastructure did not immediately occur in all three operations necessary to provide basic needs and services and jump-start the economy. There are three main differences between the Balkans' operations and the effort in Afghanistan that are striking and obvious.

First, whereas the Balkans interventions were executed under a NATO blanket authority, the military operation in Afghanistan was a military coalition coordinated by the United States, excluding formal NATO authority, with Americans holding every key command position. The intervention was designed with a small force in mind; therefore, unlike the Balkans, security and stability throughout the countryside were not established immediately upon entry into the theater. While NATO forces in Bosnia and Kosovo immediately began the process of disarming and demobilizing the former warring factions under the auspices of a brokered agreement, the U.S. forces that deployed to Afghanistan arrived not as peacekeepers, but as combatants with the mission to hunt down and destroy the Taliban and al Qaeda terrorist network.

The second main difference that set it apart from the Balkans was the governmental structure established in Afghanistan. Although the governmental leaders in the Balkans and the regions that they controlled were readily identifiable, it was much more difficult to define the friendly and enemy organizations in Afghanistan. Three groups came to control much of the country following the Soviet withdrawal. First was the Taliban, the Afghan rogue government. After Soviet forces departed Afghanistan in 1989 and the Moscow-installed government collapsed three years later, a coalition of tribal-based *mujahideen* assumed control of the country. The coalition quickly fell apart and its factions engaged in a civil war that ravaged the land. Out of this chaos emerged the Taliban, consisting largely of young students from the religious schools in neighboring Pakistan, led by Islamic teachers headed by Mullah Omar. Rooted in the southern Pashtun tribe, the Taliban moved northward in 1994, determined to bring order to Afghanistan and create a pure Islamic state based on an extremely strict reading of the Koran. Capturing Kabul on September 26, 1996, the Taliban initially had a measure of acceptability and support among the Afghanistan populace. However, the regime's repression, particularly against women, its abysmal human rights record, cultural excesses, coercive imposition of radical Islam, and provision of a safe haven for terrorists, global arms dealers, and drug peddlers quickly made the Taliban an international pariah.[2]

The second group was the non-Pashtun force that quickly formed as the Northern Alliance, organized loosely under ousted president Burhanuddin Rabanni, an ethnic Tajik. The alliance was composed of commander Ahmed Shah Massoud's Islamic Society of largely Tajik forces and General Abdul Rashid Dostum's ethnic Uzbek National Islamic Movement. The forces of the Shi'a Hazara tribe, which maintains close relations with Iran, and those of the Turkmen tribe also joined the Northern Alliance.

The third governing authority in Afghanistan was Osama bin Laden's al Qaeda organization based in more than sixty countries around the world.[3] Although deferential to the Taliban—some U.S. counterterrorism officials even saw it as a partner of the Taliban—al Qaeda consisted almost exclusively of Arabs. Prior to October 2001, Afghanistan formed the nerve center of their activities and also served as the main base for their ideological and terrorist training. The result was a country with three functioning "governments," far from being an integrated unit. It was a country at war with itself.

The third main difference between the Balkan and Afghan interventions concerns infrastructure. As the initial intervention force entered Afghanistan, it quickly determined that little infrastructure could be used as the basis for operations. If the force required infrastructure for support, it had to be built. Unlike the Balkans, where the infrastructure was somewhat damaged from neglect and war but still repairable in most areas, Afghanistan's infrastructure had been decimated by a combination of twenty-three years of war, neglect, oppressive rule, and extended drought. Massive humanitarian relief was the initial order as Afghanis struggled to obtain even the barest of necessities; however, infrastructure to move relief supplies to areas outside Kabul did not exist. Many Afghan villagers were forced to stock food stores during winter, as the lack of infrastructure precluded any resupply reaching the village during the cold months. Roads initially built in the 1960s by the United States and the Soviet Union were worn and damaged through to the sub-base. Elevations in excess of 6,000 feet inhibited even the sturdiest of vehicles from traveling during snowy conditions.

THE STATE OF AFGHANISTAN
AT THE CESSATION OF HOSTILITIES

Afghanistan's level of development and decrepit infrastructure bring up perhaps the greatest difference between intervention in the Balkans and the case of Afghanistan. Infrastructure was a definite factor in planning the military campaign against the Taliban and al Qaeda, but it was also a major factor in the long-term effort in the Bush administration's War on Terror. In fact, rebuilding Afghanistan soon became a top priority for the Bush administration, if only to support President Hamid Karzai's efforts to govern the country effectively and reverse Afghanistan's fortunes as a failed state and thus a breeding ground for terrorists. U.S. Secretary of State Colin Powell told Karzai, the interim Afghan leader, that the United States would make substantial financial commitments at the international donor's conferences and that U.S. forces would be relentless in pursuing the remnants of al Qaeda and the Taliban. Secretary Powell said: "This country needs everything. It needs a banking system. It needs a sanitation system. It needs a phone system. It needs road construction. Everything you can imagine. We don't want to leave any contamination behind. That is in the interests of the Afghan people and certainly the mission we came here to perform."[4] President Karzai responded: "The Afghan people have been asking for a staying commitment, a staying partnership, from the United States to Afghanistan in order to make the region safe, in order to make Afghanistan stand back on its own feet and continue to fight against terrorism or the return of terrorism in any form to this country."[5]

The linkage among national reconstruction, the unification of the nation around a central government, and the elimination of aggressive factions was made explicit by President Bush just a few months after Powell's trip. Speaking at Virginia Military Institute (VMI) in mid-April 2002, the president likened Afghanistan's reconstruction to the Marshall Plan, named after VMI graduate and author of the reconstruction plan for postwar Europe, former secretary of state General George C. Marshall. Said the president:

> We know that true peace will only be achieved when we give the Afghan people the means to achieve their own aspirations. (Applause.) Peace— peace will be achieved by helping Afghanistan develop its own stable government. Peace will be achieved by helping Afghanistan train and develop its own national army. And peace will be achieved through an education system for boys and girls which works. (Applause.)

> We're working hard in Afghanistan. We're clearing minefields. We're rebuilding roads. We're improving medical care. And we will work to help Afghanistan to develop an economy that can feed its people without feeding the world's demand for drugs. (Applause.) . . .
>
> By helping to build an Afghanistan that is free from this evil and is a better place in which to live, we are working in the best traditions of George Marshall. (Applause.) Marshall knew that our military victory against enemies in World War II had to be followed by a moral victory that resulted in better lives for individual human beings.[6]

The nature of this long-term commitment is evolving. The military situation remains tenuous and the long-term commitment of U.S. forces will continue to be debated. However, the concrete, indisputable facts concern the state of the Afghan infrastructure. More than two decades of conflict and four years of drought led to widespread human suffering and massive displacement of people. Many parts of the country remain vulnerable to famine, the infrastructure base was destroyed or severely degraded, and human resources were depleted. State institutions were largely nonfunctional and the economy increasingly fragmented. The social fabric was weakened considerably, and human rights were undermined, with women and minorities as the principal sufferers. UN humanitarian agencies did much to alleviate the situation, wrestling with the Taliban who attempted to block foreign aid from flowing into the country. On September 12, 2001, however, the World Food Program, as well as a score of NGOs, all of which served as the principal lifeline for millions of Afghans, withdrew from the country in light of anticipated U.S. retaliation, leaving behind 5.5 million hungry people. According to the World Food Program, about 15,000 tons of stockpiled food remained in the country at the time of the group's departure, enough to last only two weeks.

Afghanistan will need major reinvestment in all sectors. Significant resources will be needed not only to rebuild the human and physical capital destroyed over the past two decades, but also to move Afghanistan onto a higher trajectory of growth and human development for the medium term. In the short term, there remains a pressing demand to meet the humanitarian needs of a war-weary population and to help ensure that the transition to peace is as smooth as possible. The Bonn Agreement, which established the Afghan Interim Government, provides clear political markers that the country needs to meet in order to sustain international support. It is essential that early assistance provide a stake in the peace process for ordinary Afghans in addition to those who might otherwise engage in conflict or illicit activities. Prior to 1979, Afghanistan was among the poorest and least developed countries in the world. Since then, its economic and social indicators have only deteriorated further. The international community must determine what level of reconstruction will constitute mission success in a country with very limited preconflict infrastructure and resources.

The Economy

Afghanistan is a landlocked, mountainous, geographically remote, sparsely populated, ethnically diverse, yet geopolitically important country. According to the World Bank, it has long been one of the poorest countries in the world, falling near the bottom in terms of average per-capita income and the UN Human Development Index (169th out of 174 countries in 1996). Afghanistan's prewar economy was mainly based on agriculture and animal husbandry. The country had a low population density because of difficult topographical and climatic conditions (high mountains covering most of the country, extremes of temperatures, and arid to semi-arid climate). In 1978—the last year of peace—Afghanistan was largely self-sufficient in food and was a significant exporter of agricultural products. Agriculture, however, was largely concentrated in the narrow river valleys and plains where irrigation water from snowmelt was available. Industry was largely undeveloped, with only a few plants established in the areas of textiles, medicines, and cement. Nevertheless, macroeconomic policy was surprisingly balanced, with budget surpluses, a market-based competitive exchange rate, and modest foreign and domestic debt.[7]

Economic conditions were sacrificed to political and military upheavals during two decades of war, including the nearly ten-year Soviet military occupation. During that conflict, one-third of the population fled the country, with Pakistan and Iran sheltering a combined peak of more than six million refugees. The drought, the long drawn-out war of Soviet occupation, and the subsequent internecine conflict severely damaged Afghanistan's economy. By the mid-1990s, the state and civil society had broken down over time and there was a progressive erosion of institutions—both modern and traditional—that had governed the prewar society. Given the breakdown of the state and civil society, a four-year drought led to famine. Crop production was halved and livestock herds heavily depleted, more than erasing the modest gains of the early to mid-1990s. Increasing numbers of people lost their means of livelihood and were displaced, either internally or to neighboring countries. Malnutrition significantly worsened, with starvation occurring with increasing frequency.

The Taliban, in a positive move, banned opium poppy cultivation; however, this ban sharply reduced the incomes of those small farmers and rural wage laborers who were dependent on poppy cultivation and related work. Government-provided social services, which never had a strong outreach into the rural areas, atrophied and to a large extent stopped functioning. NGOs and UN agencies took up the task of providing essential social services to parts of the population, building on community-based efforts in various parts of the country. Agricultural output came down sharply, livestock herds were depleted, and large-scale industries almost ceased functioning.[8] In early 2000, two million Afghan refugees remained in Pakistan and about 1.4 million in Iran, while the Afghanistan economy was in a state of collapse.

The Transportation Sector

Long-term conflict not only devastated Afghanistan's infrastructure but also deprived the country of new investment that would have raised services above prewar levels. Most Afghans have little or no access to decent basic services and must either go without or rely on costly alternatives. Among the most serious costs, particularly for women and children, are the costs in terms of health (from unsafe water and sanitation, and indoor air pollution from burning traditional biomass fuels) and time (required for fetching water and fuel). It is difficult to overemphasize the low base from which reconstruction will begin. The national road network is in poor condition, with significant numbers of bridges and causeways damaged or destroyed. According to the Asian Development Bank's Preliminary Needs Assessment, 128 kilometers of the 227 kilometer Torkham-Jalalabad-Kabul road (crucial both for trade and for relief shipments) are so seriously damaged that it takes four days for a truck to make a return trip between Peshawar and Kabul, a journey that used to take less than a day. Twenty-five years ago it took three hours to travel from Kabul to Kandahar; in December 2002 it took fourteen. Few rural villages have all-weather road access, and it is estimated that much of the primary road network of 2,500 kilometers needs rebuilding. In addition to destruction and underdeveloped physical infrastructure, public institutions (national and municipal) nominally responsible for service delivery were severely weakened through loss of experienced staff and lack of funding for even routine maintenance.[9]

For a mountainous, landlocked country like Afghanistan, roads and airports are vital for transport, for international trade, to facilitate national integration, and to avoid supply bottlenecks that create inflation. In light of this, forty-one airports augmented the poor road network; however, only one of the airports can adequately handle the wide-body jet aircraft prevalent in today's commercial air fleets. The largest and most important airport was Kabul International Airport, where traffic doubled to over 100,000 passengers annually between 1969 and 1976. Topographical conditions, however, limited the airport's capacity to handle wide-body jets, resulting in several expansion projects by both the Soviets and the United States to fix the problem. The Soviets lengthened the Kabul air strip for use by larger aircraft, with new terminals and hangars, pushing up passenger movement to 127,000 in 1982.[10]

There is an almost nonexistent rail network. The total length is 24.6 kilometers of mixed gauges connecting Turkmenistan to Towraghondi and Uzbekistan to Kheyrabad—not sufficiently developed to aid significantly in Afghanistan's redevelopment.[11] Road rehabilitation and upgrading will focus on the core highway network comprising the national Ring Road and border links, most of which was originally built by the U.S. Army Corps of Engineers and the Soviet Union in the early 1960s. Fast-track projects throughout the country are required to remove all bottlenecks such as collapsed bridges, disintegrated pavements, and damaged tunnels. Subcontracting can be used to generate employment through extensive labor-intensive methods in projects such as extensive drainage, erosion protection, and routine maintenance works.

Water Supply, Sewage, and Solid Waste

Access to adequate and safe water and sanitation facilities is limited, although in some areas NGOs and communities have improved conditions. Piped water and sewage networks are few in number and in poor shape because of a lack of maintenance and war damage. There is heavy reliance on on-site water and local sewage solutions. These solutions, together with severely diminished water resources caused by four years of drought, have led to high levels of groundwater pollution. Currently an estimated 77 percent of the population does not have access to safe water, although this masks wide differences among provinces and districts, and less than 20 percent of urban households have access to piped water. Rampant waterborne diseases are a major cause of the prevailing high infant and child mortality rates, with approximately 85,000 children under age five dying annually from diarrheal diseases. Few residential or public buildings in Afghan cities have sewage systems, and those that do have systems discharge wastewater directly into rivers without treatment—and downstream users suffer the

**Figure 3. Mortality Rate (per 1,000 live births) in
Afghanistan and South Asian Region**

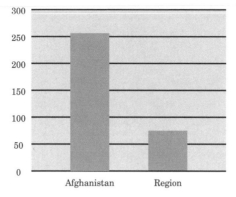

Source: The World Bank, "Afghanistan"; n.d.; available from <http://www.export.gov/
afghanistan>; Internet: accessed February 6, 2003.

consequences. In 1997, the World Bank estimated that sanitation coverage was 23 percent of the urban population and 8 percent of the rural population. Hygiene education accompanying
water supply installation has been introduced by some NGOs,
but coverage remains extremely limited.[12]

Energy

What energy production existed before the conflict has since
ceased. War has resulted in a shift back to traditional biomass
fuels (firewood, crop residues, animal waste) for cooking and
heating, which are likely to be a major contributor to respiratory
diseases, especially among women and children. Prewar electricity
was available only in the cities—about 6 percent of the population
had access to electricity supply; because of severe damage to electrical facilities and a lack of any routine maintenance, this supply
is limited to a few hours a day. The electricity production in 1999,
for example, was limited to 420 million kilowatt hours, with fossil
fuel producing 35 percent of the available electricity. Even though
little or unreliable data is available, the output now is only a small

percentage of the 1999 level. In addition, petroleum storage facilities around major urban centers were destroyed, and transport costs of imported fuels were inflated by the high costs of road transport. Natural gas used to be a major export, but gas fields ceased to operate and the wells were capped.[13] The final tally is that there is little energy production for a country that has twenty-three million inhabitants. The combined effects of the war, the drought, hyperinflation, and population displacement result in a country that now exists by scavenging for items to burn for residential uses.

Telecommunications

Communications facilities are seriously underdeveloped, with limited telephone and telegraph service. Access to telecommunications is one of the lowest in the world, with only two telephones per 1,000 people. In 1997, limited domestic telecommunications links were established among Mazar-e Sharif, Herat, Kandahar, Jalalabad, and Kabul through satellite and microwave systems. In addition, there are two international links: one Intelsat linked only to Iran and one Intersputnik link for the Atlantic Ocean region with a commercial satellite telephone center in Ghazni.[14] There is no mobile service or Internet service in the country. Because Afghanistan's telecommunications sector was so underdeveloped even before the conflict, reconstructing the telecommunications sector will require a determination of what constitutes success and mission completion. Although communications reconstruction in Bosnia and Kosovo was considered a key to stimulating the economy and establishing normalcy, Afghanistan's prewar telecommunications state may lend itself to a different approach by the international community.

Mine Threat

Afghanistan, a country slightly smaller than Texas, is the most mine- and UXO-affected country in the world, a situation that has been exacerbated by the increase in open conflict and coalition military operations. Villagers attempting to disarm and recycle land mines continue to be maimed and killed, even though seven million of the approximately twenty-six million inhabitants have received some form of mine awareness education. According to Donald "Pat" Patierno, head of the U.S. Department of State Bureau of Political-Military Affairs Humanitarian Demining Assistance Program, "Desperation causes some folks to engage in amateur demining even though they know the danger and may have received mine awareness training. This behavior is not unique to Afghanistan."[15] Land mines were first introduced to Afghanistan during the Soviet occupation (1979 to 1989) and were widely sown by Soviet troops, their Afghan cohorts, and mujahideen freedom fighters. When the Soviets withdrew, the mines remained and the warring factions continued to plant more. In addition, unknown quantities of UXO litter the country. These contaminants infest agricultural and grazing fields, irrigation canals, urban areas, homes, roads, power stations, airfields, and other facilities. UN estimates place the number of mines in the country at between five million and ten million. The sheer number of land mines throughout the country is even more staggering in light of the fact that only 11 percent of the total land area is contaminated with mines, and over half the country's terrain does not even lend itself to effective mining.[16]

Prior to these recent hostilities, the total economic loss to the country over the past twelve years as a result of mines and UXO was estimated by the United Nations at more than $550 million; the limited data available suggest a casualty rate of 150 to 300 per month, with 200,000 remaining survivors of mine and UXO accidents. Pre–September 2001 assessments indicate 732 square kilometers of known mined area, of which an estimated 100 square kilometers are mined in former frontline areas and 500 square kilometers of UXO in contaminated battle areas. Recent events added to the problem in Afghanistan, with new areas being contaminated by coalition UXO. Similar to Bosnia, the significant shifts in frontline military positions created new areas impacted by UXO from ground fighting, and ammunition depots in major towns, when hit, spread UXOs over as much as a five-kilometer radius. In addition, mine and UXO injuries escalated because of new contaminations and increased population displacement, often in unfamiliar areas.[17]

In addition to the human toll and the loss of valuable livestock, mines and UXO are obstacles to the return of internally displaced persons (IDPs) and refugees. They deny people access to farm and grazing land, shelter, and water, and prevent the rehabilitation of essential infrastructure such as roads, bridges, irrigation systems, schools, and other public buildings. At least 60 percent of the mine- and UXO-contaminated areas are in such locations, resulting in major losses to both the Afghan economy and society. Prewar mine action in Afghanistan, however, was extremely cost-effective based on experienced UN and NGO mine clearance teams and large-scale use of mine detection dogs. The United Nations estimated that each dollar spent yielded $4.60 in economic returns. The annual yield for one square kilometer of clearance was as much as $2,000 for grazing land and from $13,500 to $520,000 for farmland. Cleared roads provided $250,000 in economic benefits per fifty kilometers. In addition, prewar mine action resulted in an estimated 50 percent reduction in civilian mine victims and facilitated the return or resettlement of approximately 1.53 million refugees and IDPs.[18]

THE MILITARY RESPONSE
TO POSTCONFLICT RECONSTRUCTION

Postconflict reconstruction in this war-torn country takes on a different meaning than it did in the Balkans. Unlike in the Balkans, military forces in Afghanistan, except for Civil Affairs teams and SOF forces, are more centralized in the cities and do not venture far from their established safe havens unless actively engaged in ground operations. Roads are in some cases nonexistent, and the roads that do exist are replete with banditry and theft and are avoided by the military. The military footprint in Afghanistan is not all-encompassing. U.S. and coalition forces are not present on every street corner, and there are no well-established confrontation lines or zones of separation for coalition forces to monitor. Because the physical infrastructure is so lacking, most resupply for coalition forces arrives daily by air. There has not been a designation of an off-base MSR network as there was in both Balkans operations, so engineer-funding streams were couched in force protection and force bed-down, rather than in reconstruction. Given this scenario, is there a military piece in Afghanistan's reconstruction?

United States Engineering Effort

> Deploy rapidly to multiple locations in a contingency area of operations and conduct base camp construction. On order conduct airfield repair, sustainment, survivability, and general engineering as needed in support of theater combat operations.
>
> —*United States Engineer Mission Statement*

The engineer mission statement was clear: there was to be no postconflict infrastructure reconstruction executed by military engineers in Afghanistan.[19] All missions would be to support the deployed combat force and would adhere, again, to minimum military requirements. However, there were sufficient military tasks the engineer task force was required to complete in order to fully carry out its assigned mission. On September 11, 2001, CENTCOM Engineering Division and its equivalent engineer staffs within its component commands proceeded to direct military engineer efforts toward specified tasks that required engineer support, including contingency planning, engineer unit deployment, airfield repair and upgrade, mine and UXO clearing, and base camp construction. In the immediate wake of the terrorist attacks, engineers evaluated the condition of available infrastructure in the area of responsibility and compared this information with available engineer assets and capabilities. The initial deployment of SOF units into the theater did not include supporting engineers—an omission that became obvious when the demand for engineers quickly escalated. In immediate response, some engineer forces already in the area revised their deployments to support early Enduring Freedom requirements. An Air Force RED HORSE unit, for example, diverted from a programmed project in one country to a contingency tasking in another.

As Operation Enduring Freedom progressed past the initial SOF stage, the flow of forces into the area significantly increased. Air Force RED HORSE and PRIME BEEF (airfield construction) units, Army engineer and prime power units, and Navy Seabee units deployed to contingency installations to repair and upgrade airfields, construct base camps, and provide electrical power. Subsequent Army engineer units relieved Air Force and Navy Seabee units to continue base construction, maintenance, and repair, and coalition partner engineers deployed into the area to support runway repair, well drilling, and mine clearing. Dividing the engineer mission into five categories—mobility, countermobility, survivability, general engineering, and Explosive Ordnance Disposal/Mine Action Center—it becomes readily apparent that engineer support to the deployed forces was an all-encompassing job, considering the limited amount of military engineers (a few battalions of various engineer specialties) deployed into the theater.

Mobility. Mobility operations are designed to facilitate the ease of movement for the military force and to enable rapid response and rapid resupply for combat forces whether in enemy contact or in day-to-day operations. The three mobility tasks that the engineer force accomplished in the first year of operations in Afghanistan were route and airfield reconnaissance, airfield repair, and MSR maintenance and upgrades. Because there were no robust ground lines of communications in the area of operation, maintaining the air line of communications became a high priority. To adequately support the deployed forces in Afghanistan, war-fighters needed airfields in several surrounding Central Asian countries and eventually within Afghanistan itself; the airfields would support fighter operations, logistical hubs, and force bed-down. Because U.S. and coalition forces had conducted only limited operations in the region before September 11, the only airfields and bases available quickly enough to support Operation Enduring Freedom were several fighter air bases built by the Soviets. The Soviets hastily constructed or expanded these airfields during their 1980s Afghanistan campaign, using precast concrete slabs without reinforcing bar, emplacing them over roughly graded ground without a sub-base—a recipe for airfield failure and disaster. Years of neglect and conflict, as well as Enduring Freedom air strikes, damaged and deteriorated the airfields, supporting utilities, and ground transportation infrastructure.[20]

Initially, rapid runway repair was the high-priority mission for engineers. To get forces and logistics in theater quickly, they patched numerous bomb craters, repaired spalled and cracked pavement, and laid steel airfield matting. A more innovative approach was the Navy Seabees' use of acrylic copolymer soil stabilizers to suppress dust and stabilize soil for a desert air strip. But there were problems. Traditional concrete repair techniques necessitated closing sections of runways for days to wait for freshly placed concrete caps and patches to cure to full strength. As a time-saving alternative, engineers harvested undamaged slabs from unused areas of the airfields to replace the unserviceable slabs. Small patches of damaged runway were cut out, the sub-base was replaced and compacted, and the area was capped with the harvested slabs. These slabs were replaced during consecutive nights so airfields could remain operational with minimal disruption while undergoing pavement repair.

In addition, a team from the Air Force Civil Engineer Support Agency completed pavement evaluation studies at Kandahar and Baghram. These studies provided analyses on airfield characteristics such as pavement strength, the number of passes a runway could endure before failing, and recommendations on runway, taxiway, and parking apron usage. The teams generally overestimated the capacity of the airfields. For example, the assessment of the Kandahar airfield stated that it could support 50,000 passes by C-17s and 50,000 C-130 passes after several craters were repaired and that the Baghram airfield could support 15,000 passes by C-17s and more than 50,000 C-130 passes. Engineer planners relied on the assessments and were relieved that the airfields could support this amount of heavy traffic.

For various reasons, however, the assessments were inaccurate. Once the initial repairs were completed in accordance with the assessments, the runways started again to deteriorate, requiring daily maintenance. The premature failure of the Baghram airfield was attributed in part to several passes made by Russian IL-76 and AN-124 aircraft—the first being about the size of a C-17 and the second being among the largest airframes in the world. The assessments did not project the use of these large airframes on the airfields, but there was no way to limit the use of large aircraft until the airfield failed and the Kabul airfield opened. As a result, friendly forces expanded their operations and used airfields built by the Soviet Union, the United States' Cold War adversary.[21]

Concentrating on Kandahar and Baghram, engineers conducted initial rapid runway repair assessments to determine the requirements to make the airfields operational for military aircraft. Upon completion of the assessments, the U.S. Air Force's 200/201st Expeditionary RED HORSE Squadron, with help from the Italian and Slovakian air forces and Polish engineers, completed concrete repairs to the runway, rewired the air traffic control towers, and constructed "clamshell" aircraft maintenance hangars.[22] In addition, members of the 92nd Engineer Battalion (Combat Heavy) and the 326th Engineer Battalion (Air Assault) completed more than sixty other concrete repairs to the airfields at Kandahar, Baghram, and Mazar-e Sharif. These repairs totaled more than 110,000 cubic yards of reinforced concrete and hundreds of cold patch asphalt repairs. In an effort to streamline resupply operations to the deployed force, additional assessments were executed at various ports and airfields in surrounding countries throughout Central Asia. All MSRs in the base camps in Central Asia, Baghram airfield, and Kandahar airfield were upgraded and maintained for military traffic; however, it is notable that no MSRs were repaired external to the base camps. To lessen construction times, U.S. engineers attempted to obtain materials from local quarries or else contract the delivery of suitable material from the limited local capacity. Materials were difficult to obtain early on in the operation because of the austere infrastructure and limited suppliers available, but this situation gradually improved. For example, Type I cement was the only kind available in Afghanistan, so all Type III cement (needed for proper repair of the runway) and all cold patch (needed to repair the asphalt at the Kandahar runway) had to be flown in. Keeping an adequate supply of these repair materials on hand was a constant challenge.[23]

Countermobility. The intent of all countermobility operations was to provide force protection to the deployed force while in the base camps and deter unwanted enemy movement upon a friendly force. This was a tough mission to execute because the enemy does not necessarily wear uniforms or operate as a traditional military force. Upon entry into theater, combat engineers constructed 8,000 meters of concertina wire fencing around Kandahar Air Base to keep local nationals and stray animals from conducting unauthorized entries onto the airfield. Six log cribs (an obstacle created from two parallel walls of railroad ties filled with dirt) were constructed at the base camp entry control points to facilitate vehicle movement, with two high blast walls made of 25,000 cubic yards of soil constructed for vehicle inspection. To secure the entry control point and provide cover for those soldiers conducting the vehicle inspections, two concrete bunkers were constructed and installed. To adequately guard the base camp perimeter, soldiers needed to be in a position higher than the ground that they were defending. In response, engineers constructed sixteen guard towers to help provide perimeter security. Finally, 800 meters of antitank ditch (a bulldozer-wide ditch designed to stop vehicle movement) were built on both the northeast and south sides of Kandahar airfield in order to adequately secure the coalition aircraft. With force protection always remaining a high priority, the determination of to what extent countermobility measures would be employed was always a judgment call based on the perceived threat.

Survivability. Survivability operations were designed and built to provide both vehicle and personnel with covered fighting positions from which to conduct combat operations. To enhance and protect the coalition force intelligence-gathering ability, engineer forces first built hull-defilade positions (deep enough so that only the vehicle turret is exposed above the ground) around the Kandahar perimeter for the Canadian Coyotes (intelligence vehicles), and vehicle-fighting positions for American Humvees equipped with TOW (tube-launched, optically tracked, wire-guided) missiles for perimeter defense. The engineers then used their small emplacement excavators (small tractors with a small scoop blade on one end and an excavator arm on the other) to dig bunker positions for the dismounted infantry, vehicle positions for the mortars, and 2,000 feet of force protection trenches for personnel throughout the Kandahar life support areas.

Logistics assets, because of their immobility and vulner-ability, required protection from direct and indirect enemy fire; therefore, engineer forces constructed twelve-foot earthen berms around the ammunition supply point and the bulk fuel point. The berms not only protected these logistics services from enemy fire, but also protected the rest of the base camp if an explosion occurred during refueling or rearming operations. In addition, it is common practice in a combat zone for Apache helicopters to rearm and refuel with the engines and blades turning in order to decrease the aircraft turnaround time and limit the amount of time spent exposed to enemy fire on the ground. To support that mission, engineer forces constructed berms for "hot" rearming/ refueling points throughout Central Asia and Kandahar. Again, these berms not only protected the Apaches from external gun-fire, but also served as protection for others in the base camp if an aircraft exploded while undergoing this somewhat dangerous logistics operation.[24]

These survivability missions were labor, material, and equip-ment intensive and required large quantities of lumber, plywood, and sandbags for overhead bunkers and covers. In addition, the austere environment and rocky soil conditions necessitated heavy digging machinery requiring extensive maintenance sup-port. Because engineer parts are not readily available in the

Army inventory because of the low density of the equipment, engineer units, as a normal course, usually establish contracts at local commercial dealers (for example, Caterpillar or John Deere) in order to procure parts. This scheme was executed both in Pale, Bosnia, and in Pristina, Kosovo, in order to ensure ongoing maintenance support for engineer parts. In Afghanistan, however, the lack of a local vendor base led to difficulties in contracting for spare parts for commercial engineer equipment. Once the airfield was established for military aircraft, engineer parts were procured through vendors in the Middle East and Europe and then flown to Afghanistan on available military aircraft.

General Engineering. Realizing that there was not much in Afghanistan to exploit for the coalition force facilities, the engineer task force, as in Bosnia and Kosovo, spent a considerable amount of its energy constructing the base camps for the 6,000-man deployed force. However, unlike the Balkans operations, the planning time available to develop the scheme for base camp operations was greatly curtailed. Initial bed-down facilities for the first units arriving in Baghram consisted of a mix of old Russian barracks, standard general-purpose medium tents, and force provider tents (contained in U.S. Army pre-positioned logistics sustainment packages). Instead of designing and building SEAhuts as was done initially in Kosovo and ultimately in Bosnia, troops in Operation Enduring Freedom deployed to Tier II tents (canvas tents with wooden floors and wooden frame walls). The engineer task force employed horizontal assets to prepare the gravel site layout for 350 Tier II tents, followed by vertical construction with electrical lighting and outlets. As the camp expanded, more force provider facilities were added, and several buildings were renovated for use as offices and limited sleeping quarters. Elements of the United States Army's 249th Prime Power battalion—the same unit that was able to repair and provide power to the New York Stock Exchange six days after September 11—provided 2.5 megawatts of power in Central Asia and an additional 3 megawatts of power at Kandahar. Initially, units depended on their own tactical generators for their power needs; however, because the existing power distribution systems at both camps were deemed to be unsafe, the utility detachment and other engineer personnel installed underground power lines.

Providing an adequate supply of potable water at Baghram was also challenging during its rapid expansion. Initially, bottled water was flown in—an acceptable solution when the camp consisted of fewer than 300 people. It was soon apparent, however, that as the population expanded, bottled water would not be adequate to meet dining, laundry, and hygiene requirements. As a solution, on-site wells were established both at Baghram and at Kandahar to provide 80,000–100,000 gallons per day; 6,500 feet of pressurized service lines for showers, laundry/bath units, and dining facilities were emplaced; and 3,000 feet of a gravity flow sewer line was constructed in order to transport both the gray and black wastewater to a local leach bed within the camps' perimeters—again, the only sewage treatment system operating in Afghanistan.[25]

Because the local jails were no longer functional, the engineer task force had to create a short-term holding facility at Kandahar to handle all prisoners or detainees. This facility consisted of four guard towers, a small shower facility, 3,000 feet of eight-foot-high chain-link fence with razor wire, floors and lighting for thirty cells/tents, and thirty custom latrines for the detainees. In some cases, these were better conditions than where the detainees had been living before their capture. In addition, engineer forces built several wooden frame headquarters buildings—one for the brigade headquarters, one for the Joint Special Operations Task Force, and three others for support elements. For all construction, the engineers developed an adequate drainage plan, despite the ongoing drought, and adequate concrete pads for vital tent facilities and aircraft parking. Again, the lack of available local sources to contract for material considerably slowed the construction times at Kandahar and Baghram; all material had to come from sources outside of Afghanistan.[26]

Explosive Ordnance Disposal and Mine Action Center. Because of the pervasive mine and UXO situation in Afghanistan, there was a heavy requirement to support the deployed forces with Explosive Ordnance Disposal (EOD). Engineer units were tasked to clear thousands of mines and UXO from thousands of square kilometers of ground to make the immediate area safe for occupation and use by coalition forces. The Soviets operationally used antipersonnel minefields to protect the airfields and then left them in place when they departed. These minefields were fenced and generally well marked. Subsequently, however (as in Bosnia), the locals lifted many of the mines and placed them in areas outside of marked minefields. Both the Taliban and Northern Alliance forces, for example, were suspected of lifting mines and planting them in unmarked fields during their battles in and around the Baghram airfield. Coalition engineer and EOD units conducted clearance operations to make designated areas safe for use by coalition forces. It is important to again highlight that Title X, United States Code, prohibits U.S. soldiers from conducting humanitarian demining operations. However, demining, executed by civilian deminers, and area clearance, conducted by military engineers for the coalition forces, significantly differ in that area clearance renders an area only reasonably safe for operational use, while demining provides a very high level of assurance that all mines and UXO have been removed from a designated area.

The procedures chosen to clear areas in Afghanistan were based on several factors, such as the estimated threat, the purpose of clearing, the type of terrain to be cleared, the type of clearing resources available, and the time available. Generally, there were three methods of neutralizing mines in Afghanistan: manual, explosive, and mechanical. The least preferred method, manual clearing, involves moving or lifting mines or UXO by hand. U.S. soldiers do not manually lift mines by doctrine; as this method involves the greatest amount of risk, it is not the preferred method of many coalition force engineer units either. Clearing mines and UXO with explosives involves placing additional explosives in close proximity to the mines or UXO without disturbing them and destroying them in place. U.S. Army EOD units and the Norwegian engineer unit coupled this technique with a method of shooting the mines with a sniper rifle. The intent was to separate the fuse from the explosive material before the fuse became activated; however, the munition often exploded during this uncertain process. The final method and that which was most used in Afghanistan was the mechanical method using the Mine-Clearing Armor-Protected (MCAP) bulldozer. The MCAP dozers were effective at clearing mines to a depth of about six to eighteen inches and could withstand blasts from antipersonnel mines with little or no damage. However, the enclosed cab intensified the blast effects from the detonation, and if operators detonated several mines in rapid succession, they were relieved because of the concussion effects they experienced.

The area-clearing results were impressive. In the immediate vicinity of Kandahar airfield alone, EOD cache-clearing operations found more than eighty weapons caches. In the first year, EOD personnel destroyed more than 120,000 munitions, totaling more than 350,000 pounds of explosives. EOD provided support to conventional and SOF forces for all operations and provided an emergency response for minestrikes and UXO. Using the MCAP bulldozers, Norwegian Hydrema mine flails, and Jordanian Aardvark mine flails, coalition engineer forces cleared more than three million square meters in Baghram, Kandahar, and Mazar-e Sharif. The MCAP dozer alone detonated more than seventy mines and uncovered in excess of 700 UXOs. In addition, eight teams of "sniffer" dogs and their handlers were brought in from Bosnia and used successfully to proof Baghram and Kandahar for UXO. A drawback of using dogs for mine detection, however, is that the method is significantly slower than mechanical methods and the dogs' olfactory sense is greatly affected by environmental conditions—hot weather, dust, and the residual odor from recent detonations.[27]

As in the Balkans, the military Mine Action Center provided mine products to the task force for the Kandahar area of responsibility. Upon entry into the theater, there was little information on specific minefield locations. As an initial guide, engineer task force soldiers relied heavily on old Soviet maps for minefield locations; however, upon establishing a link with the UN Mine Action Center, which had been operating in Afghanistan for several years before Operation Enduring Freedom, engineer forces in each task force were able to track UN clearance operations, reports of areas that had been completely cleared and deemed safe, and reports where mines and UXO were newly discovered. In some circumstances, unfortunately, military area clearance procedures were not tracked in enough detail to allow the areas to be turned over to a humanitarian demining center upon conclusion of military clearance operations—something that the UN humanitarian deminers needed to determine if further demining actions were required in order to certify that the area is cleared to UN demining standards. Despite some initial problems, the engineer forces were able to establish an adequate database in an effort to protect coalition soldiers during combat operations. As of July 2002, the task force had endured ten mine and UXO incidents in Afghanistan, which resulted in several deaths and severe injuries; although one incident is too many, this is a relatively low number when compared against the pervasive threat.

Coalition Joint Civil-Military Operations Task Force Effort

At the grassroots level, there was a military effort that concentrated on the Afghan population, but mainly in the humanitarian assistance realm and not in postconflict recon-struction. Campaigns for hearts and minds have been conducted in other operations, but there was a two-pillared approach in Afghanistan that was truly unique. During the mission analysis, General Franks emphasized that simultaneous with combat operations, the coalition had to demonstrate that the War on Terror was never directed specifically against the Afghan people. It was important to the establishment of a safe and secure environment that soldiers were seen to be doing beneficial things to help the locals overcome their present adverse situation. This military presence was key in spreading the security umbrella from the large cities into the villages and was not an attempt by the military to usurp the traditional NGO role of humanitarian assistance. In previous operations, units conducted civil-military operations, but there never was the overt designation of a Coalition Joint Civil-Military Operations Task Force (CJCMOTF). There were some possible disadvantages: lack of synchronization between the joint force and CJCMOTF commanders; duplication of effort; and increased force requirements. But in the case of Afghanistan, the advantages of a CJCMOTF—consolidation and coordination of civil-military operations, unity of command and effort for civil-military operations, and freeing the combatant commander from civil-military tasks—significantly outweighed the disadvantages. With coalition forces remaining for the most part in the large towns, no other organization would be in a position to demonstrate to a good portion of the Afghan people that the war was not a war against them.[28]

In early October 2001, CENTCOM ordered the creation of the CJCMOTF; however, it did not specify its mission or give it specific tasks upon which to develop the mission statement, as would normally happen for a subordinate element. The initial guidance covered a broad range of possibilities regarding the humanitarian assistance and support to the coalition commander's area of operations, but the overriding stipulation was that the CJCMOTF was to take its lead from the United Nations and other civilian relief agencies. However, IOs and NGOs refused to plan or speculate on future requirements without the definition of a specific need. Thus, the CJCMOTF staff had to organize and plan against an unknown requirement. The first elements of the CJCMOTF deployed to Camp Doha, Kuwait, in November, and Brigadier General David Kratzer of the 377th Theater Support Command assumed command in early December. In absence of CENTCOM guidance, Brigadier General Kratzer and his staff developed the following mission statement:

> CJCMOTF facilitates continued good relations with local authorities and populations, identifies and coordinates civil-military projects, continues support to Coalition commanders, and facilitates emer-

gency humanitarian relief operations in Afghanistan. On order, CJCMOTF transfers responsibility of projects and missions, as appropriate, to IO/NGOs, Department of State (DOS), International Security Assistance Force (ISAF), and the Office of Military Cooperation–Afghanistan (OMC-A) and redeploys from Afghanistan.[29]

This was a good start for a mission statement, but it was not enough guidance for Brigadier General Kratzer's subordinate commanders to fully carry out their jobs. With the establishment of a broad mission statement, the commander needed to establish his mission intent so that his subordinates would have adequate direction—an intent that subordinates could refer to for guidance when unforeseen events occurred. Again, with a country that needed everything, some priorities had to be established in order to better focus the limited civil-military assets in theater. After much discussion, the CJCMOTF Commander published his intent (see table 8).

Operationally, the CJCMOTF made some progress, although funding was a constant issue. Under its self-designed mandate, the CJCMOTF attempted to identify, coordinate, and conduct quick-fix humanitarian projects throughout the country that were not being accomplished by the civilian humanitarian assistance community. The task force was careful to coordinate its efforts with Afghan agencies and the IO/NGO community, seeking out the projects that would have the greatest impact on the Afghan people, such as the National Impact Projects proposed by the interim government.[30]

Once a National Impact Project was identified, CJCMOTF had to establish that the project met certain criteria. First, the project had to comply with Overseas Humanitarian Disaster Civil Aid (OHDCA) guidelines—not a simple task because OHDCA guidelines are quite extensive. Also, CJCMOTF ensured that the project supported the Afghan Transitional Authority. Last, the CJCMOTF coordinated its efforts with the various government ministries to ensure that the project was good for the task force and good for Afghanistan; one of the most important parts of the task force's mission was to support the transitional government and the choices the government made for the rebuild-

Table 8. CJCMOTF Commander's Intent—Key Tasks

- Establish Coalition Humanitarian Liaison Cells (CHLCs) where the United Nations has humanitarian centers to enable IO/NGO-led humanitarian assistance operations.

- Establish CHLCs where specific SOF teams are operating to augment their humanitarian assistance and situational awareness capabilities.

- Provide civil-military operations to support local coalition commanders to facilitate military operations.

- Synchronize civil-military operations as conducted by all actors in order to avoid confusion or duplicative efforts among all parties.

- Establish links to embassy, USAID, UN offices, ISAF, OMC-A, and other relevant actors in Kabul to provide situational awareness and recommendations for future U.S. action.

- On order, CJCMOTF transfers projects and missions to IOs/NGOs, the Department of State, and ISAF in order to set conditions for redeployment of CJCMOTF from Afghanistan.

Source: CJCMOTF, "Coalition Joint Civil-Military Operations Task Force" (briefing slides with scripted commentary, CJCMOTF, Kabul, March 17, 2002), 15.

ing of Afghanistan. After the approval process was complete, the project was offered to local contractors for bidding. Upon acceptance of a bid, Afghan labor was hired and local materials were used to maximize the benefit to the local economy.[31] During the construction phase, coalition engineers, public health professionals, and local contractors met periodically to ensure that the projects were completed to an exacting standard and to answer any ongoing questions about the current project or any future projects.

All of the National Impact Projects were in Kabul. They ranged from a power and water complex decimated by decades of war, to pharmaceutical companies that provide medication to the multitudes of the sick and injured. There were ten National Impact Projects in progress throughout Kabul, including a teachers training college, an artificial insemination farm, the restoration of the Kabul Dental Hospital, and the repair of 266 kilometers of irrigation canals. According to Major Jeff Coggin, chief of the task force's public health department:

> Whatever we do here will affect the rest of the country. A good example of that would be the teachers college. If fixing a school for children helps one community, then fixing a school that instructs teachers will help an entire nation. The Afghan workers take a great deal of pride in their work. They realize that what they're doing is for everyone.[32]

Funding for CJCMOTF projects came from a variety of sources. Primarily the task force received funds from OHDCA—Title X funding that is fenced annually by Congress. OHDCA funds were previously used in peace operations for quick impact, high-profile projects to jump-start humanitarian civic action. However, until Operation Enduring Freedom, there was never such an organizational focus from as high as the Office of the Secretary of Defense on the spending of these funds. Given the archaic peacetime rules that governed their use, this became somewhat problematic. The rules demanded intense involvement of much of the CJCMOTF and CHLC staffs—something the organizations were not tasked to do. The CJCMOTF slowly turned into a monetarily poor military NGO and sacrificed its traditional core competencies of community assessment, information coordination, and military civil action activities. Coalition engineer assets were too few in number to spread across Afghanistan, and CENTCOM was never going to use operational funds for civilian infrastructure reconstruction. The initial $2 million of OHDCA funds was the only funding that the military had for humanitarian assistance, requiring interagency approval before the money was released; it did not arrive in theater until February 2002. Despite the funding problems, the CJCMOTF estimated that considering the Afghanistan economy, its cost of living, exchange rate, daily labor, and material costs, the management of these projects and funds would be similar to managing a project of $20–$30 million.[33]

However, such projects have always been secondary to the coalition's main objective: fighting remnants of the Taliban and al Qaeda. As the United States reached the one-year anniversary of deploying forces into Afghanistan, three quarters of Afghanistan was considered relatively secure, leading to a slight shift in emphasis away from combat operations and toward reconstruction efforts. General Richard B. Myers, chairman of the Joint Chiefs of Staff, asserted that the United States should change its priorities in Afghanistan and de-emphasize military operations in favor of more support for reconstruction efforts. General Myers suggested that it may be time for the military to "flip" its priorities from combat operations aimed at hunting down al Qaeda and Taliban fighters to "the reconstruction piece in Afghanistan," a notable shift in priorities for a Pentagon that has eschewed nation-building exercises.[34] These remarks were quickly reflected in CJCMOTF operations on the ground. Colonel Phil Maughan, the commander of the CJCMOTF in Kabul, said that the new focus of coalition activities using regional teams was designed to help Afghanistan's new government establish its authority, make it easier for aid organizations to carry out their work, and allow coalition forces to go home. According to Colonel Maughan:

> Eventually, what we envision with these regional teams is getting the central government out to the regions, giving them the legitimacy they need to support Kabul. But, we are also trying to get the NGOs and the UN to start working together. Once they start doing that, there will no longer be a need for the U.S. military and we can go home.[35]

Until the fall of 2002, civil-military operations in Afghanistan were modest, with a budget of $6 million supporting scattered teams of six reservists each. Working from U.S. bases in half a dozen Afghan cities, the teams contracted local workers to rebuild war-damaged schools, clinics, wells, and other public structures. Under the new program, the budget doubled and large professional Civil Affairs teams, including engineers and veterinarians, were deployed and stationed at regional bases in the cities of Herat, Mazar-e Sharif, Kunduz, Jalalabad, Kandahar, Gardez, and Bamian.[36] A coalition of private agencies operating in Afghanistan criticized the expansion of the military civic action program, calling it "risky and premature," and suggested that uniformed troops taking a major role in providing aid might undermine their efforts to bring about stability and development. But as word of the American plan spread, local officials and residents welcomed the news, partly because the added foreign troops meant greater security and partly because the projects would provide work for hundreds of people in areas flooded with returning refugees and idle former combatants.

Shortfalls

The security situation in Afghanistan has changed remarkably since September 11; however, the state of the physical infrastructure has only gotten worse. The military reconstruction approach taken thus far in Afghanistan falls short of what was required in the first year. Military engineers did not have the mandate to execute any postconflict reconstruction. Although their list of accomplishments is laudable, their efforts, by design, were solely in support of the deployed military force, with no effort dedicated to projects that specifically benefit the Afghan people. The CJCMOTF worked hard to initiate and complete several humanitarian projects—projects that were both job-creating and beneficial to a specific local need—but there were problems. These projects did not address the large-scale reconstruction of the physical infrastructure; the creation of the first-ever CJCMOTF was rife with organizational problems; and the jungle of archaic rules and procedures that the CJCMOTF had to wade through in order to accomplish any projects, regardless of the size, greatly limited the number and types of projects that it was fortunate enough to complete. The CJCMOTF served essentially as a military NGO, trying to fill humanitarian aid gaps that seemed to exist among the civilian NGOs that were deployed on the ground; however, even that was problematic. The CJCMOTF was charged to work with the civilian NGO community to determine the existing gaps, but met with little cooperation or sharing of information, often resulting in duplicative efforts.

A year after the formation of an interim government, Afghanistan in many ways has been transformed. The Taliban's harsh Islamist regime has been swept away. Schools, especially for girls, have reopened across the country. A large vote took place in June, electing an administration that is charged to prepare a democratic constitution. In Kabul, violence has diminished so much that the murder rate is half that of Washington, D.C. But basic needs are not being met, even in Kabul. According to Lieutenant Colonel Michael Stout, deputy commander of the CJCMOTF, power cuts by the city's feeble stations are frequent. Many middle-class Afghans, who last winter had electricity most of the night, found that in fall 2002 they can get power only a few hours a day. Only a few organizations have nonstop power: the presidential palace, government ministries and ministers, peacekeepers (self-supplied with generators), hospitals, and places such as the airport, radio stations, and ambassadors' homes. The rest must accept it in limited quantities. According to Fariduddin Wafik, the director of power for Kabul:

> The biggest problem is the lack of water. The dams are empty—one in three doesn't have even a drop of water in it—and most of the country's energy is hydroelectric. Our machinery is so old. The winter will be even worse. Everyone comes here asking for [electricity], but it's impossible. We simply can't provide it to everyone twenty-four hours a day. Personally, when there's a light on in a house, I feel happy.[37]

To compound the problem, the international aid agencies still haven't arrived in force within the first year—similar to Bosnia and Kosovo. According to Afghanistan's minister of reconstruction, Amin Farhang, the reconstruction process at the one-year mark is not satisfactory. Promises made in accordance with the Tokyo reconstruction conference held in January 2002 have yet to be fulfilled. In total, the donor countries promised $4.5 billion for the next five years for Afghanistan, including $1.8 billion for 2002; however, of this $1.8 billion, $600 million was given to the

United Nations, $600 million to the NGOs, and only $90 million to the government of Afghanistan. In terms of the projects that the government was working on, progress has been slow.

As a measure of comparison, if the countries that have recently received the most aid per head by the international community were listed from the most to the least, the order would be Bosnia, Kosovo, East Timor, Rwanda, and then Afghanistan. Afghanistan is at the bottom of the pile, receiving just $75 per person per year, against an average of $250 for the other four countries. In addition, only 40 percent of the aid that arrived was going to long-term development; the rest was for short-term feeding programs. In demanding reconstruction funds at the Tokyo conference in January 2002, UN secretary-general Kofi Annan requested that the new money should be "separate from and additional to" short-term humanitarian assistance.[38] Afghanistan's foreign minister Abdullah Abdullah visited many Western countries, including the United States, making his case for additional money. Though the world already pledged billions in aid, the war-ravaged country's needs are still enormous. Afghanistan says that it needs up to $20 billion over the next five years to rebuild a country devastated by decades of conflict and that, without more aid, extremists will take opportunities to destabilize the nation. According to Abdullah:

> In the Tokyo conference, neither Afghanistan nor the international community had an assessment close to the scale of the problem. The needs of Afghanistan are enormous and reconstruction is a large part of security. If you can change the lives of people, for example in poverty, electricity, etc., you will have a great impact on the security situation. Tokyo pledged $4.5 billion over two and a half to four years, but we have three problems. First, considering the situation, this is a small number and is not in the scale of the problem. Second, the composition of the money is not known—some, about 70 percent, went to the humanitarian situation. And, third, countries have not defined the money. Some of it is listed as credits and some are slow in disbursements. People expect us to deliver—otherwise, the situation will turn negative.[39]

As far as the government is concerned, its main priority is road reconstruction. Because Afghanistan is landlocked, it is dependent on the roads for the transport of goods throughout the country. But the government has no money and is dependent on the international community for help. According to Farhang:

> As of yet, we haven't undertaken any real large-scale projects for the Afghan people—projects that give the people confidence in what the government is doing. We have done some visible projects to demonstrate to the people that we are doing something, but these have been small in nature. Such projects might include road reconstruction and the erecting of street lights, but we need to undertake larger projects. While the international community knows and understands our efforts, at the same time they have strong reservations and concerns, particularly in the area of security. They want a 100-percent secure Afghanistan, which is not possible. Keep in mind, Afghanistan has been at war for twenty-three years. It's simply not possible to ensure that [security] at this point.[40]

The shortfalls in Afghanistan at the one-year mark are great and there has been no viable effort, except for pledges and promises, from either the military or the international civilian community to address the large-scale physical infrastructure reconstruction so vital to Afghanistan's prosperity. This lack of effort at physical infrastructure reconstruction has exacerbated the security problem, thus affecting the overall economy. Standards in some of the cities are slowly improving, but the situation outside of the cities remains tenuous at best.

THE INTERNATIONAL CIVILIAN RESPONSE

Prewar Efforts

Total international assistance to prewar Afghanistan (in the range of $200–$300 million annually in recent years) overwhelmingly went to humanitarian relief purposes, much of it in the form of food aid and other in-kind assistance. Another major program was demining, funded mainly through a United Nations–managed trust fund. However, key development sectors such as education and infrastructure accounted for only a small proportion of total prewar assistance, resulting in the poor state of infrastructure found in Afghanistan today. The dominance of humanitarian assistance to a large extent reflected donor restrictions against the provision of funding for explicit development purposes to a country without a legitimate and recognized government. The distinction between humanitarian and development activities is very much blurred, however, in the context of a country that has been facing conflict and a "complex emergency" situation for many years. Regardless, the Loya Jirga should have taken care of that specific bureaucratic anomaly.

Funding of assistance for Afghanistan was spread across a large number of bilateral donors, of which by far the largest has been the United States, followed by the EU. Most international assistance to Afghanistan continues to be delivered by about forty sizable (that is, annual spending of $1 million or more each) NGOs, along with numerous small and tiny entities. In the absence of effectively functioning government service delivery or leadership, NGOs are the main actors in many areas, such as primary education (especially for girls), rural water supply, basic health units, demining, and others.[41]

Before the recent conflict there were some improvements in NGO coordination in the field, and promising steps toward what could be called sector strategizing and programming among some NGOs (for example, in the case of rural water supply). However, aid delivery remained highly fragmented and unco-ordinated. There were cases of duplication, working at cross-purposes, and "crowding" on the part of both UN agencies and NGOs in response to donor demands. The logistics of getting assistance to Afghanistan was a difficult, high-cost endeavor. Rugged terrain and poor transport resulted in high transport and delivery costs; large parts of the country were inaccessible during winter, with NGOs stockpiling foodstuffs to avert a crisis. In addition, aid management occurred at four different levels: the field; regional hubs in Afghanistan; Pakistan, where most agency country offices are located; and New York and other UN agency headquarters and donor capitals. This greatly com-plicated the decision making and raised overhead costs. The UN system's regular air transport operations (using chartered aircraft), together with the ICRC's plane, constituted the only safe and reliable air transport in the country, but they were very expensive. The difficult and volatile security situation further added to costs and aid-delivery bottlenecks.

International Demining

There has been a bright spot, however. The Mine Action Program for Afghanistan (MAPA) has operated under the coordination of the UN Office for the Coordination of Humanitarian Assistance to Afghanistan since 1989, and was composed of the UN Mine Action Center for Afghanistan (MACA), the UN Regional Mine Action Centers (RMACs), and fifteen NGOs working as implementation partners. The RMACs were responsible for the field-level management, coordination, and oversight of mine action activities in their respective regions. The fifteen NGOs implemented most of the physical activities associated with mine action, including awareness, technical training, survey, and clearance, under the coordination of the MACA. In the absence of an indigenous national coordinating body, the MACA planned, managed, and supervised all mine action activities for Afghanistan. It also provided technical support, ensuring the proper integration of mine action into wider humanitarian assistance programs. In total, MAPA employed more than 4,700 Afghan personnel. MAPA operations were disturbed by the military operations in late 2001, with damage from air strikes, widespread looting, and the threat to the safety of mine action personnel forcing it to significantly curtail its operations. In the face of this new situation, it was still required to develop and implement a comprehensive response to the emergency. One of the new aspects of this response was the retraining of deminers to deal with the threat from new types of coalition UXO.[42]

Prior to the recent conflict, MAPA managed one of the most effective demining programs in the world. Mine awareness briefings to more than seven million people contributed significantly to lowering the land mine casualty rate by an estimated 50 percent. By the end of 2001, Afghani deminers had cleared more than 224 square kilometers of high-priority, mine-infested land and 321 square kilometers of former battlefield areas, while destroying approximately 210,000 land mines and 985,000 pieces of UXO. In spite of the current military situation, MAPA reported that clearance operations have returned to 100 percent of previous capacity, although ongoing security concerns limit operations in some areas.

MAPA is expanding its mine clearance capacities. In 2001 there were a total of 113 clearance teams; MAPA increased this number to 201 by the end of 2002. In the first quarter of calendar year 2002, mine clearance organizations coordinated by MAPA cleared 23,825,611 square meters of high-priority mine- and UXO-contaminated area. In addition, another 32,091,000 square meters were returned to various communities for productive use. This turnover stemmed from the successful survey work conducted under MAPA auspices. In the same period, MAPA reported that 751 antitank, 16,196 antipersonnel, and 251,169 UXO devices were cleared. MAPA reported that the clearance of cluster munitions continued at a rate faster than anticipated. All known cluster munition strike sites were surveyed where access was possible and are in the process of being cleared. MAPA estimated that an additional 75 million square meters were to be cleared by the end of 2002 and a further 60 million square meters were turned over as a result of survey work.

The long-term objective of MAPA is to create a situation in Afghanistan where people can go freely about their lives without the threat of mines and UXO. In the short to medium term, MAPA is working to allow reconstruction and development activities to be carried out in a safe environment.[43] Effective implementation will lead to increased repatriation, reduced casualties and fatalities, increased food production, and increased employment opportunities—including ex-combatants; increased micro- and macro-economic capacity; increased individual and national self-reliance; and enhanced access for emergency, rehabilitative, and development projects and programs. Overall, the MAPA strategy has been a great success story, although much work remains.

Postconflict Efforts

Postconflict efforts must focus on placing the direction and management of reconstruction in the hands of the Afghan government; therefore, the Working Draft of the Development Plan and Budget and the proposed six national projects represent the next logical step in a process that was started at Tokyo. At the donors' conference, a broad vision was outlined in Karzai's presentation—a vision of a prosperous and secure Afghanistan that would also bring prosperity to its trading partners and stability to the region.[44] Following extensive consultation among government ministers and senior officials, the National Development Framework was produced. The framework articulated a strategy to develop this vision and was presented to donors at the Implementation Group Meeting in April 2002. The National Development Budget was the elaboration of the framework into a series of detailed programs and specific projects within each program. It was not possible to complete a full development budget until more information on resources, particularly resource constraints faced globally and by each sector, was known. A full budget, integrated with an operating budget to cover recurrent expenditures, was to be prepared and presented to donors for consideration at the first full Consultative Group meeting in late February/early March 2003.

Three pillars of the framework were identified:

▦ Human Capital and Social Protection (45 percent)

▦ Physical Infrastructure (35 percent)

▦ Trade and Investment and Rule of Law/Security (20 percent)

The decision on expenditure shares highlights a number of issues. First, at one level, it is clear that there is a trade-off between spending on humanitarian assistance and spending on physical infrastructure. If the budget is to be the central tool of policymaking it is critical that these issues are considered together in the budget, and through this decision the government has indicated its broad disposition between spending in the two areas. Second, it highlights the fact that synergies must be exploited among different categories of spending. For example, infrastructure spending through labor-intensive programs addresses humanitarian needs, whereas effective spending on infrastructure, such as on roads, can reduce the operating costs of providing humanitarian assistance, allowing more assistance to be provided at a lower cost.

As an interim measure, pending the finalization of the National Development Budget, six priority projects were extracted from the working draft and agreed upon by the cabinet as representing the government's highest priorities for donor funding. The cabinet recognized that the needs were too urgent and the aspirations of the community too high to allow a delay of an additional five months before implementation commenced. Rather, national projects were immediately needed to increase the delivery of tangible results to ordinary Afghan men and women. Further delays would reduce the people's faith in both the government and the international community, and they would undermine the legitimacy of the government—all of which could lead to a slide back into conflict. The approved six national projects were:

■ National Solidarity and Emergency Public Works Projects: to rebuild local governance structures and nationwide community projects.

■ National Education Infrastructure Project: to rapidly rehabilitate or construct primary schools in every district across the country.

■ Urban Infrastructure Project: to bring together the management of water and sanitation facilities, power delivery, and road rehabilitation.

■ Water Resource Investment Project: to invest in medium-sized multipurpose dams to increase the water resources of the country.

■ National Infrastructure of Governance: to restore the presence and capacity of central government throughout the country so that it can deliver services in an accountable and efficient manner.

■ Transport Project: to build a ring highway linking the major urban centers, highways from the ring highway to the major border points, and a highway across the center of the country from Kabul to Herat. [45]

Other problems existed, however. Despite the interim government's attempt to prioritize work, there were concerns by some donors, such as the Asian Development Bank, that Afghanistan did not have a national engineering agency to manage the work. The Asian Development Bank can provide the money for roads and other infrastructure but questioned who would do the overall master planning, operations and maintenance, national standards, quality assurance, fiscal programming, and accounting. There is a small pool of engineers in the country who are eager to contribute, but there is no central national agency to help train and pool engineering resources. This is a significant void in a country faced with such a large reconstruction program. The Afghanistan Reconstruction Steering Committee, consisting of the United States, Japan, and Saudi Arabia, will attempt to sort out the reconstruction efforts and marry them with the efforts of the Asian Development Bank, the World Bank, the UN Development Program, the Islamic Development Bank, and various donor countries; however, the key missing ingredient is an institution with experienced senior managers that can execute and integrate these various programs.[46]

ASSESSMENT

Although it would be premature at this point to put a precise price tag on Afghanistan's reconstruction, the financial cost will be high, reflecting the toll taken by two decades of conflict on the country's infrastructure, human capital, state institutions, environment, and, increasingly, social capital. Rehabilitation of infrastructure, capacity building, and institution building; agricultural and water conservancy investments to promote food security; an expanded demining program; restoration of basic services to where they were operating before the war (mainly in the cities); bringing back, settling, and ensuring sustainable livelihoods for the large numbers of refugees and, more recently, IDPs; and other reconstruction activities will carry high costs. The overall cost of reconstruction in Afghanistan would be built from a needs assessment and costing of programs in different sectors. In some areas of activity such as demining, food security, and to a lesser extent education, previous work by the World Bank and other agencies provides a sound basis for making preliminary assessments of the likely cost of reconstruction. For example, in the case of demining, clearance of identified high-priority minefields can be roughly estimated to cost around $200 million (compared with a total of about $150 million spent on the mine action program during 1991–1999). However, with peace, large numbers of refugees would be returning and more marginal lands would be exploited, so it is likely that minefields previously identified as low priority would become higher priority and also would need to be cleared. It would cost close to $300 million to clear all identified low-priority minefields, with a price tag of around $500 million for total mine clearance. Previously undiscovered minefields are still being identified and surveyed, which would further raise the cost of mine clearance.

Moreover, reconstruction in Afghanistan cannot be separated from longer-term economic and social development. Merely restoring the pre-1978 economic situation in Afghanistan (even if that were possible) would leave the country as one of the poorest in the world in terms of both incomes and social indicators. This would make the task of maintaining political stability and promoting national integration very difficult and would leave Afghanistan vulnerable to a resurgence of conflict. Population growth since the 1970s means that the pre-existing economic base and infrastructure could not in any case support the current population if most refugees return to Afghanistan. Therefore, reconstruction will need to be combined with a major development effort. For example, basic education and health, which in the past covered only a small portion of the Afghan population even in peacetime, will need to be greatly expanded to cover the bulk of the population. In addition to being rehabili-tated, the agricultural production base will need to be expanded and improved so that it can support and provide food security to substantially larger numbers of people. The combination of reconstruction with urgent development needs will further raise the cost of reconstruction in Afghanistan.

International experience also suggests that the cost of infra-structure reconstruction will be high. For example, in the West Bank and Gaza, a total of $3 billion of reconstruction assistance was proposed in the first two years, for an area with a popula-tion of less than two million and with at least some function-ing basic infrastructure and services. In the case of Lebanon, external assistance for reconstruction was in the range of $400 million per year over a period of ten years, for a population of four million. In the Balkans, reconstruction costs have also been high—in the case of Bosnia, with a population of about five mil-lion people, total pledges (including humanitarian as well as reconstruction assistance) were $5.4 billion during 1995–1999. And East Timor, with a population of less than half a million, is receiving $350 million of reconstruction aid over a three-year period. These comparisons indicate that for Afghanistan, a coun-try of twenty-five million people (including refugees currently in other countries)—more than ten times the combined population of Kosovo and East Timor—the cost of reconstruction will be quite high, even taking into account the much lower level of per-capita income in Afghanistan.[47]

In practice, what will constrain the level and cost of recon-struction assistance are domestic absorption capacity and the need to avoid excessive domination by foreign firms and staff of the reconstruction implementation process. However, Afghan private-sector capacity in neighboring and nearby countries is substantial and can and should be brought into the reconstruc-tion effort, which will increase domestic absorption capacity. The high cost of reconstruction and likely constraints on the avail-ability of external funding mean that a private sector–oriented approach is called for. At first glance, Afghanistan would not appear to be a prime candidate for private investment. Nevertheless, prewar Afghanistan was known for its entrepreneurs in trade, currency exchange, and other activities. A sizable group of Afghan businesspeople has developed in neighboring countries with considerable financial resources, particularly in Pakistan. The reconstruction strategy should try to attract back to Afghanistan the large groups of Afghan businesses, entrepreneurs, and skilled and unskilled workers currently in Pakistan and Iran. Moreover, Afghanistan has a positive prewar history of cost recovery for key infrastructure services such as electric power, telecommunications, energy, and oil/gas pipelines. It is extremely important that such services start out on the right track during reconstruction. Options for private investment in infrastructure should be actively pursued.

It is abundantly clear, however, that very little postconflict reconstruction in the physical infrastructure arena for Afghanistan occurred in the first year after the cessation of hostilities. Some blame it on the tenuous security situation, others blame it on the poor record thus far of receiving the promised pledges from the Tokyo Conference, and still others blame it on a new Afghanistan administration with little capacity to handle and process those donations that have been offered. Regardless, until these types of problems are discovered and solved, there needs to be an external interim ability available and capable of starting the country's reconstruction until the international civilian community can sort out funding and organization. Afghanistan is once again an example of a war-ravaged country where little progress was made in the first year, except for the quick overthrow of the Taliban regime and the creation, through a Loya Jirga, of an Afghan interim government. These are small steps forward to be sure, maybe even large steps forward in an institution-building sense, but much more could have been reconstructed to help jump-start the economy and give the interim government additional legitimacy while the long-term interveners and government took the time required to become properly established.

5

A POSTCONFLICT
RECONSTRUCTION
TEMPLATE

BEFORE SEPTEMBER 11, 2001, and the international response in Afghanistan, it was obvious that peace support operations were beginning to consume increasingly greater numbers of military forces from the international community. Despite comments that military peace operations would degrade the armed forces' ability to fight and win the nation's wars, U.S. peacekeeping operations increased significantly in the last half of the 1990s. It was clear that as a result of their valuable capabilities, the U.S. and European militaries would continue to have an important role to play and would be requested to participate in future peace support operations.[1]

Despite the unique characteristics of the military interventions in Bosnia, Kosovo, and Afghanistan, several common threads could form a foundation upon which to build a postconflict reconstruction template. The case similarities under the broad headings of planning, culture, and infrastructure provide a stage upon which the template can emerge. The task is straightforward—develop a system that captures what is good from these recent interventions, yet change the current system to respond to what is currently dysfunctional.

CASE REVIEW

Planning

A general lack of planning for postconflict reconstruction characterized all three cases. It should be possible to find some
postconflict guidance in the Political-Military (POL-MIL) Plan
that is normally developed, written, and promulgated by the U.S.
Department of State. But for these cases, only one POL-MIL
plan was approved. No POL-MIL Plan was written for Bosnia,
and general guidance for stability operations was issued as the
operation progressed. Civil Affairs planning and organization was
immature at the IFOR level at the time of deployment and did not
fully exist in any country other than the United States. NATO
had no established mechanism to execute contingency engineering missions—this capability had to be developed while IFOR was
deployed in theater. In addition, it was believed that all tasks,
both military and civilian, were sufficiently outlined in the Dayton
Agreement, negating the requirement for additional coordination.
Thus IFOR relegated its efforts to executing the military-desig-
nated tasks, while the other tasks were delegated across several
civilian agencies. Because the Dayton Agreement did not foresee
or seemingly encourage a mixing of the two, the military mission
was executed quickly and efficiently; however, with little initial
civilian organization, the civilian tasks languished.

The military did not envision or thoroughly develop the civilian postconflict reconstruction tasks. Military engineers were
limited by the minimum military requirement imposed by
NATO and planned only for the one-year mandate that was
given to IFOR. As late as November 1, 1996, the IFOR staff was
not allowed to develop plans to hand over the military operation to a follow-on force. They were allowed to plan only for a
complete withdrawal and redeployment that was to occur in
December 1996. Only when the U.S. presidential election was
completed was the SFOR concept proposed. This gave IFOR
planners a little more than three weeks to plan, rehearse, and
execute a turnover to a modified SFOR staff, commanded by a

completely different military organization. Thus little thought was given to the military development of a postconflict reconstruction plan; the planners adhered to the delineation of tasks provided in the Dayton Agreement, which left that task to civilian organizations.

In Kosovo, NATO tried to learn from its mistakes in Bosnia. Early project design was completed before the air war, using the same contingency engineering approval methods developed in Bosnia. NATO approved early money devoted to projects that AFSOUTH engineer planners believed would be necessary to support the military mission in theater. Without the benefits of a solid infrastructure baseline, planners developed generic projects in order to establish some kind of method for immediate execution of projects. But, again, the engineers were limited by the minimum military requirement. Their plans could not extend beyond those tasks that would support the military mission. The State Department drafted and approved a POL-MIL plan; however, that plan was never fully operationalized in the U.S. brigade at Camp Bondsteel.

At a higher level, the EU attempted to learn from mistakes made in Bosnia and initially formed the European Commission Task Force for the Reconstruction of Kosovo, quickly followed by the European Agency for Reconstruction, whose focus was the rehabilitation and repair of key infrastructure and public utilities—one of the four pillars promulgated by the UN Administration in Kosovo. These agencies, however, were not formed until the summer of 1999 and February 2000, respectively. This late formation with no prior planning resulted in little reconstruction progress during the first year after hostilities ceased. The initial program was not announced until March 2002, and basic needs throughout the rural parts of Kosovo were still not met by the end of 2002.

Afghanistan provided an even bigger challenge. Without a UN mandate or a combined international headquarters such as NATO sponsoring the intervention, coalition planning with a U.S. lead was essential. The State Department developed a POL-MIL plan for Afghanistan, but the plan was never approved. Draft copies were furnished to the CJCMOTF so that the Civil Affairs soldiers in theater would have the benefits of the planning that had occurred; however, without approval, the POL-MIL plan had no authority to task other agencies for support. The engineer plan evolved as the mission unfolded. Because the initial intent was to try to execute the operation with SOF and airpower, little advanced planning for postconflict infrastructure was conducted. As the force grew in Afghanistan, CENTCOM engineers scrambled to find forces sufficient to complete the military support mission on base and at the airfields but did not extend the engineer reconstruction mission beyond the limits of the military base. MSRs were never designated, with the command encouraging military personnel to stay off Afghanistan's roads because of extensive damage and mines. Civil Affairs soldiers, who were more dispersed throughout parts of the country, executed several quick-impact, high-profile projects with funds provided by the assistant secretary of defense for stability operations, but this funding source was limited and its effects on the overall state of infrastructure in Afghanistan were minimal.

State Department officials appear wary of developing plans for potential contingencies for fear that their planning could inadvertently commit the United States to an inadequately vetted foreign policy. But, because the world is a most uncertain place and all needs cannot be adequately anticipated, policymakers should accept this uncertainty as a given and, instead, devise an alternate method to accommodate the uncertainty and the startup time required for civilian intervention, yet still provide a mechanism to start the postconflict reconstruction phase of an operation immediately upon the cessation of hostilities. The first priority of the template, therefore, must be the development of an enhanced planning mechanism to plan for postconflict reconstruction. Planning must begin during the preconflict phase of an operation in order to sufficiently coordinate the military and civilian resources necessary to execute the challenging mission.

A high-level coordination group that can establish necessary working relationships between the military and the civilian agencies is essential so that reconstruction can begin quickly and be maintained to transition to local authorities.

Cultural Differences

Responses by the United States to recent crises demonstrate an important but false dichotomy between civilian and military roles in postconflict reconstruction. In contingencies such as Somalia, Haiti, Bosnia, and Kosovo, uniformed services have created a safe and secure environment and have also set the conditions for the reconstruction of war-torn societies through their expertise in logistics, engineering, policing, and support for humanitarian needs—but only to a point. Artificial limitations have been placed upon the military to avoid the image of nation building and have limited the military's response to truly humanitarian emergencies or only military support. Many civilian policymakers and agencies continue to think of peace operations in a linear fashion, insisting that a determination of specific civilian and military tasks in the postconflict phase provides them with a bright line delineating specific roles and responsibilities in different stages of conflict. Maybe the intent is to be able to assign credit or blame for progress in the various areas; however, this linear thinking falls short in a place like Afghanistan, where some areas of the country are ripe for recovery while other areas remain mired in Afghan-on-Afghan conflict. The record of the past decade's crises provides the proof: postconflict reconstruction requires integrated security and social, economic, and political development efforts, not separate tracks that diverge.

The three cases highlight the cultural differences and inherent capabilities found between the military and the international civilian community. In all three cases, the international civilian community held early donor conferences. The conferences verified the need to fund postconflict reconstruction, resulting in large amounts of money pledged by interested governments and international agencies. The conferences were highlighted by passionate pleas by the secretary-general of the United Nations, encouraging nations to pledge money for reconstruction, in addition to the money already pledged and spent for humanitarian assistance. However, the donations were slow to materialize. Some money that was initially pledged for reconstruction was later tied to specific projects, hampering the local government's ability to apply the money to its highest priorities for reconstruction. Other pledges were never actually received, affecting the IOs' ability to organize and deploy to execute the reconstruction mission. These problems highlight a cultural reality that must be recognized at the beginning of the planning process: Most international organizations do not have an established staff ready to deploy into a country with little notice. The organizations require time to develop a staff, organize their deployment, gather funding, and deploy. Because of a continuing uncertainty for funding, this intense effort will not begin until there is an established requirement to deploy. This causes an immediate gap in the reconstruction effort once the conflict has ceased.

Many of the reasons for this rapid-response gap go beyond a simple lack of capability and involve a lack of clarity about the time frame for such postconflict assistance. Civilians in the diplomatic and development communities do not plan for short-term contingencies, something in which the military specializes, and often lack significant experience working with military counterparts. Military planners, uncertain about missions that exceed traditional security functions, debate whether the involvement of soldiers for such long periods of time dilutes the war-fighting capacity of the armed forces—something that military officers will continue to debate in their respective war colleges for many decades. Finally, the providers of development assistance are still unclear about how to integrate humanitarian emergency response with immediate postconflict reconstruction and later transition into the broader strategic vision of long-term reconstruction. Unless the international community develops sufficient rapid civilian response capacity, the military will continue to be the force available to accomplish "civilian" tasks, greatly reducing its ability to redeploy and potentially degrading the ability to engage in high-intensity conflict and the ongoing campaign against terrorism.

The military culture is on the other end of the civil-military continuum. Because of its overall mission to "fight and win our nation's wars," the military has the capability to rapidly deploy to various regions around the world and has the inherent logistics capability to sustain itself once it is deployed in a theater. Organizationally, the military has the in-place chain of command and organization to implement immediate action. The military missions in the three cases were somewhat different, but all had the overall priority to establish security and stability throughout the region. The primary differences in the security missions were their goals. In the Balkans, the military had two agreements upon which to base its security mission. As peacekeepers, the military was to separate and disarm the former warring parties, discouraging organized criminal activities and encouraging the pursuit of legitimate alternative employment. With routine patrols and military checkpoints, the goal was to establish a safe and secure environment so that the civilian agencies and local nationals could re-establish the economy and local forms of governance. The military part of the mission was hugely successful.

In Afghanistan, however, the military was a combatant force instead of a peacekeeping force. The goal was to search and destroy the Taliban and al Qaeda cells wherever they were found in order to limit their abilities to conduct terrorism throughout the world. The assumption was that by destroying these organizations, a legitimate government would develop in Afghanistan through self-determination, increasingly providing the basic needs for its citizens as it became established. This mission was also rapidly accomplished with few Taliban and al Qaeda remnants still remaining in Afghanistan; however, the endstate of the security mission was not to establish patrols across the breadth of the country, as in the Balkans, but to target specific Taliban and al Qaeda cells for destruction. Afghanistan has never been effectively ruled from a central location. It does not have a sufficiently developed infrastructure to allow a central government to effectively rule across the entire country. Therefore, the Bush administration proposed a limited force without the same massive patrolling found in the Balkans. Nor did the mission target the reconstruction of Afghanistan's infrastructure. However, realizing that the development of viable infrastructure is a key to establishing and maintaining security in Afghanistan, DOD shifted its priority at the end of 2002 from the establishment of a secure environment to that of reconstruction using the Civil Affairs Provincial Reconstruction Teams (PRTs). Once the PRTs conduct the initial damage assessment, it will still be up to the international civilian community and the local government to execute the projects, as there is no residual military engineer capability in theater to execute postconflict reconstruction. Comprehensive and joint civil-military planning during the preconflict stage might have spurred this change in military priority at an earlier moment after the initial deployment.

The postconflict reconstruction template must address the cultural differences and logistical capabilities that are found in the military and civilian communities. Neither side can successfully execute a postconflict reconstruction plan by itself. As the mission requires the military for the short-term rapid-response capability and the civilian long-term development capability, a mechanism is required that will successfully mesh the advantages and mitigate the disadvantages of each organization. Clearly, the slow civilian rapid-response capacity does not apply to humanitarian assistance, which is currently well handled by the international community; however, the key civilian response gaps are in the area of the immediate postconflict assistance that allows for reconstruction to begin. Because the future is always cloudy, all operations are contingencies in one form or another, which prevents the international civilian community from having the proper startup time and funding to respond rapidly. Anything less than a rapid response may lead to further violence and loss of life. Suppression of renewed conflict demands, at its most basic level, imaginative coordination and execution of all aspects of the peace accords; therefore, postconflict reconstruction must be an activity that engages both military and civilian actors, demanding careful thought and execution.

State of Infrastructure

The greatest similarity among the three cases is their state of infrastructure. Despite the differences in government—province, republic, or independent country—the future for each region is heavily dependent on having a viable infrastructure. Each case required a viable physical infrastructure to enhance the freedom of movement. Freedom of movement leads to increased trade and commerce, greater interaction among former warring parties leading to the development of common goals and ideas, and enhanced governmental development allowing for the provision of basic needs. At the cessation of hostilities in each case, no viable infrastructure existed that could support freedom of movement or even support the ability to get farm goods to market in a reasonable time. Restricted infrastructure provided little connection to neighboring countries, seriously impacting the region's ability to conduct external trade—which is key to jump-starting an economy that has stagnated during a conflict. Each country had considerable war damage to its infrastructure, compounded by numerous years of insufficient maintenance. In some instances, the physical infrastructure could be repaired, whereas in others the infrastructure was so degraded that complete reconstruction rather than repair was the order. Regardless of the extent of damage, each region did not have the ability to begin its reconstruction internally. The stimulus must come externally until the local capacity can be built and assume the task.

The third thread that the postconflict reconstruction template must address is a mechanism to provide immediate recovery of basic needs, followed by detailed project management, with an ultimate transition to local authority control and execution. The template must establish a flow of assistance commensurate with both the abilities of the external agencies and the extent of damage.

A POSTCONFLICT RECONSTRUCTION TEMPLATE

Principles

For future operations, if the postconflict reconstruction gap is to be closed in order to take full advantage of the relative calm that exists immediately after the cessation of hostilities, the international community must develop a more holistic approach, integrating not only the international civilian community in its overall plan for reconstruction, but also the military community, which has the capability to mobilize and quickly establish reconstruction centers of excellence. There is a way to successfully integrate the quick-start abilities of the military without compromising the neutrality of the IO and NGO community. The post–Cold War world has continued to emphasize the capability gap between the military and civilian organizations by creating events that force the military to remain in theater performing nonmilitary missions simply because no civilian agencies can rapidly deploy. Ongoing missions in Bosnia, Kosovo, and Afghanistan reflect the changing demands being placed on U.S. military forces in postconflict environments and serve as a reminder that civilian agencies still lack the basic capacity to provide immediate, rapid support to supplement, and ultimately replace, a military ground presence once fighting has stopped. Former CENTCOM commander General Anthony Zinni asserted that the U.S. military has become the "stuckee," the force that gets stuck with all the cleanup because no other alternative exists to fill the emergency gaps.

Clarity of Mission. Efforts to suppress renewed conflict can succeed only if there is a clearly stated mission for the postconflict reconstruction program as a whole and specific, intermediate objectives that are attainable for each organization and institution. As the primary source, this mission and these intermediate objectives should derive from a thorough understanding of the agreement that serves as the foundation for the entire military intervention. These missions and objectives are further supplemented by specific tasks for each participant—tasks that point to the completion of the overall objective and tasks by which progress can be measured. In addition, missions and objectives must be not only clear but also achievable. In practice, this may mean accepting solutions that are incremental in nature, allowing for sufficient flexibility to facilitate required modifications as the operation proceeds. Leaders must build in periodic reviews or assessments to modify missions or develop new missions if that is required. Part of the reconstruction template must include a civil-military reconstruction working group to provide immediate planning and support for impending crises. Such planning will significantly help to clarify the postconflict reconstruction mission and develop an execution plan that all parties can agree to, accept, and implement.[2]

Unity of Authority and Integration of Effort. Conflict suppression is a multidisciplined operation, requiring a thorough integration of complex functions that are executed by diverse organizations. Therefore, the establishment of an overarching integrating structure is a key step in carrying out the practical, day-to-day management of postconflict reconstruction operations, as well as establishing local capacity and management. Yet the creation of an integrating structure is the most daunting challenge that the international community confronts, as autonomous organizations must surrender a measure of independence to achieve cooperation. Civilian and military leaders must overcome the hostilities and suspicions that often separate them to work toward the common goal of recovery.

The establishment of a common mandate of authority is fraught with suspicion—posed not only by the states and IOs involved but also by members of the military community. Most of the organizations that participate in conflict prevention operations—particularly NGOs and elements of the private sector—have no obligation to respond to any national or international authority, including the United Nations. NGOs, in competition for scarce resources, balk at the sharing of information and are reluctant to cooperate. Moreover, civilian agencies strongly resist any requirement that they subordinate themselves to—or even cooperate with—a military chain of command for fear of compromising their neutrality. At the same time, military leaders are reluctant to place themselves under the direction of a civilian organization, particularly one that has an international membership, and bristle at what they may consider to be ill-informed and ill-advised civilian guidance.[3] It simply takes too long to put together a new civilian structure to deal with the immediate need to prevent conflict. In recognition of this fact, the postconflict reconstruction template must adequately address the obstacles to civil-military cooperation and the problem of how to respond immediately to primarily civilian reconstruction tasks when civilian reconstruction agencies do not have the standby capacity.

Timely Political Decisions and International Commitment. Postconflict reconstruction operations generally occur in a fluid environment, requiring rapid decisions framed in the context of the overall objective. Such operations demand that an often cumbersome decision-making process be shortened, streamlined, and responsive. Moreover, each participating organization must have a complete understanding of what political and resource commitments will be required to meet its intermediate objectives. This understanding provides the foundation for the commitment and the conditions under which the commitment may terminate. Arbitrary deadlines for the withdrawal of peacekeeping forces or other international organizations are counterproductive; commitments must be made to the satisfaction of predetermined objectives, not to dates on a calendar. According to General Joulwan, any system that induces or permits excessive delays in reaching political decisions will condemn itself to irrelevance, no matter how clear the mission objectives may be, how unified and effective the civil-military working group may be, or how committed the actors may be.[4]

In successful postconflict operations there is a long-term commitment that every organization and institution involved must understand to ensure a constant source of funding during project execution. The willingness of donor nations in particular to maintain their support is of fundamental importance. The fact that peacekeepers and peacebuilders must be able to react quickly to the changing postconflict environment puts a premium on systems that streamline the process of political decision making. Therefore, an integrated and coordinated approach to postconflict reconstruction produces a web of activities, each of which supports a subsequent range of other activities. If one activity on the critical path to recovery disappears, the entire pattern is in danger of losing its coherence and its effectiveness and could be significantly delayed.

Relying on Joulwan's principles, the following template for postconflict reconstruction incorporates the military process for course-of-action development to provide a logical, step-by-step mechanism for plan development. The model examines all facts bearing on the problem, determines the mission for postconflict reconstruction, determines the available capability and capacity for execution, determines the executable strategy in which all actors can readily agree and can identify their roles and responsibilities, and determines the phasing of control. The intermediate goal is to return the primary civilian tasks back to civilian implementation at the earliest feasible opportunity, with the ultimate goal of building local capacity, local management, and local control. With this objective, the result is a postconflict reconstruction template developed into four phases:

■ Phase 1: Preconflict Planning and Strategy

■ Phase 2: Emergency Response

■ Phase 3: Subsequent Recovery and Project Management

■ Phase 4: Transition to Local Capacity

Phase 1: Preconflict Planning and Strategy

What distinguishes rapid response from humanitarian aid is that it goes beyond the saving of lives and extends to develop the foundation for postconflict reconstruction of a war-torn region. It has become more difficult, however, to define where humanitarian assistance ends and who is ultimately responsible for moving the transition forward. Whereas it is certain that immediate response activities often require international actors to hand programs over to local nongovernmental authorities or other international actors, such transitions can be difficult. Most problematic is the absence of a clear timeline and planning process that bridges rapid-response initiatives and developmental initiatives. The cultural divide between short- and long-term efforts is exacerbated by archaic rules that allow for flexible assistance on the front end of a crisis but do not enable it as the crisis matures.

Similarly, some tasks that are performed at the cessation of hostilities may not be needed after the crisis, such as demobilizing and disarming soldiers or UXO removal. Follow-on programming to support long-term reconstruction may not be considered or may be set aside for a later discussion—a discussion that may never occur once the immediate crisis is resolved. It is evident that no clear interagency process exists to ensure a seamless transition from short-term rapid response to long-term reconstruction in order to meet the future needs of an affected country.

At USAID, for example, a rapid response capacity for complex emergencies was formed in 1992, when USAID's OFDA consolidated interagency personnel, grant mechanisms, and contracts to work with NGOs and other specialized organizations, ensuring the delivery of humanitarian aid and short-term quick relief at the community level. Furthermore, in 1994, USAID established an Office of Transition Initiatives to provide immediate programming in the area of political development in countries emerging from conflict. This initiative has grown to a larger, more established effort to address the re-emergence of violence as well as postconflict reconstruction efforts, but funding and staffing remain inadequate. This relatively small response to an ever-growing requirement to provide immediate, on-the-ground programs in war-torn societies is severely limited by resources, staff, and capacity to address the complex situations that currently affect the national interest. Moreover, this program functions outside of the traditional development culture and is funded from a separate appropriations account. These factors, however mundane, complicate the goal of moving from short-term assistance to longer-term reconstruction.[5]

Recent terrorism events have opened a window of opportunity to revisit the inherent lack of rapid civilian response so that government agencies, civilian and military, can realize the complexities of this type of effort and develop operational capacities to fill the postconflict reconstruction gap. After more than a decade of U.S. involvement in multinational peace operations and complex emergencies, it is readily apparent that the civilian capacity to respond rapidly is uneven, lacks specific legislative authorities, and is resource starved. In addition, the lack of an integrated interagency strategy and planning guidance contributes to the squandering of comparative advantages, the clouding of priorities, and the inefficient use of resources. Instead of the current ad hoc nature of reconstruction response, an integrated civil-military framework would provide clear direction for the broad range of agencies involved in both the emergency response phase and the subsequent recovery and project management phase to ensure seamless support for the transition from war to peace. Furthermore, any strategy or planning for rapid response must realize the importance of preventing the re-emergence of conflict as a central tenet.

Documentation and Mandate. First, Phase 1 requires official documentation, a National Security Policy Directive (NSPD) on postconflict reconstruction. Different from the current NSPD on strategic planning, the reconstruction NSPD would identify key gaps and clarify roles and responsibilities of different agencies at the operational level to fill not only the long-term reconstruction needs of a war-torn country but also the emergency response gap that currently exists. There have been few attempts in the past to resolve this issue. In May 1997, President Clinton signed Presidential Decision Directive 56 (PDD-56) on "Managing Complex Contingency Operations," which attempted to institutionalize the lessons learned and best practices from past experiences. PDD-56 called for:

- The Deputies Committee to establish an interagency Executive Committee to assist in policy development, planning, and execution of complex contingency operations.
- The development of a political-military implementation plan as an integrated planning tool for coordinating U.S. government actions.
- An interagency rehearsal or review of the plan's main elements prior to execution.
- An after-action review of each operation.
- Interagency training to support this process.[6]

PDD-56, despite its good intentions, was never fully implemented. There were pockets of resistance to interagency political-military planning for crises, reflecting both an "antiplanning" bias on the part of some agencies and a miscalculation of the time and resources needed to execute full-time planning. President Clinton's model was centered around the National Security Council (NSC) but had a serious, crippling byproduct: it offered no direction for sustained leadership below the president, who often is distracted by a host of competing concerns on a daily basis. There were no levels below the Deputies Committee to further advance the planning and cooperation for impending crises. The national security adviser or a representative might have provided leadership but would risk losing their status as honest brokers. Even the most conscientious and candid official has difficulty balancing the roles of an honest broker, who encourages all views to be heard, and a leader, who must promote the policy he or she advocates. Yet personal leadership has proven to be essential, both inside and outside Washington. To ensure this leadership, the U.S. government turned in practice to a different model.

In practice, the U.S. government has delegated exceptional powers to one individual, either informally or formally, as a special representative of the president within a particular domain. Two examples of such individuals were Richard Holbrooke, who facilitated an end to the Bosnian war and brokered the Dayton Agreement, and Robert S. Gelbard, who oversaw the implementation of the agreement and served as a special envoy abroad. Both were from the Department of State, the agency that would normally produce individuals delegated with such powers. The motive for appointing a special representative is the recognition that the interagency process does not work, is tediously slow, and is characterized by lack of cooperation—perhaps detrimental enough to be a hindrance to developing long-term peace. In such circumstances, the special representative has little interest in promoting the normal interagency process, anticipating that it would only make a difficult mission even harder to execute. They may increase their leadership power by encouraging the interagency process to atrophy, paving the way to coordinate directly with relevant agencies through their department and personal staff. Interagency working groups may approach irrelevance while the special representative assumes the central role in making and implementing policy. There may be little harm in this arrangement if the special representative is an extraordinary person, but a system that depends on finding such people is unsound.

The Tower Commission supports the view that the organization most capable of managing the interagency process is the office of the national security adviser, provided that the NSC is sufficiently empowered by the administration to fully exercise this management. The commission concluded that the present system operates better when chaired by the individual with the greatest stake in making the NSC system work.[7]

Upon taking office, the Bush administration developed NSPD-XX (the unnumbered designation signifying that it is still in review), which builds upon PDD-56 but expands its scope, providing guidance on advanced warning, planning, prevention, and response options for complex emergency operations. NSPD-XX establishes an NSC-chaired Contingency Planning Policy Coordination Committee at the assistant secretary level to develop the interagency contingency plans for emerging crises, focusing on U.S. objectives, endstate, policy options, interagency responsibilities, resource issues, and strategies for all aspects of the operation.

There are two problems with this proposal. First, the NSC must be empowered by the president to fully coordinate and manage the interagency process. The NSC must be able to speak for the president and to serve as a task manager in the interagency deliberations. Different administrations use their NSC in various ways—President Clinton's NSC enjoyed adequate power to play the lead role; President Bush's NSC is a shadow of its former self and does not have the interagency power required to head the coordination committee. Second, NSPD-XX languishes in an executive branch inbox awaiting a presidential signature, and in the case of Afghanistan no person or entity was in charge of interagency planning and coordination below the Deputies Committee—the specific disadvantage of the PDD-56 model.[8]

Using the representative levels of effort available outlined in figure 4, a new NSPD should codify the roles and control mechanisms for each phase of reconstruction. Aggregate levels of activity will grow as governmental functions approach normalcy.

To solve the problem of the civil and military components being unfamiliar with each other and to enhance the strengths that each brings to the peacebuilding process, the NSPD would create at the strategic level a standing Civil-Military Reconstruction Working Group (CMRWG) to provide immediate support for impending crises. Ideally headed by a strong NSC director or someone delegated from the State Department, the CMRWG would coordinate planning, identify resources, refine government policy, and expedite logistical support. With more than twenty-four countries facing long-term, intractable conflicts, such standing and ongoing planning efforts would yield better interagency coordination and a clear understanding of the existing capacities that each type of situation requires.

Additional language in the NSPD, focused more specifically on how the government should organize its participation in postconflict reconstruction operations, would further enhance the unity of effort. Fundamental to any interagency process is

Figure 4. Phases and Levels of Effort of Local, Civilian, and Military Operations

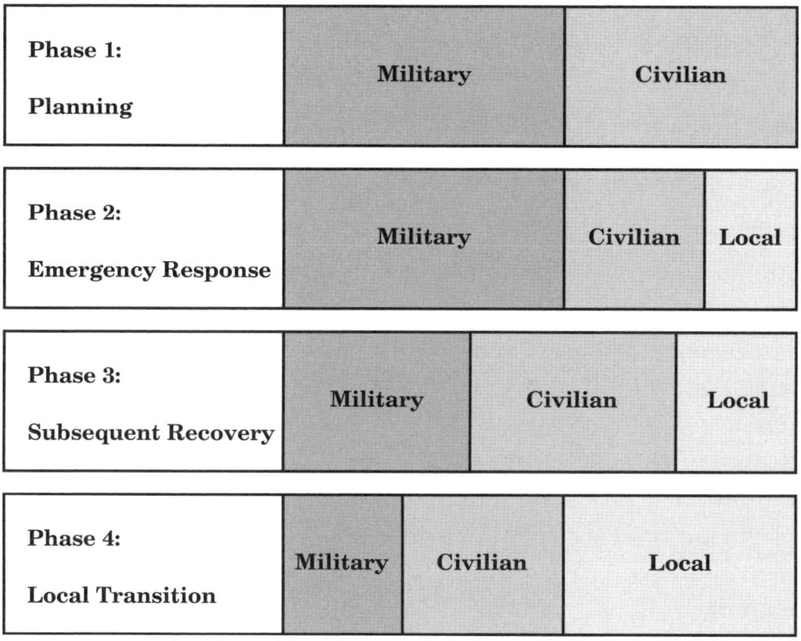

Phase 1: Planning	Military	Civilian

Phase 2: Emergency Response	Military	Civilian	Local

Phase 3: Subsequent Recovery	Military	Civilian	Local

Phase 4: Local Transition	Military	Civilian	Local

eliciting well-considered advice. Each agency in the process has its own expertise and its own outlook on the situation and, preferably at an early stage, the relevant agencies should articulate their positions in a frank and open manner. Usually these broad positions will be at least compatible and a broad consensus will develop, with disagreements emerging during the discussions on specific implementation. Serious disagreements should illuminate important policy issues requiring resolution at the highest level. A sound interagency process should promote resolution and minimize the opportunities to defer or circumvent issues that need to be resolved. During the planning and the execution of postconflict reconstruction, the interagency process should help integrate a combined effort by providing channels of communication among relevant agencies from the working level to the highest level. In addition, it should harmonize U.S. efforts with non–United States agencies, including IOs and NGOs.

The strongest solution would be to combine the NSC-centered model and the special representative model—pairing a robust, NSC-managed interagency process with a person wielding the extraordinary powers of a special representative. Carefully applied, the elements of this combined approach would complement, not thwart, each other. A special representative would benefit, as the president does, from an interagency process that encourages differences of opinion until a decision is reached and then expects agencies to close ranks. The NSC would benefit from a special representative who has the power to implement the policy choices reached and supported through a rigorous interagency process. Some obstacles remain, however. Institutional cultures that do not value planning are a fundamental and persistent obstacle that must be overcome if the United States is to succeed in postconflict reconstruction operations. Success will primarily require sustained leadership on the part of the national security adviser to ensure that strategy development and planning are conducted according to the president's guidance, and will also require specific steps in some agencies to change their "antiplanning" culture.

Working Group Dynamics. The success of the CMRWG and a successful strategy development and planning process require a high degree of capacity—particularly trained and available personnel—in all participating agencies. In the past, such efforts have been hampered by the fact that each agency representative in the process was essentially a one-person show, and most had additional responsibilities completely unrelated to planning, which was usually a secondary responsibility. In contrast, this working group must be a standing organization, with individuals dedicated full time to contingency planning and immediate crisis response. Thorough planning requires devoting quality personnel to the process on a full-time basis. In agencies where planning is not a routine or a valued endeavor and where other priority areas may already be understaffed, building the internal capacity necessary for success will require leadership and culture change initiated at the highest levels.

Developing planning expertise and capacity in key offices that are likely to play important roles in postconflict reconstruction operations is critical to improve the response time at conflict termination. Currently, little strategic planning expertise exists outside the U.S. military and little training is conducted on the civilian side. President Clinton's PDD-56 established interagency training programs to develop a cadre of professionals capable of planning complex contingency operations; however, these training programs have not been fully implemented. There are valuable planning skills that can be perfected in advance, and a planner should have the opportunity to make mistakes and learn lessons in a training environment, without the pressures and high stakes of real-world operations. Training also builds familiarity with and acceptance of shared frames of reference, but will require additional funding. Personnel selected for training should be assigned to positions classified as planners, where their training will have the most beneficial impact on the planning process. In addition, this training should be opened to NGOs to develop a common planning standard across all of the applicable agencies. In times of relative peace, these personnel would be used to support deliberate planning and promote interagency coordination and training efforts; whereas in times of crisis, these planners will be sufficiently trained and familiar with one another to produce a coherent postconflict reconstruction plan that can be executed by the immediate responders, taken over by the long-term agencies, and transitioned to local control once local capacity is developed.

It is paramount that all key players, including those outside the government, be involved in the ongoing planning for postconflict reconstruction. The government must be able to determine what others central to the postconflict reconstruction effort plan on doing, as their actions may directly affect the United States' ability to achieve its objectives in an operation. NGOs involved in humanitarian assistance lie specifically outside of the reconstruction planning parameter because their mandate is concentrated on providing emergency humanitarian relief; however, the government must have a concept of NGO action in order to avoid duplication of effort. One solution would be to organize the most senior NGOs (those with an operating budget of more than $1 million) into a coordinating committee to work out a subplan in coordination with the NSC. This idea addresses the need for NGOs to develop their own plans, as opposed to having the military or government agencies impose a plan on them, while at the same time cutting through the problem of dealing with hundreds of independent NGOs. As one participant at a National Defense University workshop stated, "You cannot regulate or enforce the NGOs to follow a plan. They must see the clear-cut advantage to following it."[9] By having the NGOs create the plan themselves, the assumption is that the process would be closer to achieving coordination with the government plan.

Another approach may be to create the coordinating committee solely out of the donor organizations. Because there are far fewer donor agencies than NGOs, it may be simpler to get donors involved in a standing planning committee for humanitarian assistance. Should the donor agencies concentrate on postconflict reconstruction rather than on humanitarian relief, it is imperative that they be integrated into the CMRWG. These are the agencies to which the military will hand over the control of the postconflict reconstruction efforts; therefore, their views and capabilities must be included in the agreed-upon plan. It may also be in the government's interest to invite key non-U.S. participants to a review of the U.S. plan. In addition, the United States should consider including its closest allies as partners in the U.S. planning process. Although there could be legitimate operational security concerns with all of the actors, these can be managed, as they currently are in the U.S. interagency process. Figure 5 graphically depicts the CMRWG.

Although the CMRWG accomplishes out-of-theater planning, the creation of a Civil-Military Operations Center (CMOC) at the operational and tactical levels is the key to the effective use of diverse organizations and resources in theater as well as to the conduct of the day-to-day management of conflict

Figure 5. Civil-Military Reconstruction Working Group (CMRWG)

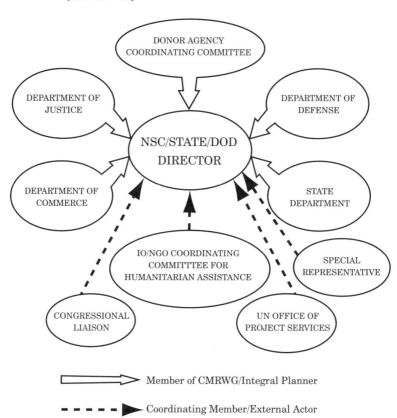

prevention. The CMOC is an implementing and integrating body designed to operationalize the terms of a peace accord or other international agreement. It establishes policies for and coordinates the management of implementation, not only for postconflict reconstruction but for all postconflict operations. Clearly mandated authority for the CMOC must be promulgated by an organization with the standing and clout to make such a mandate legitimate. The United Nations is an obvious source, but for certain operations an appropriate regional organization, such as NATO, can also provide the necessary authority. Whatever its origin, the mandate must identify the basis for the action, the locus of authority, and the objectives that the operation is designed to achieve. If endowed with such authority by the United Nations or other appropriate organizations, the CMOC can then develop its structure, membership, operational procedures, and management system. According to Ambassador Robert Oakley, "The center (civil-military operations center) was an effective innovative mechanism, not only for operational coordination, but to bridge the inevitable gaps between military and civilian perceptions. By developing good personal relationships, the staffs were able to alleviate the concerns and anxieties of the relief community."[10]

Through the CMOC, each participant becomes aware of the objectives and activities of other participants. But the CMOC has no authority to direct action by any organization. It will be successful largely because the basic objectives of each of the participants have been negotiated and agreed to by their more senior members in the CMRWG. Ideally, a CMOC would integrate all postconflict recovery activities in theater; in practice, however, this is difficult to achieve. Thus a CMOC may be able to focus only on integrating functions related to a series of specific events. These events, which should themselves be integrated into the overall scope of the operation, may be widely diverse and include elections, the return of refugees, major economic initiatives, visits by major figures in the international community, the withdrawal of peacekeepers, and, for the purposes of postconflict reconstruction, the repair of key infrastructure assets.

The authority of the CMOC would derive from the parent organization that is commanding the overall mission. For example, the authority of the CMOC in Bosnia would derive from the North Atlantic Council. However, each participant would coordinate directly with its parent organization within the strategic-level working group. This parallel reporting chain would ensure that coordination occurs both vertically—along formal organizational lines—and horizontally—along functional lines. Active participation by the former warring parties is highly desired.

The leadership of the CMOC would depend upon the phase of the operation. During transformation and in the first stages of stabilization, the senior military commander is the head of the CMOC. When conditions allow for the primary focus to shift to civilian implementation, and only when the civilian staff is firmly in place, the leadership would pass to the SRSG or High Representative if it is a UN operation, or to a State Department representative if it is a unilateral operation. During normalization, leadership would remain with the civilian representative until such time as the local government can assume the full range of its responsibilities. Then, during the final stages of normalization, the local government would assume full responsibility and the military and civilian international organizations would be reduced and withdrawn.

Clearly there are issues of subordination that must be addressed proactively and decisively; the need for integration, coordination, and unity of effort is too important to be left to ad hoc arrangements. Ad hoc arrangements did not work well in Bosnia, Kosovo, or Afghanistan and thus should be firmly established prior to any future contingency. The civilian representatives must be prepared to subordinate themselves to the military during implementation and stabilization, and the military must be ready to subordinate its activities to the civilian representative in the last stages of stabilization and normalization. As a solution, the deputy chairman of the CMOC should always be a civilian if the chairman is a military officer, and vice versa; this will help mitigate the tendency for one agency or the other to assume total primacy in the postconflict operation. Essential to the success of the CMOC would be a completely integrated staff—a combined joint task force that includes civilian and military representatives at all levels, with key civilian and military staff officers within each staff section. Each participant would be assigned to a section depending upon individual and organizational expertise. At the tactical level, coordination teams should be formed under the aegis of the CMOC and placed in appropriate locations for the necessary duration.

Figure 6. Civil-Military Operations Center (CMOC)

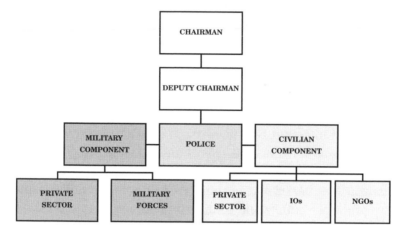

There is one sector, however, that is not represented in either the CMRWG or the CMOC. Unlike participating nations, IOs, and many NGOs, the business sector has no overarching, integrating structure and is motivated by goals and objectives (such as profit) that may or may not be consistent with those articulated by the United Nations and endorsed by the relevant players. Especially challenging is the coordination of the activities of private industry as it seeks investment opportunities. Although investment should be encouraged and supported, the CMOC would have to coordinate such private-sector activity early in the operation—and ensure that it contributes to the overall promotion of peace—until the national government is fully in place. For this reason, the CMOC's economic development staff and Infrastructure Recovery Office (outlined in Phase 2) will be pivotal. A proposed CMOC is presented in figure 6.

Formed under one chairman, the CMOC would encourage cooperation and discourage conflicts among competing organizations. Because all organizations would have a voice at the CMOC, individual agendas could still be pursued. Duplication of effort would also be avoided.

Planning Template. Once the working group is established, the CMRWG needs a planning template for reconstruction—a process that the working group uses to comprehensively analyze the postconflict reconstruction mission in advance and develop an executable plan, thus narrowing the time required for planning while embroiled in crisis. Several mechanisms can be used to get participants working from the same plan, including a comprehensive interagency assessment of the crisis situation. This begins, and should begin, well before a crisis takes shape in the minds of policymakers. Such an assessment can focus the strategy and planning effort from the outset by aiding the development of a common appraisal of what needs to be done on the ground to achieve the desired policy objectives. It can establish avenues to share information during the planning process. Although any such assessment is a living document that will certainly be revised over time, it provides an invaluable foundation for developing a common view of policy aims, strategy, and plans. In addition, if at all possible, this process should include the "reality check" of perspectives from personnel already in the field.

The establishment of a common template or generic plan will enhance the strategy development and planning process. Equally important is that the CMRWG must identify a set of standing interagency arrangements for government postconflict reconstruction efforts (similar to arrangements agreed to in the Federal Response Plan used by the Federal Emergency Management Agency for domestic disasters). Such a template will be tailored by the particulars of each operation and will depend on factors such as the complexity of the operation and the level of U.S. involvement. However, its benefit is that it focuses analysis and debate on key issues that must be resolved at the strategic level, giving those at the operational level the overall guidance required to achieve rapid success on the ground. It provides a shared foundation on which individual agencies can build their own operational responses.

The template to follow during postconflict reconstruction planning is relatively straightforward and can loosely follow the Operation Plan development process developed and taught by the U.S. Army, but with a few modifications. Once the standing working group is formed, the operation plan is written under the direction of the NSC director, using the following eight-step process:

■ Step 1: Develop available facts.

■ Step 2: Develop specified tasks.

■ Step 3: Develop unspecified tasks.

■ Step 4: Determine any constraints on the operation.

■ Step 5: Develop the mission statement.

■ Step 6: Develop the plan of execution.

■ Step 7: Promulgate the execution plan through individual agencies.

■ Step 8: Execute the plan.

Step 1: Develop available facts. Determine all available facts bearing on the problem. Determine what infrastructure damage is present in the country and document it for further action. Depending on the contingency, these facts may be difficult to obtain. Some applicable information may include items as simple as a list of the key towns and villages, a list of counties or regions upon which to organize a response, the extent of local engineering capacity or engineering materials, or the stability of the local ministries. This first step can and should begin well before conflict erupts in a region, taking advantage of all available time before the contingency proceeds to the crisis stage. As this is a standing working group, planners should develop the ability to anticipate hot spots and trouble regions in the world. As part of this anticipation, planners should begin to develop a basic information database of each area, updating as necessary when new information becomes available. It is a continuing process that does not stop even upon the receipt of an execution order. Because of the interagency nature of the working group, members should be able to provide specific expertise in certain areas and collectively be able to comprehensively analyze and determine the initial facts on the operation. Sharing information among agencies is key. Artificial firewalls established to protect areas of information must be breached so that a full and complete appreciation of the possible mission requirements can be gained.

Step 2: Develop specified tasks. Determine the specified reconstruction tasks given to the working group by higher agencies. These tasks will define the reconstruction problem and allow the working group to better focus its effort. Many of these tasks may come from a peace agreement that was negotiated, and many tasks will come from specific goals that the higher agency requires for postconflict reconstruction. The delineation of specified tasks may establish limits upon reconstruction that the higher agency wants to impose; however, many times the higher agency is unable to identify an endstate and may rely on the working group to figure it out. Although not an ideal situation, it is realistic in today's chaotic international environment.

Step 3: Develop unspecified tasks. Determine any unspecified reconstruction tasks that must be accomplished or planning parameters that must be established in order to execute the specified tasks. Often, specified tasks will require the completion of a preliminary subtask in order to be successful. It is plausible that the higher agency simply does not spell out all the tasks for brevity and speed, or omits a required task in its contingency planning. The reconstruction working group must comprehensively flesh out these "hidden" tasks so that the logistics, materials, human resources, and funding can best be allocated with priority. The result of failing to define parameters is that there is no established point that determines mission success—it goes hand-in-hand with establishing an appropriate exit strategy. It is also during this step that the working group comes to an agreement regarding what sectors the group will concentrate on for reconstruction. Basic needs such as electricity, water, heat, road and bridge infrastructure, and telecommunications may be a way to organize the plan. But rather than simply state that the country's electricity will be restored to twenty-four-hour service, when prewar conditions do not suggest that level of development, the working group must consciously determine what level of reconstruction is appropriate based on the country's history. Did the country have twenty-four-hour electrical power before the conflict, was central heat available in the cities before the conflict or did the inhabitants heat themselves with biomass fuels, was there a central water system or did the country subsist on well water, and did the country have an established sewage system or were local methods used and were they appropriate?

The working group must take into consideration the likelihood that the local government can continue to promote its country's growth once the basic level of reconstruction is accomplished. If the answer is no, then a higher level or standard for reconstruction must be considered, giving the country a higher starting point to promote continued human growth and potential. If the working group had been established for Afghanistan, for example, it would have quickly determined that reconstructing Afghanistan to its prewar state would not have brought the country into any condition for future growth, thus limiting its chances for long-term peace. Because of the neglect of more than twenty-three years of warfare since the Soviet invasion, Afghanistan's infrastructure was reduced to rubble and required much more than a re-establishment of the conditions that the Americans found in December 2001. In addition, the country must now support a much larger population than in 1978, and requires an infrastructure expansion commensurate with its twenty-first century requirements. If little information is available on the working infrastructure, such as in the case of Kosovo, the working group should establish the basic reconstruction criteria and allow the CMOC, working through the Theater Emergency Recovery Office (TERO, outlined in Phase 2), to determine through an area assessment what areas require certain reconstruction tasks and what areas already meet the standard established by the working group. Obviously, accurate information is desirable, but in the absence of accurate information, establishing a cutoff line for reconstruction standards will go far toward establishing the reconstruction endstate for the international community.

Step 4: Determine any constraints on the operation. During this step, the working group determines any constraints that will curtail the scope of the operation or prevent the operation from occurring at all. Constraints could include a lack of funding, lack of or overcommitted human resources, or even the absence of political will. If the constraints are surmountable or can be successfully mitigated, the working group continues to develop a mission. If the constraints are determined to be insurmountable, discussion with the higher authority must occur to redefine the reconstruction task into something feasible, acceptable, and suitable.

Step 5: Develop the mission statement. Once the tasks are analyzed, the postconflict reconstruction mission should be restated. Discussion must narrow the scope of the mission to what is necessary to jump-start the country in conflict. Although very short, this mission statement will serve as the principle that will guide all reconstruction efforts. It is the mission statement that gives the member organizations power to procure material and logistics in support of the mission. Instead of pouring money into a situation without a fully developed plan on how to use the funds, the mission statement gives the working group a foundation upon which to request resources from donor agencies and governments. The agreed-upon mission statement provides the working group with an authorized mandate upon which to pursue successful execution.

Step 6: Develop the plan of execution. During this step, the working group determines the realistic sequencing of organizations into the theater. If the pace of the contingency operation denies the NGOs and IOs the ability to deploy rapidly, an initial executive agent that can rapidly deploy must be chosen and agreed upon by the working group. Because of the inherent logistical advantages that the military has, there is a strong case for establishing the military as the executive agent in Phase

2. The plan should reflect the organizing structure and should also establish levels of reconstruction in order to establish first priorities. For example, the military under Phase 2 may concentrate during Reconstruction Level One on the rapid establishment of basic electricity, water, roads, and initial demining in order to forestall a humanitarian disaster and allow freedom of movement to promote peace. Reconstruction Level Two may concentrate on the refurbishment of electricity and water to make these systems more efficient for the future and safer for the environment, may concentrate on the resurfacing of roadways in order to promote the market economy, and may focus on a mine awareness program to limit the number of casualties to land mines. Regardless of the reconstruction levels, it is in the strategic working group that these decisions must be made, reconstruction levels defined, and an execution plan with an initial executive agent established.

Step 7: Promulgate the execution plan through individual agencies. Using the guidance and direction of the congressional liaison and the power and influence of both the NSC director and the special representative, the individual members promulgate the agreed-upon plan within their own agencies. The members of the working group should be able to come to the group with the ability to speak with authority for their agency. Once the reconstruction plan is completed, the members take the execution plan back to their agencies so that they can further develop its course of action in line with the overall coordinated plan. Ideally, individual agencies should be developing a parallel plan with the working group so that it will not require much effort for the agency to establish its execution plan once the working group publishes its document.

Step 8: Execute the plan. The executive agent receives an execution order to deploy and establishes the TERO in country under the auspices and coordination of the CMOC. The CMOC connection is important: Because the CMOC coordinates all activities for postconflict reconstruction, the emergency response office, which handles the infrastructure-specific aspects of the reconstruction plan, must be well integrated into the CMOC to avoid duplication of effort and to enhance on-the-ground execution. Until this order is received or the region is no longer considered a possible contingency, planners must continue to refine the plan based on the most recent information available. As in Afghanistan, time may be a precious commodity in later stages of plan development and execution, so planners must take advantage of all time available during any slow periods to continue plan refinement. Although strategy obviously drives planning, in practice planning also helps to refine strategy by framing and assessing alternative approaches, identifying negotiated tradeoffs, and highlighting interagency policy conflicts for decision makers. The result of this is more than just a set of documents; it encourages key players to build working relationships, resolve differences, identify potential inconsistencies and gaps, synchronize their actions, and better understand their roles and responsibilities. Smoothing out such wrinkles is much less costly in terms of lives and resources before an operation begins than during its execution.

Phase 2: Emergency Response

Once the reconstruction plan is successfully promulgated throughout the government agencies, the IOs, and the NGOs, an execution order to deploy into theater and establish a TERO is the trigger for the postconflict reconstruction template to enter Phase 2. In the immediate aftermath of hostilities, an external body, possibly a body suggested by the United Nations, will take the lead in establishing a viable government in theater. However, the newly established government will not be able to provide for all, if any, of its own recovery needs. With that assumption, external countries will play a crucial role in the immediate restoration of the physical infrastructure that will be vital to the development of the local government, economy, and security. Because of the short response time involved, the military takes the initial lead as the execution agent for Phase 2. According to Ambassador Robert Oakley:

There are growing doubts by some influential members of Congress and by individuals in senior defense positions on the advisability of military involvement in such situations. This is especially true as the number of operations and size, duration, and cost of military participation have all increased. They would rather equip, plan, and train for the big ones and avoid what they perceive as essentially civilian ops. U.S. military capabilities such as logistics, strategic lift, intelligence, engineering, and organizational planning mean that we are the only nation with the capacity to deploy rapidly enough to respond to major emergencies. These capabilities, coupled with the military prowess to deal with high intensity conflict, are why the U.S. has been called upon in the past and why it will continue to be called upon in the future. Even when there is a lack of enthusiasm, there may be no alternative other than inaction. The military is called upon too frequently because it is too easy, and because not enough has been done to develop greater civilian capabilities.[11]

For Phase 2, the emergency response phase, there must be two organizations to effect rapid emergency reconstruction: the National Capacity-Building Coordination Office and the TERO.

National Capacity-Building Coordination Office. The first organization required for Phase 2 is the DOD-led National Capacity-Building Coordination Office. This office would be responsible for coordinating all capacity building, including DOD reconstruction/construction assistance activities, and providing command and control for the operation and interface with U.S. agencies, foreign governments, and international aid organizations. It may seem redundant to establish an office separate from the executing reconstruction office; however, previous reconstruction efforts, such as post–Desert Storm, show that many aspects of reconstruction must occur that do not necessarily happen on the construction site and for which there may not be the appropriate facilities in most areas of the theater. This DOD office would initiate agreements, process letters of assistance, assist in international legal process reviews, coordinate explosive ordnance removals in accordance with international law, coordinate DOD humanitarian activities, assist in funding transfers and processing, and coordinate overall program management.

The National Capacity-Building Coordination Office would require personnel with specific international programs skill sets. These personnel would include:

■ Program managers familiar with regulations and require-ments relative to the development of international programs, such as foreign military sales, Section 607(a) of the Foreign Assistance Act for Technical Assistance, agreements with international aid organizations, and the United Nations.

■ Lawyers familiar with regulatory requirements associated with international agreements and contracting.

■ Resource management and budget officers familiar with the acceptance of various classifications of money, foreign military sales, Section 607 technical assistance, burden sharing, and letters of credit.

The initial staffing level needed for this type of office would be in the range of thirty-five to thirty-eight U.S. members and about fifteen host nation employees to act as expeditors and partners to learn and help execute the program. A National Capacity-Building Coordination Office is outlined in figure 7.

Theater Emergency Recovery Office. The second office required to effect rapid emergency reconstruction is the TERO. The TERO has four specified tasks. First, to determine the scope of the reconstruction effort, comprehensive damage assessments of the critical infrastructure must be rapidly completed. The assess-ments include the determination of building structural safety and pavement evaluations; completion of environmental baseline studies to document hazardous sites (other than minefields) to be used in the eventual turnover of modified infrastructure to local authorities; thorough evaluation of damages to power generation and distribution systems, water and sewage treatment facilities, airfield facilities, and water resources infrastructure; and deter-mination of the reconstruction efforts for heat, communications, medical facilities, and schools—the minimal facilities to return life to some sense of normalcy. Local nationals will integrate into Damage Assessment Groups (DAGs) as team members to assist

Figure 7. National Capacity-Building Coordination Office

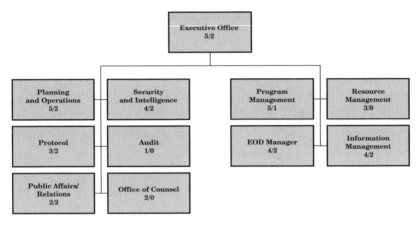

Numbers are suggested staffing ratios of U.S. to host-nation personnel.

with the surveys, solutions, and execution of the reconstruction work. Commercial contractors, under contract to the U.S. government through delivery-type contracts, would also be members of the DAGs. The DAGs would assess the damage, design a remedial solution/fix, negotiate with the contractor, and award the contract, usually the same day, to execute the repairs. This would expedite the return to normalcy with basic life-support services.

DAGs can be formed in two ways. First, the teams can be formed quickly using uniformed members of the United States Army Facility Engineer Group, an organization of 410 officers and noncommissioned officers who are mostly degreed and registered professional engineers. The full organization, which can be tailored to meet any contingency, is organized during peacetime into:

■ Thirty Facility Engineer Teams (FETs) with seven members each.

■ Four Facility Engineer Centers providing staff assistance to the FETs.

■ Six fifteen-member detachments.

■ A Mobilization Planning Support Cell.

■ A group headquarters to provide expertise, guidance, and policy review to support all activities.

The expertise within the Facility Engineer Group is extensive and allows the organization to leverage assets across the nation and to render high-quality, professional results in various engineering disciplines including architectural, civil/ structural, electrical, environmental, and construction management.[12]

However, because of political realities, military force ceilings may be imposed on a peace operation, precluding the deployment of additional uniformed personnel into the theater for reconstruction. Force ceilings were stringent in Bosnia, Kosovo, and Afghanistan, for example, and uniformed members who wanted to come into the theater for short periods were thoroughly reviewed before they were given clearance to enter the theater in order to maximize the work potential of every uniformed slot available. In addition, perception problems with the local nationals may preclude the use of uniformed military personnel in reconstruction. The local government's acceptance of any "foreign," especially Western, assistance will be difficult. This sensitivity could be eased somewhat by creating a predominately civilian organization. Therefore, the second way DAGs can be formed is by using civilian engineers from the United States Army Corps of Engineers or from the United States Navy's Civil Engineer Corps to preclude the appearance of a U.S. military organization. The project management, contracting, and logistical infrastructure could all be civilian positions, without resulting in degradation in the ability to deploy rapidly.

The second TERO task is to expedite construction and repairs in order to promote rapid recovery of the local economy. The response would identify national and regional engineering and construction capabilities and material resources that could contribute to quick emergency recovery. The initial priority is to contract for repair and emergency construction of national infrastructure using local and regional capabilities. This would spur rapid development and recovery of the local engineer capacity, provide jobs for unemployed locals, and inject much-needed revenue into the fledgling economy. If this capability is not immediately available, the second, less desirable option would be to bring in contractors from neighboring countries who have experience working within the environment and constraints of the region. The last option is to bring in international contractors from developed countries. Although this course of action would most likely provide quality engineering, the program costs would be greater because of the requirement to pay international consultant prices, and the long-term development of the local engineering capacity would hinge on the ability to hire and train local nationals. Sources for local material would follow the same course—efforts to use local vendors to provide material of acceptable quality would be maximized. Resources would be applied to meet the priority national needs, and technical assistance would be provided to local officials in their repair and reconstruction efforts.

For three major reasons, the third task is to develop a system to track the reconstruction effort. The primary reason is that during this effort a critical infrastructure data base would be developed, providing the basis to facilitate the organization of further political, cultural, and economic development. This data base goes far in helping the newly formed government establish legitimacy and helping the new government completely frame the reconstruction problem in order to develop long-term construction solutions. Second, the TERO must be able to show to donor governments and agencies that the money donated to the postconflict reconstruction program is being used with prudence and maximum long-term impact. As seen in Bosnia and Kosovo, funding audits do not stop simply because the implementing organization is deeply involved in a contingency operation. The third reason, although with less direct impact, affects the political will of the governments that have agreed to provide human resources, money, and equipment. If reconstruction progress is well documented, the ability to sustain the external political will in the postconflict reconstruction phase will be enhanced, even

Figure 8. Theater Emergency Recovery Office

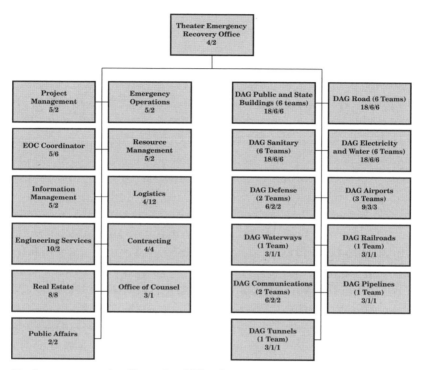

Numbers are suggested staffing ratios of U.S. to host-nation NGO/contractor personnel.

if other world events attempt to deflect attention away from the reconstruction efforts occurring in theater.

The final specified task is to train local technical personnel in maintaining and improving infrastructure. Using local nationals as part of the recovery process not only puts the population back to work rebuilding their own infrastructure but also leverages their knowledge and experience of the environment. Figure 8 depicts a TERO initially established in theater. This initial organization would evolve into Phase 3, a more typical planning, design, construction management, and contracting organization (similar to a forward-deployed engineer district found in peacetime overseas locations).

Authorization and Funding. Any national capacity-building/reconstruction effort will take from five to ten years or longer, depending on the specific needs of the country and the funding stream. Capacity building and reconstruction projects should be prioritized based on the desires of the local government and those projects having the greatest benefit to the widest range of the population. The minimum level of funding required to create a noticeable benefit would be dependent on the infrastructure conditions but would potentially require funding in the range of $200 to $300 million for the first year, with subsequent years (four to five minimum) funded at the $350 to $500 million level. This level of funding would not complete the capacity building but would make a noticeable improvement in the general population's quality of life. Money alone, however, will not necessarily make a noticeable change; the funding must be utilized for its intended purpose and not be diverted to other purposes, with an honest broker in charge of disbursements and program/infrastructure construction quality oversight.[13]

DOD can generally respond under the legal authorities of other agencies in providing infrastructure assistance in response to overseas disasters. Initially, Section 607(a) of the Foreign Assistance Act of 1961 (Public Law 87-195, as amended, 10 U.S.C. 2357) would be used to provide for the restoration of civil infrastructure. This provision of law permits any U.S. government agency to provide commodities and services to friendly countries and nongovernment and private volunteer organizations on an advance-of-funds or reimbursement basis. Section 607 agreements are typically executed between the Department of State and the host government or IOs so that DOD is not the actual signatory. In the case of postconflict reconstruction, IOs would be the major source of money under Section 607 authority.

Normally, DOD components may participate in foreign disaster relief operations only after a determination is made by the Department of State. However, under 10 U.S.C. 404, "Foreign

Disaster Assistance," and DOD Directive 5100.46, "Responsibilities for Foreign Disaster Relief," the military commander at the scene of a disaster may undertake disaster relief operations without prior approval of the ambassador/chief of mission when the emergency is so acute that immediate action is required to save life and property. Although primarily targeted toward humanitarian relief, there may be circumstances when the repair of physical infrastructure would be considered vital to the saving of lives. In addition, under the Army Technical Assistance Program (authorized by Title 33, U.S.C. 2314[a]), DOD can provide technical assistance to U.S. private firms that bid or execute overseas projects, including disaster response and recovery work.[14] This act could come into play when the DAGs complete the damage assessment and require U.S. firms to complete the emergency repairs because of lack of local engineering capacity.

Several authorities are available for DOD to support other federal agencies. These include the Economy in Government Act (31 U.S.C. 1535), the Corps of Engineers' Economy Act (10 U.S.C., 3036[d]), and, specifically, Section 234 of the Water Resources Development Act of 1996 (33 U.S.C. 2323a, "Interagency and International Support Authority"), which authorizes the United States Army Corps of Engineers to accomplish work directly for federal agencies and IOs. It is under these authorities that DOD can provide technical assistance to USAID and OFDA.[15] Finally, another authority provides limited funding for troop unit construction. DOD receives an annual appropriation under Title 10, U.S.C. 401, Humanitarian and Civic Assistance (H/CA) to promote U.S. and host nation security interests. It is intended that the deployed U.S. military personnel will exercise their operational and readiness skills while improving the condition of the host nation. The Joint Staff administers the program and the secretary of state must approve the application of H/CA in any given country. Conceivably, H/CA could be used in support of a recovery project; however, the use of these funds in the past has been quite limited and of little value.

Phase 3: Subsequent Recovery and Project Management

The postconflict template is split into four phases, but some of these phases are not always neatly separated. Although the emergency response phase is developed for a ninety-day anticipated duration, the distinction between the emergency response phase and the subsequent recovery and project management phase becomes blurred. There may be cases where emergency repairs occur in one area while more substantial, long-term repairs begin in other areas. The emergency response organization developed in Phase 2 closely resembles an emergency management structure that could be used in responding to natural disasters.

The response organization consists predominately of structural engineers, who can conduct damage surveys quickly and provide detailed estimates for repairs, rather than contract-management and quality-assurance specialists. The goal of emergency response is to restore facilities and services to their prewar condition, not to make massive improvements. However, during the subsequent recovery phase, emergency management, using the rapid assessment DAGs, shifts to a more traditional project management structure using a commodity-centered structure based on region analysis. This revised structure, the Theater Project Management Office (TPMO), can administer large contracts and complete projects to established quality standards; however, the structural design of the TPMO is based on the ability of the international aid agencies to deploy and assume the reconstruction mission. As the footprint of the aid agencies grows, the importance of the TPMO diminishes and the local national involvement in the TPMO can switch to assuming key roles in the internal ministries of the local government.

The recovery and project management phase includes additional repairs to the electrical and water supply systems, government and public buildings, and transportation networks. As the various local government ministries resume operations, the requirement for additional work by the TPMO is expected to increase temporarily. The ministries will identify additional requirements but will begin to take on some of the responsibility that the TERO had initially held. Although the TERO base structure provides a skeleton on which to easily transition to project management under the TPMO structure, primary responsibility for the operation is transferred from emergency services to the project management division.

The project managers serve as the primary link with individual local ministries and each project manager handles the full range of projects associated with a particular ministry, in a specific region, across all functional areas. The project managers are assigned to each regional sector to coordinate with the appropriate local official responsible for that sector, establishing solid rapport, trust, and confidence between the manager and the local entity. Each manager develops a program to administer all projects for that sector, from early design conception through to project completion, when the TPMO turns the finished product over to the ministry. The project managers establish priorities, develop budgets, and determine project features and quality standards. They monitor and report progress through the design, contracting, and construction phases and supervise turnover of the project to the local nationals. Their staff is determined by the amount of work required in each region; the assessments by the DAGs drive this staff organization as it determines the required scope of work.

For example, in region A, the project manager may require resources to complete projects in all areas—public and state buildings, roads, sanitation, electricity and water, defense, airports, waterways, and communications; however, region B may be landlocked and may not need resources to support waterway reconstruction, but it may have a greater role in the reconstruction of roads because of the region's landlocked dependence. The staffing is all situation-dependent and is driven by the result of the initial damage assessments. Because of the lead time to fill engineering positions, it is critical that the damage assessments be conducted quickly and accurately so that there will be a seamless transition between emergency response and project management.

As the role of the project management division expands, the role of the emergency management section, complete with the DAGs, decreases. Eventually, the emergency management division is dismantled, with their few remaining functions placed within the project management division. As prudence dictates, the military staff members are replaced initially by expatriate civilians and subsequently by local nationals as the situation stabilizes and matures. The model in figure 9 depicts the final structure that represents a gradual decline in contractor representation and an increase of local nationals in the TPMO staff, assuming that external contractors will decrease their presence as local nationals become stabilized and assume the reconstruction role for their own country.

Phase 4: Transition to Local Capacity

The ultimate goal of the postconflict reconstruction strategy is to reach Phase 4 and transition all reconstruction functions to local capacity for construction and to local ministers for management. The outside agencies must never lose sight of the fact that the purpose of external nation assistance during postconflict reconstruction is to help the host nation develop its own capabilities and its own public and private institutions. According to Lieutenant General Henry J. Hatch, chief of engineers during the Persian Gulf War, "You don't do that by going in and just building projects; it is a training, imparting of information, a building of a capability in the country."[16] Thus integrating local nationals is a key element of this concept of postconflict reconstruction. By incorporating local engineers into the organization from the TERO through TMPO and giving them hands-on experience, the recovery effort will encourage the development of improved facilities, expanded engineering expertise, and stronger personal relationships.

A second key to the success of the postconflict reconstruction effort is the ability to bridge the cultural gap between the interveners and the host country. A lack of understanding—such as when Eastern culture meets Western values—can cause strains initially until the emergency responders and the locals learn to

Figure 9. Theater Project Management Office

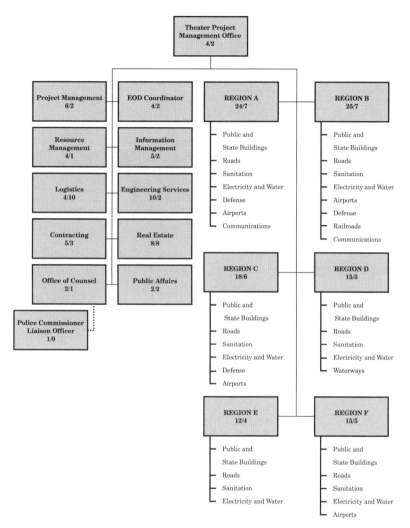

Numbers are suggested staffing ratios of U.S. to host-nation/contractor personnel.

understand each other's methods and mores. Cultural awareness on the part of the interveners is essential to establish and maintain a tangible bond focused on the rebuilding of a warravaged country. In addition, the interveners must withdraw before the host government loses enthusiasm for their presence. From the beginning, U.S. policymakers must recognize the need

to hand over responsibility for the recovery of the local infrastructure to the local government as expeditiously as possible.
Recovery efforts must visibly take into account the wishes of the
local government and rebuild the country within the managerial auspices of the newly formed local government. Initially,
as demonstrated in Bosnia, Kosovo, and Afghanistan, the local
government may require significant help to decide what the
priorities should be for reconstruction, but as the capacity builds
and proves to be competent, the external assistance must fade
into the background and redeploy. The ability for the interveners to accomplish this handover successfully will significantly
affect how war-torn countries will view the benefits of outside
help. There may always be the perceived danger that the goal of
the interveners is to assume control of the local government and
its affairs. Such accusations have surfaced in both Bosnia and
Kosovo. But the interveners had no postconflict reconstruction
plan to successfully guide their actions. Therefore, planning for
the handover during preconflict operations and demonstrating a
strong resolve to hand over operations at the earliest point possible during reconstruction will significantly affect the willingness and ability of governments to accept future help.

Although the reconstruction of Kuwait after Operation Desert
Storm was an anomaly because the local government was able to
pay for its own reconstruction and the locals had a fully functioning government almost immediately at the cessation of hostilities, some valuable insights can be garnered from that recovery
operation. The result of the operation was that the Kuwaiti
government and people appreciated the efforts of the United
States Army to repair the civil infrastructure; without the work
of the postconflict reconstruction force, the Army would not have
been able to transfer responsibility to the Kuwaiti government
nearly as fast. According to Janet McDonnell, a historian with
the United States Army Corps of Engineers:

> The Civil Affairs soldiers and the Corps of Engineers members not only
> played a critical role in planning and executing the recovery operations
> but also left behind an enduring spirit of goodwill. In large part through
> the efforts of the United States Army, not a single Kuwaiti died from

lack of food, water, or medical care. Within thirty days, primary power in Kuwait was restored and roads were cleared. Within forty-five days, the water supplies were replenished. Within ninety days, the airport was reopened. The country's civil infrastructure was restored within nine months. The United States Army was able to make a rapid transition from offensive ground force to nation assistance, successfully translating its victory on the battlefield into an environment of political and social stability and economic recovery.[17]

By the end of the recovery period, the prewar status quo had been restored in Kuwait—both politically and economically. In addition, the bond between the two nations was solidified enough that the Kuwaiti government asked the United States to station a small force temporarily in Kuwait and agreed to periodic joint military exercises, something that would have been unheard of a year earlier. Again, Kuwait was an anomaly, but it serves as an example of what can be quickly accomplished during reconstruction when the funding, organization, and political will coincide.

Phase 4 does not suggest an organization chart for the transition to local capacity as each country's government and internal ministries are developed in accordance with their culture and traditions. The new government must develop the resulting organization with a close eye on the methods that will give the country the greatest possible chance at continued growth and prosperity.

FINAL THOUGHTS

If the U.S. government plans to intervene militarily into a region as peace enforcers and then peacekeepers, such as the ongoing military role in the Balkans, or if the plan calls for military operations as a combatant in response to a perceived threat, such as the military role in Afghanistan, the planning process not only must take into account the conduct of military combat operations but must also succinctly plan the rebuilding of the country into an entity that can competently manage its internal affairs and develop its economy without perpetual external aid—otherwise, the intervention will have a high probability of failure. An approved State Department POL-MIL Plan that outlines

the operation through the recovery and reconstruction phase
is essential to provide guidance to the interagency community;
however, it is also essential to develop and execute a postconflict
reconstruction plan, carefully unifying the government agencies
with the IOs and NGOs that are so essential to completing the
recovery of a war-torn country. Although at times there is much
animosity between the aid agencies and the military, there is a
concrete way in which to build relationships and accommodate
all interests into a coherent plan that will provide maximum
benefit to the host country and its people.

History is on the side of those advocating postconflict reconstruction. The most well-known and widely successful reconstruction
venture was the Marshall Plan to rebuild Europe after World War
II. Much of Europe was in a shambles, characterized in many
instances by physical devastation and political instability, making
the continent vulnerable to the expansive goals of the Soviet Union.
As a result, Congress approved Secretary of State George C. Marshall's plan in 1947, to provide financial support for reconstruction
programs developed by participating European countries.

However, the advantages of having a rapidly deployable civil-
military engineer organization were better demonstrated when
the United States decided to help Greece recover from the devastation of war. Soon after the end of World War II, Greece was torn by
a civil war between Communist guerrillas and government troops.
President Harry S Truman and the U.S. Congress believed it to
be in the national interest to prevent a Communist takeover. To
strengthen the anti-Communist forces, a program of economic aid
was developed under the auspices of the State Department, with
the underlying view that a Greece on the road to economic recovery would be less likely to fall to Communism. President Truman
appointed Dwight P. Griswold, a former governor of Nebraska, as
the administrator of the recovery program—an early example of a
special representative appointed by the president for recovery and
reconstruction. Upon receiving Griswold's report on the country's
extensive damage, the State Department decided that the reconstruction and rehabilitation of roads, railroads, bridges, ports, and

the Corinth Canal, one of Greece's main waterways, were the primary concerns. The prevalent view was that once the country's transportation system was restored and the ports were in operable condition, economic recovery would be more rapid.[18]

The State Department received more than a hundred letters from construction firms interested in doing the work. The department, unfamiliar with executing construction and letting contracts, and having no organization to manage the job, sent representatives to the Office of the Chief of Engineers to gather information regarding the selection of contractors, the types of contracts that could be used, and the amount of fees to be paid. The State Department, concluding that it was unsuited to manage the reconstruction effort, asked the engineers, who had a far-flung civil works and military construction organization, to do the work. Formally, the secretary of state requested the secretary of war to assume responsibility for the job; assigned to the Corps of Engineers in late July 1947, the project was to be completed within a year.

Organizing in a fashion similar to a TPMO, the corps reconstructed about 900 miles of highway, rebuilt three major ports, restored railroad bridges and tunnels totaling two miles, and upgraded ten airfields. After about one million cubic yards of earth and debris had been removed, the Corinth Canal was reopened. Construction exceeded the one-year schedule by half a year, mainly because of guerrilla attacks, unusually severe winter weather, and chronic resupply delays; however, the engineer civil-military organization enabled the efficient accomplishment of the postconflict reconstruction mission and established several major precedents. First was the creation of an engineer organization to administer and supervise large-scale infrastructure reconstruction in a foreign country. Second was the provision of technical assistance in conjunction with economic aid. Third, the practice of training local contractors to perform as much of the actual work as possible began in Greece. And, fourth, the commitment to help a friendly nation to help itself was manifested in projects aimed at restoring the Greek economy.[19]

Since the end of the Cold War, the spread of Communism is no longer the key tenet that drives U.S. policy. Instead, the prevention of inter- and intraethnic conflict and rapid conflict resolution should war emerge have become central to the U.S. foreign response. No longer can the United States pick and choose its reactions to conflicts based solely on national interest or its desire to not get involved. With the advent of enhanced global information technology, the opinions of Americans who earlier did not have a resonant voice and of internationals urging American intervention have become equally strong in affecting the direction of U.S. foreign policy. Therefore, the prevention of human suffering and the provision of aid to help a people recover from war have become equal in importance to the actual conduct of military operations and require the same effort in their planning and execution. Also, because the number of military operations has grown exponentially since the end of the Cold War, exit strategies and preconflict developed endstates must be integral to every military intervention. As the military reduces its size and as the requirement for military forces for peace operations increases, developing methods that will enable the military to rapidly redeploy upon completion of the emergency response and recovery missions is imperative.

The United States has seen the effects of not having a post-conflict reconstruction plan in Bosnia, Kosovo, and Afghanistan. If there is no vetted plan, there is no real measure to determine if the intervention is successful or to determine the point when the interveners can withdraw. Only when a host country has the four qualities outlined in the opening chapter—internal security, external security, a viable economy, and a working infrastructure—can intervening forces declare mission success and an endstate. But until the initial planning is accomplished to determine the endstate, the United States will either be required to apply more money and resources over a longer period of time than is necessary to pursue a stable situation in a peace operation or risk losing significant allies and influence built up through years of engagement and diplomacy.

The postconflict reconstruction template is a guide. It outlines one way to accomplish the planning and execution for postconflict reconstruction. There may be other ways to accomplish the same endstate; however, other proposals must include four basic principles to be successful:

■ *Preconflict planning to determine endstate, to achieve approval and acceptance by both governmental and nongovernmental agencies, and to determine the structure required for immediate response.* Planning facilitates rapid response. If the civilian aid agencies cannot provide a rapid response, the government must decide to provide a rapid response through its own resources, to be handed over at the earliest moment. If the postconflict response mirrors that used in Bosnia, Kosovo, and Afghanistan, there is a high probability of inter- and intraethnic rivalries re-emerging into conflict during the first year after the cessation of hostilities. In the first year, the local government does not yet have the resources to rebuild; these must come from external sources in order to help build the economy, to give the locals work that is productive and not destructive, and to establish local government legitimacy early in the reconstruction process.

■ *An organizational structure to accomplish immediate damage and infrastructure assessment.* One of the downfalls in Bosnia, Kosovo, and Afghanistan was the inability to quickly ascertain the reconstruction mission. Assessments were late in development, driving a reconstruction gap that could not be overcome. Whether it is organized as a TERO or as a Civil Affairs Provincial Reconstruction Team, as was eventually created in Afghanistan, the effect must be to have accurate damage assessments and quick turnaround contracts to restore the basic needs of life as quickly as possible.

■ *An organizational structure to effect long-term infrastructure reconstruction.* Until local capacity is developed, there must be an agency that can competently manage the external assistance required to jump-start a conflict-ridden country into economic viability. If the aid agencies cannot respond because of organizational and funding delays, the civil-military model is an approach that would adequately jump-start the reconstruction effort until the major aid organizations can deploy.

■ *The overarching goal is to transition to local capacity and management at the earliest possible moment.* It must be the goal of every reconstruction intervention to build capacity and support local control. A reconstruction mission's success will be largely dependent on the ability of the host country to continue with the reconstruction effort in the absence of external help. Whether it is through the development of ministries of transportation and infrastructure or through the development of regional administrators who manage all aspects of governance in their province, local control is the desired endstate so that external interveners, military and civilian alike, can return to their countries of origin.

The focus on external resources may risk overemphasizing the role of the military and the donors in a war-torn country's successful recovery from violent conflict. It is vital for all concerned to understand that the critical determinants of successful peacebuilding and sustainable recovery will always be *internal*. The good intentions of the military with a seamless transition to civil agencies supported by the donor community cannot serve as a substitute for the willingness of local actors to renounce violence and to devote domestic resources to reconstruction. But the value of this approach is that it will jump-start the economy of the host nation, giving it a rapid start to recovery with a goal of self-sufficiency. A corresponding rise in self-sufficiency will thus advance the redeployment of the intervening military forces and civilian agencies and lead to possible long-term peace.

The reconstruction of a country's physical infrastructure will not guarantee long-term peace; however, the absence of a viable infrastructure places a burden upon a fledgling government and people that cannot be internally overcome, and it will prevent any chance of long-term peace from developing to its full potential.

NOTES

1. The New Security Environment

1. Janet A. McDonnell, *After Desert Storm: The U.S. Army and the Reconstruction of Kuwait* (Washington, D.C.: Department of the Army, 1999), 5.

2. J. Lewis Rasmussen, "Peacemaking in the Twenty-First Century," in *Peacemaking in International Conflict: Methods and Techniques,* ed. I. William Zartman and J. Lewis Rasmussen (Washington, D.C.: United States Institute of Peace Press, 1997), 30.

3. From a Lexis-Nexis summary of "The Johnson Administration and Pacification in Vietnam: The Robert Komer–William Leonhart Files, 1966–1968." Online. Available: http://www.lexisnexis.com/academic/guides/military_history/vietnam/vietnam_pacification.asp. (Accessed September 24, 2003.) Deputy National Security Adviser Robert Komer and his assistant, William Leonhart, were charged by President Johnson to consolidate and hasten "all U.S. nonmilitary programs for peaceful construction relating to Vietnam."

4. Ibid.

5. Michael Mandelbaum, "Foreign Policy as Social Work," *Foreign Affairs,* January/February 1996.

6. General Anthony Zinni (ret.) appearing on *The News Hour with Jim Lehrer,* September 30, 2003. Online. Available: http://www.pbs.org/newshour/bb/military/july-dec03/zinni_09-30.html. (Accessed October 6, 2003.)

7. From "The Military's Role in a Changing World: Conversation with General Anthony C. Zinni," Institute of International Studies, University of California, Berkeley, March 6, 2001. Online. Available: http://globetrotter.berkeley.edu/conversations/Zinni/zinni-con2.html. (Accessed October 6, 2003.)

8. Monica Toft, press briefing on terrorism, Kennedy School's Joan Shorenstein Center on the Press, Politics, and Public Policy, Washington, D.C., November 15, 2001.

9. Brigadier General Claude DeWilde, Chief of Engineers, IFOR, "Request the Gift of Bailey Bridges to Bosnia," memorandum to the NATO Infrastructure Committee, Sarajevo, Bosnia, 19 July 1996. Garland H. Williams CHENG7@ifor.mil, "Request the Gift of Bailey Bridges to Bosnia," electronic mail message to Colonel Ernesto Maglia emaglia@nato.mil, 20 July 1996. In July 1996, there was a series of e-mail correspondence between the Chief IFOR Engineers in Sarajevo, Bosnia (signed by Brigadier General Claude DeWilde [FR]) and the Engineering Section of the NATO Infrastructure Committee in Mons, Belgium [Colonel Ernesto Maglia (IT)], conveying the initial request to "gift" the bridges to Bosnia. The request was favorably endorsed by General George Joulwan, Supreme Allied Commander Europe, and then sent to the United States Department of State in Washington, D.C., in July 1996. The negative reply to IFOR was transmitted by telephone from Colonel Maglia to Captain Terry Tull, IFOR Deputy Chief of Engineers (U.S. Navy) in September 1996 (exact date unknown). Note: NATO e-mail communications are classified under the CRONOS communications system and cannot be retrieved by non-NATO serving officers. All addresses under IFOR have been changed to reflect the changed staff organization. The original e-mail server in Sarajevo has been replaced and attempts have failed to recover all of the original e-mail correspondence. In addition, the original document requesting the gift of the bridges was electronically destroyed during the staff transition between IFOR and SFOR, and paper copies were not kept in IFOR Headquarters (because of limited space in Sarajevo). Attempts to locate the original document at the IFOR parent headquarters, Allied Forces Southern Europe, also failed. The account of this incident is based on the author's notes because he was the staff officer who prepared and coordinated the correspondence.

10. Brigadier General Steven Hawkins, "Bosnia Bailey Bridges," e-mail correspondence to Lieutenant Colonel Garland H. Williams November 25, 2002. Brigadier General Hawkins confirms that the request was made; however, he redeployed from Bosnia before the issue was settled using NGO money during the first year of SFOR.

11. Boutros Boutros-Ghali, *An Agenda for Peace* (New York: United Nations, 1992).

12. George A. Joulwan and Christopher C. Shoemaker, *Civilian-Military Cooperation in the Prevention of Deadly Conflict: Implementing*

Agreements in Bosnia and Beyond (New York: Carnegie Corporation of New York, December 1998), 12–15.

13. Ibid., 14.

14. Ibid., 14–15.

15. Claudia Gonzalez-Vallejo and Giselda Garroso Sauveur, "Peace Through Economic and Social Development," in *The Psychology of Peacekeeping,* ed. Harvey J. Langholtz (Westport, Conn.: Praeger, 1998), 26.

16. The Challenges Project, *Challenges of Peace Operations: Into the Twenty-First Century—Concluding Report 1997–2002* (Stockholm: Elanders Gotab, 2002), 255.

17. Ibid.

18. Jason Morrow, "Greater Intervention and Military Cutbacks are a Deadly Combination," *National Policy Analysis,* no. 249 (June 1999): 1.

19. Thomas F. Lippiott, James C. Crowley, and Jerry M. Sollinger, *Time and Resources Required for Postmobilization Training of AC/ARNG Integrated Heavy Divisions* (Santa Monica, Calif.: RAND, 1998), 9.

20. Center for Army Lessons Learned, *The Effects of Peace Operations on Unit Readiness,* (Fort Leavenworth, Kan.: CALL, February 1996), A-7.

21. Army forces can be divided into three categories: *Deployable,* or operating, forces are those soldiers assigned to units that can deploy. *Institutional* forces do not deploy but support the operating forces in fields such as acquisition and training. The third category of soldiers includes those who are moving from one assignment to another, are in training, or are medically unavailable. All soldiers are assigned to one of those categories, but the actual numbers in each category change daily. For 1999, the Army assumed that operating forces constitute 63 percent of the active Army; institutional forces, 24 percent; and trainees, transients, holdees, and students, 13 percent.

22. General Accounting Office, *Peace Operations: Heavy Use of Key Capabilities May Affect Response to Regional Conflicts* (Washington, D.C.: GAO, March 1995), 4.

23. G. E. Willis, "Army Leaders Seek More Funds for '98," *Army Times,* March 23, 1998, 8.

24. That rotation base would allow one-third of the units to be deployed while one-third prepared to deploy and one-third recovered from just having been deployed. For a more detailed treatment of the relationship between the size of the rotation base and the deployment cycle, see

Ronald E. Sortor, *Army Forces for Operations Other Than War* (Santa Monica, Calif.: RAND, 1997).

25. Adam B. Siegel, *Requirements for Humanitarian Assistance and Peace Operations: Insights from Seven Case Studies* (Alexandria, Va.: Center for Naval Analyses, March 1995), 88–89.

26. Claire M. Levy, Harry Thie, and Jerry M. Sollinger, *Army PERSTEMPO in the Post–Cold War Era* (Santa Monica, Calif.: RAND, 2000), 37.

27. Congress, House of Representatives, Subcommittee of the House Services Committee, *Hearing of the Military Readiness Subcommittee of the House Armed Services Committee.* "Statement by General Thomas A. Schwartz, Commander, U.S. Army Forces Command, Fort McPherson, Georgia," 106th Cong., 1st sess., March 22, 1999.

28. Ibid.

29. Fionnuala Ni Aolain, "The Fractured Soul of the Dayton Peace Agreement: A Legal Analysis," in *Reconstructing Multiethnic Societies: The Case of Bosnia-Herzegovina,* ed. Dzemal Sokolovic and Florian Bieber (Aldershot, UK: Ashgate, 2001), 68.

30. The delegation, however, also included members of each of the national groups in Kosovo (Roma, Gorani, "loyal" Albanians, and Turks), whose legitimacy and degree of representation were doubtful.

31. The status of Kosovo is left ambiguous to the extent that it is not possible to determine clearly whether the province is autonomous with Serbia or Yugoslavia.

32. Paul R. Kimmel, "Cultural and Ethnic Issues of Conflict and Peacekeeping," in *The Psychology of Peacekeeping,* ed. Harvey J. Langholtz (Westport, Conn.: Praeger, 1998), 61.

33. Pamela Aall, Lt. Col. Daniel Miltenberger, and Thomas G. Weiss, *Guide to IGOs, NGOs, and the Military in Peace and Relief Operations* (Washington, D.C.: United States Institute of Peace Press, 2000), x.

34. Ibid., 189.

35. General Dennis J. Reimer, *Soldiers Are Our Credentials: The Collected Works and Selected Papers of the Thirty-Third Chief of Staff* (Washington, D.C.: Department of the Army, 2000), 126, 146.

36. General John M. Shalikashvili, *History of the U.S. Army War Reserve Support Command,* n.d. Online. Available: http://www.osc.army.mil/fsc.History.asp. (Accessed August 19, 2002.)

37. Nina M. Serafino, *Peacekeeping: Issues of Military Involvement* (Washington, D.C.: Congressional Research Service, August 1, 2002), 13.

38. Paul S. Killingsworth et al., *Flexbasing: Achieving Global Presence for Expeditionary Aerospace Forces* (Santa Monica, Calif.: RAND, 2000), 40.

39. United States Army Transportation School, *Division Trans-portation Officer's Guide, Reference 01-1* (Fort Eustis, Va.: Department of the Army, June 7, 2001), section 3-1. The Strategic Mobility Program was developed in response to the Mobility Requirements Study.

40. GlobalSecurity.org, "Combat Prepositioning Ships Army Prepositioned Afloat," September 16, 2002. Online. Available: http://www.globalsecurity.org/military/systems/ship/sealift-cps.htm. (Accessed February 3, 2003.)

41. Ibid.

42. General Eric K. Shinseki, *The Army Vision: Soldiers On Point for the Nation* (Washington, D.C.: Department of the Army, October 1999), 5.

43. Reimer, *Soldiers Are Our Credentials,* 126, 146.

44. Thomas R. Mockaitis, *Peace Operations and Intrastate Conflict* (Westport, Conn.: Praeger, 1999), 138.

45. Congressional Budget Office, *Making Peace While Staying Ready for War: The Challenges of U.S. Military Participation in Peace Operations* (Washington, D.C.: Congressional Budget Office, December 1999), 2–4.

46. Center for Army Lessons Learned, *Operations Other Than War, Volume IV: Peace Operations.* Newsletter no. 93-8 (Fort Leavenworth, Kan.: CALL, December 1993), V-1 to V-2.

47. Alan D. Landry, *Informing the Debate: The Impact of Operations Other Than War on Combat Training Readiness.* Strategy Research Project (Carlisle Barracks, Pa.: U.S. Army War College, April 7, 1997), 5.

48. Ibid., C-1.

49. Reimer, *Soldiers Are Our Credentials,* 22.

50. Congressional Budget Office, *Making Peace While Staying Ready for War,* 4-5.

51. Ibid., 5-1.

52. Ibid., 5-2.

53. Congress must approve any supplemental appropriations and agree with transfers and reprogramming actions of any significant amount.

That amount is set by congressional authorization and appropriation committees and can vary from year to year.

54. Congressional Budget Office, *Making Peace While Staying Ready for War,* 5-3.

55. The amount obligated could be up to one-half of that year's appropriation for O&M Budget Activity 1, which provides funds for operating military forces.

56. Congressional Budget Office, *Making Peace While Staying Ready for War,* 5-3.

57. Ibid., 5-4.

58. Pamela Aall, "NGOs, Conflict Management, and Peacekeeping," in *Peacekeeping and Conflict Resolution,* ed. Tom Woodhouse and Oliver Ramsbotham (London: Frank Cass, 2000), 123.

59. Andrew S. Natsios, "An NGO Perspective," in Zartman and Rasmussen, eds., *Peacemaking in International Conflict,* 337–41.

60. Aall, Miltenberger, and Weiss, *Guide to IGOs, NGOs, and the Military,* 8–10.

61. Aall, "NGOs, Conflict Management, and Peacekeeping," 135.

62. Aall, Miltenberger, and Weiss, *Guide to IGOs, NGOs, and the Military,* 98.

63. Ibid., 108.

64. Natsios, "An NGO Perspective," 354.

65. Michael Bryans, Bruce D. Jones, and Janice Gross Stein, "Mean Times: Adapting the Humanitarian Imperative for the Twenty-First Century" (Program on Conflict Management and Negotiation, Toronto, October 1998), 42.

66. Lisa Witzig Davidson, Margaret Daly Hayes, and James J. Landon, *Humanitarian and Peace Operations: NGOs and the Military in the Interagency Process* (Washington, D.C.: National Defense University Press, December 1996), 4-2.

67. Ibid.

68. David Last, "Organizing for Effective Peacebuilding," in Woodhouse and Ramsbotham, eds., *Peacekeeping and Conflict Resolution,* 85.

69. Ibid.

70. Aall, Miltenberger, and Weiss, *Guide to IGOs, NGOs, and the Military,* 101–102.

71. Louise Diamond and John McDonald, *Multi-Track Diplomacy* (West Hartford, Conn.: Kumarian Press, 1996), 41.

72. Annika S. Hansen, *Drawing Lines in the Sand: The Limits and Boundaries of Peace Support Operations.* Monograph no. 44 (Pretoria, South Africa: Institute for Security Studies; Boundaries of Peace Support Operations, February 2000), 6.

73. S. J. Stedman, "UN Intervention in Civil Wars: Imperatives of Choice and Strategy," in *Beyond Traditional Peacekeeping,* ed. D. C. F. Daniel and B. C. Hayes (Basingstoke, UK: Macmillan, 1995), 51.

74. Natsios, "An NGO Perspective," 348.

75. Members of the donor community include bilateral aid agencies of national governments, particularly the members of the Development Assistance Committee (DAC) of the Organization for Economic Cooperation and Development (OECD); the departments, programs, and specialized agencies of the United Nations; the international financial institutions; and numerous NGOs such as the ICRC and Oxfam. According to data compiled from the OECD's *Geographical Distribution of Financial Flows to Aid Recipients 1999,* countries emerging from conflict received aid commitments of approximately $109 billion from multilateral institutions and DAC members between 1990 and 1997.

76. The World Bank, *Conflict Prevention and Postconflict Reconstruction: Perspectives and Prospects* (Washington, D.C.: The World Bank, August 1998), 21.

77. Mark R. Walsh, "Managing Peace Operations in the Field," *Parameters* 26, no. 2 (Summer 1996), 8.

78. Michael A. Sheehan, assistant secretary-general, UN Department of Peacekeeping Operations, interview by author, Washington, D.C., September 5, 2002.

79. Joulwan and Shoemaker, *Civilian-Military Cooperation,* 21–22.

2. Bosnia

1. Laura Silber and Alan Little, *Yugoslavia, Death of a Nation* (New York: Penguin Books, 1996), 361.

2. Pearson Centre Archive, "Situation Report, Sarajevo Shelling" (Sarajevo, Bosnia, n.d.).

3. Richard Holbrooke, *To End a War* (New York: Random House, 1998), 93.

4. For an excellent account of Operation Deliberate Force, see Rick Atkinson's two lengthy articles, "Air Assault Sets Stage for Broader Role" and "In Almost Losing Its Resolve, NATO Alliance Found Itself," *Washington Post,* November 15 and 16, 1995, respectively. An official account, "Operation Sharp Guard," is available from NATO's Public Affairs Office and online from the NATO gopher.

5. Leo Tindemans et al., *Unfinished Peace: Report of the International Commission on the Balkans* (Washington, D.C.: Carnegie Endowment for International Peace, 1996), 53–54.

6. The program, called "Train and Equip," has been run from its inception by the same private company, Military Professional Resources, Inc., and provided technical assistance to the Croatian army during the war.

7. For the full text of the accords, see the General Framework Agreement for Peace in Bosnia and Herzegovina (hereafter, GFAP), finalized in Paris on December 14, 1995. Online. Available: http://www.ohr.int/gfa/ga-home.htm.

8. Ibid., Annex 1-B and Annex 1-A, Article II, 1-4. Arms control measures set a ratio of forces among the parties and their regional guarantors based on their respective populations and ostensible defense needs. From a baseline determined by the military capacity of the Federal Republic of Yugoslavia (FRY), armaments were to be reduced as follows: to 75 percent of the baseline for the FRY, 30 percent for Croatia, and 30 percent for Bosnia. Bosnia's 30 percent would, in turn, be allocated between the two entities (the Bosnian-Croat federation and the Republika Srpska) in a 2:1 ratio (GFAP, Annex 1-B, Article IV).

9. When IFOR's mandate was first renewed beyond December 1996, its name was changed to the Stabilization Force (SFOR).

10. GFAP, Annex 1-A, Article VI, para 3(c-d).

11. Ibid., Annex 2, Article V.

12. An EU administrator was established in 1994 for the city of Mostar, which was heavily damaged by Croat-Bosniac fighting in 1993 and is only marginally less divided today between its Croat western section and Bosniac eastern section than it was during the war.

13. From January 1996 to April 1997, the High Representative was former Swedish prime minister and EU mediator in Bosnia Carl Bildt. From April 1997 through August 1999, the office was held by Spanish diplomat Carlos Westendorp. It was assumed in August 1999 by Austrian diplomat Wolfgang Petritsch. Paddy Ashdown has held the office from May 2002 to the present.

14. The High Representative's authority even over his or her own office has been questionable. Most posts within OHR are seconded by member governments; particularly at high levels, these are allocated as much on the basis of political horse trading as of anything else.

15. N. D. White, *Keeping the Peace: The United Nations and the Maintenance of International Peace and Security,* 2d ed. (Manchester, UK: Manchester University Press, 1997), 127.

16. GFAP, Annex 1-A, Article I, para 1(b).

17. Steven R. Bowman, *Bosnia: U.S. Military Operations* (Washington, D.C.: Congressional Research Service, November 13, 2001), 4.

18. International Crisis Group, *The Balkan Refugee Crisis: Regional and Long-Term Perspectives* (Brussels: International Crisis Group, June 1, 1999), 4.

19. The World Bank, *Reconstruction of Bosnia and Herzegovina: Priorities for Recovery and Growth* (Washington, D.C.: The World Bank, 1995), 1.

20. The World Bank, *Bosnia and Herzegovina: Toward Economic Recovery* (Washington, D.C.: The World Bank, 1996), 3.

21. U.S. Department of State, Bureau of European and Eurasian Affairs, *Background Note: Bosnia and Herzegovina* (Washington, D.C.: U.S. Department of State, September 2001), 2.

22. World Bank, *Bosnia and Herzegovina: Toward Economic Recovery,* 3.

23. Ibid., 10.

24. U.S. Department of State, *Background Note: Bosnia and Herzegovina,* 2.

25. World Bank, *Bosnia and Herzegovina: Toward Economic Recovery,* 10. Bosnia had a GDP of about $8–$9 billion before the war. Assuming a capital output ratio of four to five, total prewar capital stock was $30–$40 billion. As nearly half of the capital stock is estimated to have been destroyed, the damage is presumed in the range of $15–$20 billion. The government's estimates of war damages include not only physical destruction but also the capitalized value of (1) unpaid wage and pension arrears since the war began and (2) the capitalized value of claims on the state such as frozen foreign exchange deposits lost to citizens and enterprises during the war.

26. Allied Rapid Reaction Corps, "ARRC Bridge Replacement Plan: Phases 1-3" (briefing slides with scripted commentary, Sarajevo, Bosnia, ARRC Engineer Branch Brief, December 30, 1996), 3.

27. Tindemans et al., *Unfinished Peace,* 96.

28. 62d Construction Royal Engineers, *Sarajevo Airport Assessment* (Sarajevo, Bosnia: 62d CRE, May 1996), 20–29. The 62d CRE, a British military unit that is similar in capability to a civilian engineering design firm, conducted a detailed assessment of the Sarajevo Airport soon after the shelling ceased. Their report outlines in minute detail the equipment that would be required to restore the Sarajevo Airport to acceptable international guidelines for civilian air traffic safety. Landing lights, runway strength, and equipment to minimally facilitate visual flight rules (VFR) landings and takeoffs were highlighted. The French contingent operated the Sarajevo Airport for military purposes only and provided portable equipment to ensure safety to NATO aircraft. Civilian traffic did not operate out of Sarajevo until late summer 1996, and then only under VFR conditions.

29. The World Bank, "Reconstruction of Bosnia and Herzegovina." Press Release (Washington, D.C.: The World Bank Group, 1995), 1.

30. Ibid.

31. Ibid.

32. European Commission and World Bank, *Bosnia and Herzegovina 1996–1998, Lessons and Accomplishments: Review of the Priority Reconstruction and Recovery Program and Looking Ahead Toward Sustainable Economic Development.* Report prepared for the May 1999 Donors Conference, n.d., Annex 6-1.

33. Ibid., Annex 4-1.

34. David Woodward, *The IMF, the World Bank, and Economic Policy in Bosnia* (Oxford, UK: Oxfam, 1998), 11.

35. Colonel Steven Hawkins, Engineer Brigade Commander, 1st Armored Division (U.S.), Oral History Interview Transcript, Bad Kreuznach, Germany, March 6, 1997, 51–52.

36. Dr. Pramod K. Sethi, remarks at the Rotary International Conference in San Antonio, Texas, June 2001. Online. Available: http://landmineconf.rotary5030.org. (Accessed October 4, 2002.)

37. Hawkins transcript, 48–49.

38. IFOR/SFOR Engineer Staff, "CJ ENGR Strategic Vision" (IFOR/SFOR, Sarajevo, December 1996), 4.

39. United States Army Task Force Eagle Headquarters, *TFE Joint Military Commission Policies, Procedures, and Command Guidance Handbook* (Rodelheim, Germany: United States Army Printing and Publications Center, May 12, 1996), 1.

40. Lieutenant Colonel Todd T. Semonite, *The Military Engineer as a Critical Peace Operations Multiplier.* Strategy Research Project (Carlisle Barracks, Pa.: U.S. Army War College, April 7, 1999), 108.

41. Hawkins transcript, 26–27.

42. Semonite, *The Military Engineer,* 68.

43. Ibid., 37.

44. Hawkins transcript, 50–51.

45. Semonite, *The Military Engineer,* 87.

46. Ibid., 99.

47. IFOR/SFOR Engineer Staff, "CJ ENGR Strategic Vision," 5.

48. General Wesley K. Clark, "Building a Lasting Peace in Bosnia and Herzegovina," *NATO Review* 46, no. 1 (Spring 1998): 20.

49. United Nations, "Mine Action in Bosnia and Herzegovina," May 2, 2002. Online. Available: http://www.mineaction.org/countries/countries_overview.cfm?country_id=252. (Accessed September 20, 2002.)

50. GFAP, Annex 1-A, Article I, para 1(b).

51. Colonel William R. Phillips, "Civil-Military Cooperation: Vital to Peace Implementation in Bosnia," *NATO Review* 46, no. 1 (Spring 1998): 25.

52. Ibid., 131.

53. GFAP, Annex 9, Article I.

54. Ibid., Annex 10, Article I.

55. Zlatko Hertic, Amela Sapcanin, and Susan L. Woodward, "Bosnia and Herzegovina," in *Good Intentions: Pledges of Aid for Postconflict Recovery,* ed. Shepard Forman and Stewart Patrick (Boulder, Colo.: Lynne Rienner, 2000), 319.

56. The "sectors" are Transportation, Electric Power and Coal, Telecommunications, Housing, District Heating and Natural Gas, Water and Waste Management, Land Mine Hazard Management, Education, Health, Industry and Finance, Employment and Labor, Agriculture, and Social Protection.

57. The objectives of the PRRP included rehabilitation of key infrastructure and social sectors to jumpstart production and ensure improved access to basic services and housing to facilitate the return of displaced persons and refugees; implementation of projects in support of employment generation and demobilization of soldiers; strengthening of key government institutions and establishment of basic economic institutions of the two entities and the state, including a new central bank, as called for under the Dayton Accords; continuation of efforts toward macroeconomic stabilization; and implementation of the demining project as an important prerequisite for physical implementation of other projects. "Chairman's Conclusions," Second Donor Conference on the Reconstruction of Bosnia and Herzegovina, n.d.

58. Senator Frank Lautenberg (D-NJ) sponsored the War Crimes Prosecution Facilitation Act of 1997 (S804, May 23, 1997), which restricts U.S. bilateral assistance and instructs the U.S. executive director to the international financial institutions (specified as the IMF, the World Bank, the International Development Association, the International Finance Corporation, the Multilateral Investment Guarantee Agency, and the EBRD) to oppose and vote against any aid or grants to countries, entities, or cantons providing sanctuary to indicted war criminals who are sought for prosecution before the International Criminal Tribunal for the Former Yugoslavia. The bill was incorporated into the Foreign Operations Appropriations Act for 1998, Section 573 of HR 2159, and became law on November 12, 1997.

59. Hertic, Sapcanin, and Woodward, "Bosnia and Herzegovina," 359.

60. The advanced industrial democracies in the Group of Seven (Canada, France, Germany, Italy, Japan, the United Kingdom, and the United States) meet regularly on the coordination of international economic policies, but their annual ministerial agendas have expanded to include common foreign policy issues as well. Russia's invitation to the 1995 G-7 summit resulted in the Group of Eight (G-8), in which international political issues close to the Russian foreign-policy realm—such as Bosnia—are discussed.

61. For example, in January and February 1996, the EC identified "official counterparts" in the Bosnian local governments that assisted in the identification of sector priorities and assisted in the coordination between EC and local activities. However, the initial identification of sectoral priorities was wrapped up in the long-term struggle between Bosnia's two entities and was not completed until late summer 1996.

62. For example, USAID contracted with the Ralph M. Parsons Company to provide overall program management of the Municipal Infrastructure and Services Program (a $265 million initiative to rehabilitate basic infrastructure in facilitating the return of refugees).

63. The degree to which donors coordinated with IFOR/SFOR varied significantly. For instance, USAID followed congressional guidance that called for the "bulk" of reconstruction resources to be confined to the U.S. SFOR sector and Sarajevo, and therefore USAID linked its mission closely with NATO.

64. Carl Bildt, "Implementing the Civilian Tasks of the Bosnian Peace Agreement," *NATO Review* 44, no. 5 (Spring 1996): 5.

65. World Bank, "Reconstruction of Bosnia and Herzegovina," 2.

66. European Commission and World Bank, *Bosnia and Herzegovina 1996–1998, Lessons and Accomplishments.*

3. Kosovo

1. Steven J. Woehrel and Julie Kim, *Kosovo and U.S. Policy* (Washington, D.C.: Congressional Research Service, July 3, 2002), 3.

2. U.S. Department of State, "The Rambouillet Agreement," n.d. Online. Available: http://www.state.gov/www/regions/eur/ksvo_rambouillet/text.html. (Accessed September 25, 2002.)

3. United Nations Security Council, letter dated June 4, 1999, from the Permanent Representative of France to the United Nations, addressed to the secretary-general, enclosing the Rambouillet Agreement, "Interim Agreement for Peace and Self-Government in Kosovo," UN Doc. S/1999/648 (June 7, 1999).

4. Steven Bowman, *Kosovo and Macedonia: U.S. and Allied Military Operations* (Washington, D.C.: Congressional Research Service, September 17, 2002), 2.

5. Wesley K. Clark, *Waging Modern War* (New York: Public Affairs, 2001), 211. General Clark reported that during the first few days of the air operation, "We were striking at the facilities of the Serb ground forces that were doing the ethnic cleansing, but we hadn't yet struck those forces."

6. William Drozdiak, "NATO Leaders Struggle to Find a Winning Strategy," *Washington Post,* April 1, 1999, A22.

7. Bruce R. Nardulli et al., *Disjointed War: Military Operations in Kosovo, 1999* (Santa Monica, Calif.: RAND, 2002), 43.

8. "Military-Technical Agreement Between the International Security Force (KFOR) and the Government of the Federal Republic of Yugoslavia and the Federal Republic of Serbia," Kumanovo, Macedonia, June 9, 1999.

9. Kosovo Force, "Background to the Conflict," n.d., p. 4. Online. Available: http://www.nato.int/kfor/kfor/intro.htm. (Accessed September 25, 2002.)

10. Ibid.

11. United Nations, Security Council Resolution 1244, UN Doc. S/RES/1244 (1999), June 10, 1999.

12. Lieutenant General Sir Mike Jackson, "KFOR: Providing Security for Building a Better Future for Kosovo," *NATO Review* 47, no. 3 (Autumn 1999): 17.

13. Ibid., 18.

14. Kosovo Force, "Background to the Conflict," 5.

15. "Undertaking of Demilitarisation and Transformation by the Kosovo Liberation Army," June 20, 1999. Online. Available: http://www.kforonline.com. (Accessed October 5, 2002.)

16. Lieutenant General Agim Ceku, Chief of Staff, Kosovo Liberation Army, "Statement," September 20, 1999. Online. Available: http://www.kforonline.com. (Accessed November 2, 2002.)

17. The Kosovo Protection Corps Commander, Kosovo Force's Statement of Principles; UNMIK/RE/1999/8, on the Establishment of the Kosovo Protection Corps, September 20, 1999. Online. Available: http://www.kforonline.com. (Accessed November 5, 2002.)

18. Dimitri G. Demeka, Johannes Herderschee, and Davina F. Jacobs, *Kosovo: Institutions and Policies for Reconstruction and Growth* (Washington, D.C.: International Monetary Fund, 2002), 5–7.

19. World Bank/Food and Agriculture Organization survey of damage in the sector, as cited in European Commission and the World Bank in Support of the United Nations Mission in Kosovo, *Toward Stability and Prosperity: A Program for Reconstruction and Recovery in Kosovo,* n.p., November 3, 1999, 7.

20. Ibid., 143.

21. Ibid., 147.

22. Ibid., 151.

23. Ibid., 76.

24. Ibid., 127.

25. Ibid., 128.

26. Ibid., 131.

27. Teledensity in the region is typically at or around 30 percent; in western Europe, it is over 40 percent.

28. European Commission, 123–126.

29. United Nations Mine Action Coordination Centre, "Kosovo Demining," September 1999, Online. Available: http://jacquesbure.free.fr/kosovo_demining.htm. (Accessed November 3, 2002.)

30. Ibid.

31. John Flanagan, interview by author, Pristina, Kosovo, June 17, 2000.

32. Richard Trow, "A Kiwi with a Mission to Clean Up Kosovo's Minefield," June 12, 2002. Online. Available: http://www.mineaction.org/countries/_refdocs.cfm?doc_ID=648&from=misc/. (Accessed October 5, 2002.)

33. United States Army Corps of Engineers—Europe District, Engineering in Europe, *Special Edition, Kosovo: The Engineers' Story* (Wiesbaden, Germany: United States Army Corps of Engineers, May 2000), 8.

34. Colonel Robert McClure, Engineer Brigade Commander, 1st Infantry Division (U.S.), interview by author, Camp Bondsteel, Kosovo, June 3, 2000.

35. Larry Wentz, "Peacekeeper Quality of Life," in *Lessons From Kosovo: The KFOR Experience,* ed. Larry Wentz (Washington, D.C.: Department of Defense Command and Control Research Program, July 2002), 383.

36. 16th Engineer Battalion, "Operations Brief" (briefing slides with scripted commentary, Camp Bondsteel, Kosovo, November 22, 2000), 16–17.

37. Lieutenant Colonel Bryan Foy, commander of 1-37 Armor Battalion, interview by author, Camp Bondsteel, Kosovo, August 12, 2000; Lieutenant Colonel Bryan Foy, e-mail correspondence to the author, November 25, 2002.

38. 16th Engineer Battalion, "Operations Brief," 8.

39. Ibid., 7.

40. United States Army Corps of Engineers—Europe District, *Engineering in Europe,* 73.

41. Ibid., 60.

42. United Nations Interim Administrative Mission in Kosovo, "Regulation Number 1999/8: On the Establishment of the Kosovo Protection Corps" (UNMIK, Pristina, Kosovo, September 20, 1999).

43. Christopher Holshek, "The Operational Art of Civil-Military Operations: Promoting Unity of Effort," in Wentz, ed., *Lessons From Kosovo,* 284–285.

44. Ibid., 287.

45. For a general discussion, see United Nations Security Council, *Report of the Secretary-General on the United Nations Interim Administration Mission in Kosovo* (New York: United Nations, 2000); International Crisis Group, *Kosovo Report Card.* ICG Balkans Report, no. 100 (Brussels: International Crisis Group, August 28, 2000); and United Nations Interim Administration Mission in Kosovo, *A Year and a Half in Kosovo* (Pristina, Kosovo: UNMIK, 2000).

46. European Commission, 4.

47. European Agency for Reconstruction. Report concerning the financial accounts of the European Agency for Reconstruction and the implementation of aid for Kosovo for the year 2000, untitled, November 12, 2001 (ECA/01/32), 1.

48. The Independent International Commission on Kosovo, *The Kosovo Report* (Oxford, UK: Oxford University Press, 2000), 124.

49. Curt Tarnoff, *Kosovo: Reconstruction and Development Assistance.* CRS Report for Congress (Washington, D.C.: Congressional Research Service, January 16, 2001), 6.

50. North Atlantic Treaty Organization, "CIMIC Reconstruction," *NATO Review* 49, no. 1 (Spring 2001): 21.

51. United Nations Mission in Kosovo, Department of Reconstruction, *Kosovo 2001–2003: From Reconstruction to Growth* (Pristina, Kosovo: UNMIK, December 2000), 2.

4. Afghanistan

1. The White House, "The Global War on Terrorism: The First 100 Days," n.d. Online. Available: http://www.state.gov/s/ct/rls/rpt/6947.htm. (Accessed December 3, 2002.)

2. Surinder Rana, "Strategic Insight: Afghanistan Military Campaign Enters New Phase" (Naval Postgraduate School, Center for Contemporary Conflict, Monterey, Calif., April 9, 2002). Online. Available: http://www.ccc.nps.navy.mil/rsepResources/si/apr02/southAsia.asp. (Accessed December 5, 2002.)

3. Michelle Boorstein, "Taliban and Al-Qaeda Fighters May Change Form of Attack, Allies Say," Associated Press, April 3, 2002.

4. Kathy Gannon, "Powell Promises to Rid Afghanistan of Terrorist Contamination," Associated Press, January 17, 2002, 1.

5. Ibid.

6. The White House, "President Outlines War Effort: Remarks by the President to the George C. Marshall ROTC Award Seminar on National Security," Virginia Military Institute, Lexington, Virginia, April 17, 2002. Online. Available: http://www.whitehouse.gov/news/releases/2002/04/20020417-1.html. (Accessed November 17, 2003.)

7. The World Bank, *Transitional Support Strategy: Afghanistan* (Washington, D.C.: The World Bank, March 12, 2002), 3–5.

8. The World Bank, "Afghanistan: World Bank Approach Paper" (Washington, D.C.: The World Bank, November 2001), 1–3.

9. Asian Development Bank, United Nations Development Program, and The World Bank, *Afghanistan: Preliminary Needs Assessment for Recovery and Reconstruction* (Kabul: Asian Development Bank, January 2002), VI-1.

10. Ibid.

11. Central Intelligence Agency, "Afghanistan" in *The World Factbook 2002* (Washington, D.C.: Central Intelligence Agency, 2002). Online. Available: http://www.cia.gov/cia/publications/factbook/print/af.html. (Accessed December 6, 2002.)

12. The World Bank, *Transitional Support Strategy,* 4.

13. The World Bank, "Afghanistan"; n.d., p. 6. Online. Available: http://www.export.gov/afghanistan. (Accessed February 6, 2003.)

14. Ibid., 9.

15. John Stevens, "Afghanistan's Hidden Killers: Land Mines," *State Magazine,* April 2002, 15.

16. Center for Defense Information, *Terrain, Taliban and Terrorists: Not Only Challenges to U.S. Forces in Afghanistan* (Washington, D.C.: Center for Defense Information, September 25, 2001), 1.

17. United Nations/World Bank, "Immediate and Transitional Assistance Programme for the Afghan People" (United Nations, New York, January 17, 2002). Online. Available: http://www.reliefweb.int/library/Afghan%20ITAP%202002_final.pdf. (Accessed December 7, 2002.)

18. United Nations/World Bank, "Afghanistan—Preliminary needs assessment for recovery and reconstruction" (United Nations, New York, January 15, 2002). Online. Available http://www.mineaction.org/countries/_refdocs.cfm?doc_ID=463&c. (Accessed December 7, 2002.)

19. 92nd Engineer Battalion (Combat Heavy), "Engineer Support to Operation Enduring Freedom" (briefing slides with scripted commentary, Fort Stewart, Ga., July 2002).

20. Colonel Jerry T. Mohr, Lieutenant Commander Frederick A. Mucke, and Lieutenant Commander Donald L. Maconi, "Operation Enduring Freedom From the Military Engineer Perspective," *The Engineer Magazine* (July 2002), 4–5.

21. Major Dennis J. McNulty, "Repairing Runways and Clearing Mines in Afghanistan," *The Engineer Magazine* (July 2002), 8–9.

22. Bobby Yettman, "RED HORSE Completes Runway Project," n.d. Online. Available http://www.centcom.mil/News/Stories. (Accessed December 6, 2002.)

23. McNulty, "Repairing Runways," 9.

24. 92nd Engineer Battalion (Combat Heavy), "Engineer Support to Operation Enduring Freedom," 8.

25. Major Dennis McNulty, "Base Camp Infrastructure Development and C2 in Afghanistan," *The Engineer Magazine* (October–December 2002), 4–6.

26. 92nd Engineer Battalion (Combat Heavy), "Engineer Support to Operation Enduring Freedom," 10.

27. McNulty, "Repairing Runways," 11–12.

28. Colonel Harold "Gene" Williams, deputy commander of the Afghanistan CJCMOTF, and Major Kimberly Field, operations officer of the Afghanistan CJCMOTF, interview by author, Fort McPherson, Ga., October 29, 2002.

29. CJCMOTF, "Coalition Joint Civil Military Operations Task Force" (briefing slides with scripted commentary, CJCMOTF, Kabul, March 17, 2002), 12.

30. Robb Huhn, "CJCMOTF Helps Impact a Nation," August 2002. Online. Available http://www.centcom.mil/News/Stories/Operation%20Enduring%20Freedom/08_02/08_07_02b.htm. (Accessed December 1, 2002.)

31. Williams, interview.

32. Huhn, "CJCMOTF Helps Impact a Nation."

33. CJCMOTF, "Coalition Joint Civil Military Operations Task Force," 29.

34. Voice of America, "US Military Shift Afghan Operations Toward Reconstruction Efforts," December 2002, p. 6. Online. Available: http://www.reliefweb.int/w/rwb.nsf/9ca65951ee22658ec125663300408599/89c64e0b539dc69d49256c8a0019fbb1?. (Accessed December 4, 2002.)

35. Ibid.

36. Lieutenant Colonel Michael Stout, deputy commander of the Afghanistan CJCMOTF, interview by author, Carlisle Barracks, Pa., January 22, 2003.

37. Ilene R. Prusher, "Afghan Refugees Strain Kabul." *The Christian Science Monitor* December 11, 2002.

38. David Loyn, "Afghanistan Struggles to Rebuild," BBC News/World Edition, November 5, 2002. Online. Available: http://www.news.bbc.co.uk/2/hi/south_asia/2405191.stm. (Accessed December 5, 2002.)

39. Interim Foreign Minister Abdullah Abdullah, "Afghanistan: Stability and Security," press briefing, Dirksen Senate Office Building, Washington, D.C., October 21, 2002.

40. Dr. Amin Farhang, "Afghanistan: Interview with Reconstruction Minister Dr. Amin Farhang," IRIN News, UN Office for the Coordination of Humanitarian Affairs, October 7, 2002. Online. Available: http://www.irinnews.org/report.asp?ReportID=30262&SelectRegion=Central_Asia. (Accessed December 9, 2002.)

41. The World Bank, *Transitional Support Strategy,* 4.

42. United Nations/World Bank, "Afghanistan."

43. U.S. Department of State, Bureau of Political-Military Affairs, Office of Humanitarian Demining Programs, "U.S. Humanitarian Demining Assistance to Afghanistan," July 30, 2002, 1.

44. H. E. Karzai, "Statement of H. E. Karzai, Chairman of the Interim Administration of Afghanistan: A Vision for Afghanistan" (Donors'

Conference, Tokyo, January 25, 2002). Online. Available: http://www.mine-action.org/countries/_refdocs.cfm?doc_ID=535&country_ID=652. (Accessed December 4, 2002.)

45. Reliefweb, "Executive Summary and National Priority Projects," October 12, 2002. Online. Available: http://www.reliefweb.int/w/rwb.nsf/vID/1EB74FFA8B0155E4C5B002AAD79?OpenDocument. (Accessed December 6, 2002.)

46. Thomas Ushijima, director of military and management, United States Corps of Engineers, Pacific Ocean Division, memorandum for record on "Trip Report - Asian Development Bank, Manila, Philippines," June 13, 2002.

47. United Nations/World Bank, "Immediate and Transitional Assistance Programme for the Afghan People."

5. A Postconflict Reconstruction Template

1. Karin von Hippel, *Democracy by Force—U.S. Military Intervention in the Post–Cold War World* (Cambridge, UK: Cambridge University Press, 2000), 5.

2. Joulwan and Shoemaker, *Civilian-Military Cooperation,* 17–20.

3. Ibid., 20–24.

4. Ibid., 25.

5. Johanna Mendelson-Forman and Michael Pan, "Post-Conflict Rapid Civilian Response" (discussion paper presented at the Center for Strategic and International Studies, Washington, D.C., March 25, 2002), 3.

6. The White House, *The Clinton Administration's Policy on Managing Complex Contingency Operations: Presidential Decision Directive,* May 1997. Online. Available: http://clinton2.nara.gov/WH/EOP/NSC/html/documents/NSCDoc2.html. (Accessed January 7, 2003.)

7. Karl F. Inderfurth and Loch K. Johnson, eds., *Decisions of the Highest Order: Perspectives on the National Security Council* (Pacific Grove, Calif.: Brooks/Cole, 1998), 350–51.

8. Michele Flournoy, "Interagency Strategy and Planning for Post-Conflict Reconstruction" (Center for Strategic and International Studies, Washington, D.C., March 27, 2002), 3.

9. Lisa Witzig Davidson, Margaret Daly Hayes, and James J. Landon, *Humanitarian and Peace Operations: NGOs and the Military in* *the Interagency Process* (Washington, D.C.: National Defense University Press, December 1996), 5-1.

10. Mark H. Sweberg, "Transitioning a Peacekeeping Operation from Military to Civilian Management" (briefing slides with scripted commentary. U.S. Department of State. Bureau of Political-Military Affairs, n.d.), 12.

11. Ambassador Robert Oakley, "Opening Remarks to National Defense University Symposium on Civil-Military Cooperation," 2001. Online. Available: http://www.dodccrp.org/ngo.html. (Accessed November 20, 2002.)

12. 416th Engineer Command, *United States Army Facility Engineer Group* (Darien, Ill.: Facility Engineer Group, n.d.), 2.

13. U.S. Army Corps of Engineers, "Proposed Model for Post Conflict Nation Capacity Building" (Transatlantic Program Center, Winchester, Va., May 8, 2002), 2.

14. U.S. Army Corps of Engineers, "Concept for Overseas Disaster Response and Recovery Operations in Afghanistan" (U.S. Army Corps of Engineers, Washington, D.C., n.d.), A-1.

15. U.S. Army Corps of Engineers, "Summary of Authorities Under Response Scenarios" (U.S. Army Corps of Engineers, Washington, D.C., n.d.), 1.

16. Janet A. McDonnell, *After Desert Storm: The U.S. Army and the Reconstruction of Kuwait* (Washington, D.C.: Government Printing Office, 1999), 239.

17. Ibid., 241–42.

18. U.S. Army Corps of Engineers, *The History of the U.S. Army Corps of Engineers* (Alexandria, Va.: U.S. Army Corps of Engineers Headquarters, Office of History, 1998), 113.

19. Ibid.

INDEX

BIBLIOGRAPHY

Aall, Pamela, Lt. Col. Daniel Miltenberger, and Thomas G. Weiss. *Guide to IGOs, NGOs, and the Military in Peace and Relief Operations.* Washington, D.C.: United States Institute of Peace Press, 2000.

Abdullah, Abdullah. "Afghanistan: Stability and Security." Press briefing at the Dirksen Senate Office Building, Washington, D.C., October 21, 2002.

Aldape, Sofia. "The U.S. Military Campaign in Afghanistan: The Year in Review." October 10, 2002. [Online.] Available: http://www.cdi.org/terrorism/afghanistan-one-year-later-pr.cfm. [December 7, 2002.]

Asian Development Bank, United Nations Development Program, and the World Bank. *Afghanistan: Preliminary Needs Assessment for Recovery and Reconstruction.* Kabul: Asian Development Bank, January 2002.

Atkinson, Rick. "Air Assault Sets Stage for Broader Role," *Washington Post,* November 15, 1995, A1.

———. "In Almost Losing Its Resolve, NATO Alliance Found Itself," *Washington Post,* November 16, 1995, A1.

Bert, Wayne. *The Reluctant Superpower: United States Policy in Bosnia, 1991–95.* New York: St. Martin's, 1997.

Bildt, Carl. "Implementing the Civilian Tasks of the Bosnian Peace Agreement," *NATO Review* 44, no. 5 (Spring 1996): 3–6.

Boorstein, Michelle. "Taliban and Al-Qaeda Fighters May Change Form of Attack, Allies Say," Associated Press, April 3, 2002.

Boutros-Ghali, Boutros. *An Agenda for Peace—Preventative Diplomacy, Peacemaking, and Peacekeeping.* Report of the Secretary-General Pursuant to the Statement Adopted by the Summit Meeting of the Security Council on January 31, 1992. New York: United Nations, 1992.

Bowman, Steven R. *Bosnia: U.S. Military Operations.* Washington, D.C.: Congressional Research Service, November 13, 2001.

———. *Kosovo and Macedonia: U.S. and Allied Military Operations.* Washington, D.C.: Congressional Research Service, September 17, 2002.

Bryans, Michael, Bruce D. Jones, and Janice Gross Stein. *Mean Times: Adapting the Humanitarian Imperative for the Twenty-First Century.* Toronto: Program on Conflict Management and Negotiation, October 1998.

Cabe, Delia K. "Nation Building," *Kennedy School Bulletin.* Spring 2002. [Online.] Available: http://www.ksg.harvard.edu/ksgpress/bulletin/spring2002/features/nation_building.html. [May 27, 2003.]

Center for Army Lessons Learned. *Operations Other Than War, Volume IV: Peace Operations.* Newsletter no. 93-8. December 1993.

———. *The Effects of Peace Operations on Unit Readiness.* Fort Leavenworth, Kan.: Center for Army Lessons Learned, February 1996.

Center for Defense Information. "Terrain, Taliban and Terrorists: Not Only Challenges to U.S. Forces in Afghanistan." Washington, D.C.: Center for Defense Information, September 25, 2001.

Central Intelligence Agency. "Afghanistan," *The World Factbook 2002.* Washington, D.C.: Central Intelligence Agency, 2002. [Online.] Available: http://www.cia.gov/cia/publications/factbook/print/af.html. [December 6, 2002.]

The Challenges Project. *Challenges of Peace Operations: Into the Twenty-First Century—Concluding Report 1997–2002.* Stockholm: Elanders Gotab, 2002.

Clark, Wesley K. "Building a Lasting Peace in Bosnia and Herzegovina," *NATO Review* 46, no. 1 (Spring 1998): 19–22.

———. *Waging Modern War.* New York: Public Affairs, 2001.

Clark, Wesley K., and Brigadier General John D. W. Corley. Press briefing on the Kosovo strike assessment. Headquarters, Supreme Allied Command Europe, Mons, Belgium, September 16, 1999.

CNN.com. "Bombing Probe Looks at Possible Tie to 1995 Terrorist Attack." June 28, 1996. [Online.] Available: http://www.cnn.com/WORLD/9606/28/saudi.probe.pm/. [February 6, 2003.]

Congressional Budget Office. *Making Peace While Staying Ready for War: The Challenges of U.S. Military Participation in Peace Operations.* Washington, D.C.: Congressional Budget Office, December 1999.

Cousens, Elizabeth, and Chetan Kumar, with Karin Wermester, eds. *Peacebuilding as Politics: Cultivating Peace in Fragile Societies.* Boulder, Colo.: Lynne Rienner, 2001.

Cox, Marcus. *State Building and Post-Conflict Reconstruction: Lessons from Bosnia.* Geneva: Centre for Applied Studies in International Negotiations, January 2001.

Daalder, Ivo, and Michael O'Hanlon. *Winning Ugly: NATO's War to Save Kosovo.* Washington, D.C.: Brookings Institution Press, 2000.

Daniel, D. C. F., and B. C. Hayes. *Beyond Traditional Peacekeeping.* Basingstoke, UK: Macmillan, 1995.

Dao, James. "The New Air War: Fewer Targets, More Hits and Scarcer Targets." *New York Times,* November 29, 2001, A1.

Davidson, Lisa Witzig, Margaret Daly Hayes, and James J. Landon. *Humanitarian and Peace Operations: NGOs and the Military in the Interagency Process.* Washington, D.C.: National Defense University Press, December 1996.

Demeka, Dimitri G., Johannes Herderschee, and Davina F. Jacobs. *Kosovo: Institutions and Policies for Reconstruction and Growth.* Washington, D.C.: International Monetary Fund, 2002.

Department of the Army. *Engineer Combat Operations.* Field Manual 5-100. Washington, D.C.: Department of the Army, February 27, 1996.

Department of Defense. *Report to Congress, Kosovo/Operation Allied Force After Action Report.* Washington, D.C.: Department of Defense, January 31, 2000.

Diamond, Louise, and John McDonald. *Multi-Track Diplomacy.* West Hartford, Conn.: Kumarian Press, 1996.

Drozdiak, William. "NATO Leaders Struggle to Find a Winning Strategy," *Washington Post,* April 1, 1999, A22.

Flournoy, Michael. "Interagency Strategy and Planning for Postconflict Reconstruction." Washington, D.C.: Center for Strategic and International Studies, March 27, 2002.

Forman, Shepard, and Stewart Patrick. *Good Intentions: Pledges of Aid for Postconflict Recovery.* Boulder, Colo.: Lynne Rienner, 2000.

416th Engineer Command. "United States Army Facility Engineer Group." Information pamphlet. Darien, Ill.: Facility Engineer Group, n.d.

Fulghum, David A., and Robert Wall. "U.S. Stalks Taliban With New Air Scheme." *Aviation Week and Space Technology,* October 15, 2001.

Gammer, Nicholas. *From Peacekeeping to Peacemaking: Canada's Response to the Yugoslav Crisis.* Montreal: McGill-Queen's University Press, 2001.

Gannon, Kathy. "Powell Promises to Rid Afghanistan of Terrorist Contamination." Associated Press, January 17, 2002.

General Accounting Office. *Peace Operations: Heavy Use of Key Capabilities May Affect Response to Regional Conflicts.* Washington, D.C.: GAO, March 1995.

General Framework Agreement for Peace in Bosnia and Herzegovina. Paris, December 14, 1995.

Glenny, Misha. "Yugoslavia: The Great Fall," *New York Review of Books,* March 23, 1995.

Global Security. "Combat Prepositioning Ships Army Prepositioned Afloat." September 16, 2002. [Online.] Available: http://www.globalsecurity.org/military/systems/ship/sealift-cps.htm. [February 3, 2003.]

————. "Operation Enduring Freedom." October 30, 2002. [Online.] Available: http://198.65.161/military/ops/enduring-freedom.htm. [December 8, 2002.]

Gordon, D. S., and F. H. Toase, eds. *Aspects of Peacekeeping.* London: Frank Cass, 2001.

Grossman, Elaine. "U.S. Challenge in Targeting Afghanistan: Is There Enough to Bomb?" *Inside the Pentagon,* September 27, 2001.

Grove Consultants International. "Creating Strategies." 2003. [Online.] Available: http://www.grove.com/services/tool_modelsv_strategy.html. [January 5, 2003.]

Hansen, Annika S. *Drawing Lines in the Sand: The Limits and Boundaries of Peace Support Operations.* Monograph no. 44. Pretoria: The Institute for Security Studies, Boundaries of Peace Support Operations, February 2000.

Holbrooke, Richard. *To End a War.* New York: Random House, 1998.

Hosmer, Stephen T. *The Conflict over Kosovo: Why Milosevic Decided to Settle When He Did.* Santa Monica, Calif.: RAND, 2001.

Huggler, Justin. "War in Afghanistan: U.S. Bombers Guided by Spy with a Phone; Our Man Behind the Lines." *The Independent* (London), December 16, 2001.

Huhn, Robb. "CJCMOTF Helps Impact a Nation." August 2002. [Online.] Available: http://www.centcom.mil/News?Stories?Operation%20Enduring%20Freedom/08_02/08_07_02b.htm. [December 1, 2002.]

The Independent International Commission on Kosovo. *The Kosovo Report.* Oxford, UK: Oxford University Press, 2000.

Inderfurth, Karl F., and Loch K. Johnson, eds. *Decisions of the Highest Order: Perspectives on the National Security Council.* Pacific Grove, Calif.: Brooks/Cole, 1998.

International Crisis Group. *The Balkan Refugee Crisis: Regional and Long-Term Perspectives.* Brussels: International Crisis Group, June 1, 1999.

———. *Kosovo Report Card,* ICG Balkans Report no. 100. Brussels: International Crisis Group, 2000.

Jackson, Mike. "KFOR: Providing Security for Building a Better Future for Kosovo." *NATO Review* 47, no. 3 (Autumn 1999).

Jansen, G. Richard. "Albanians and Serbs in Kosovo: An Abbreviated History." June 5, 1999. [Online.] Available: http://lamar.colostate.edu/-grjan/kosovohistory.html. [November 2, 2002.]

Joulwan, George A., and Christopher C. Shoemaker. *Civilian-Military Cooperation in the Prevention of Deadly Conflict: Implementing Agreements in Bosnia and Beyond.* New York: Carnegie Corporation of New York, 1998.

Karzai, H. E. "Statement of H.E. Karzai, Chairman of the Interim Administration of Afghanistan: A Vision for Afghanistan." January 25, 2002. Tokyo. [Online.] Available: http://www.mineaction.org/countries_refdocs.cfm?doc_ID=535&c. [December 4, 2002.]

Killingsworth, Paul S., Lional Galway, Eiichi Kamiya, Brian Nichiparuk, Timothy L. Ramey, Robert S. Tripp, and James Wendt. *Flexbasing: Achieving Global Presence for Expeditionary Aerospace Forces.* Santa Monica, Calif.: RAND, 2000.

Kosovo Force. "Background to the Conflict." n.d. [Online.] Available: http://www.nato.int/kfor/kfor/intro.htm. [September 25, 2002.]

———. "Kosovo Force's Statement of Principles, UNMIK/RE/1999/8: On the Establishment of the Kosovo Protection Corps." September 20, 1999. [Online.] Available: http://www.kforonline.com. [November 5, 2002.]

Lambeth, Benjamin S. *NATO's Air War for Kosovo: A Strategic and Operational Assessment.* Santa Monica, Calif.: RAND, 2001.

Landry, Alan D. *Informing the Debate: The Impact of Operations Other Than War on Combat Training Readiness.* Strategy Research Project. Carlisle Barracks, Pa: U.S. Army War College, April 7, 1997.

Lane, Charles, and Thom Shanker, "Bosnia: What the CIA Didn't Tell Us," *New York Review of Books,* May 9, 1996.

Langholtz, Harvey J., ed. *The Psychology of Peacekeeping.* Westport, Conn.: Praeger, 1998.

Levy, Claire M., Harry Thie, and Jerry M. Sollinger. *Army PERSTEMPO in the Post–Cold War Era.* Santa Monica, Calif.: RAND, 2000.

Lippiott, Thomas F., James C. Crowley, and Jerry M. Sollinger. *Time and Resources Required for Postmobilization Training of AC/ARNG Integrated Heavy Divisions.* Santa Monica, Calif.: RAND, 1998.

Loyn, David. "Afghanistan Struggles to Rebuild." BBC News/World Edition. November 5, 2002. [Online.] Available: http://www.news.bbc.co.uk/2/hi/south_asia/2405191.stm. [December 5, 2002.]

McDonnell, Janet A. *After Desert Storm: The U.S. Army and the Reconstruction of Kuwait.* Washington, D.C.: Department of the Army, 1999.

McManus, Doyle. "Clinton's Massive Ground Invasion That Almost Was." *Los Angeles Times,* June 9, 2000.

McNulty, Dennis J. "Repairing Runways and Clearing Mines in Afghanistan." *The Engineer Magazine,* July 2002.

———. "Base Camp Infrastructure Development and C2 in Afghanistan." *The Engineer Magazine,* October–December 2002.

Mendelson-Forman, Johanna, and Michael Pan. "Post-Conflict Rapid Civilian Response." Washington, D.C.: Center for Strategic and International Studies, March 25, 2002.

"Military-Technical Agreement Between the International Security Force (KFOR) and the Government of the Federal Republic of Yugoslavia and the Federal Republic of Serbia." Kumanovo, Macedonia, June 9, 1999.

Mockaitis, Thomas R. *Peace Operations and Intrastate Conflict.* Westport, Conn.: Praeger, 1999.

Mohr, Jerry T., Frederick A. Mucke, and Donald L. Maconi. "Operation Enduring Freedom from the Military Engineer Perspective." *The Engineer Magazine.* July 2002.

Morrow, Jason. "Greater Intervention and Military Cutbacks are a Deadly Combination." *National Policy Analysis,* no. 249, June 1999.

Murphy, Kim. "U.S. Bombing Spares Much of Kandahar." *Los Angeles Times,* December 13, 2001.

Nardulli, Bruce R., Walter L. Perry, Bruce Pirnie, John Gordon IV, and John G. McGinn, *Disjointed War: Military Operations in Kosovo, 1999.* Santa Monica, Calif.: RAND, 2002.

North Atlantic Treaty Organization. "Statement by Secretary General Dr. Javier Solana." Press Statement (1999)041. Brussels. March 24, 1999.

———. "Statement on Kosovo." Press Release S-1(99)62. Washington, D.C., April 23, 1999.

———. "CIMIC Reconstruction." *NATO Review* 49, no. 1 (Spring 2001).

Perl, Raphael F. *Terrorism: U.S. Response to Bombings in Kenya and Tanzania: A New Policy Direction?* Washington, D.C.: Congressional Research Service, September 1, 1998.

Phillips, William R. "Civil-Military Cooperation: Vital to Peace Implementation in Bosnia." *NATO Review* 46, no. 1 (Spring 1998).

Pirnie, Bruce R. *Civilians and Soldiers: Achieving Better Coordination.* Santa Monica, Calif.: RAND, 1998.

Prusher, Ilene R. "Afghan Refugees Strain Kabul." *The Christian Science Monitor,* December 11, 2002.

Rana, Surinder. "Strategic Insight: Afghanistan Military Campaign Enters New Phase." Monterey, Calif.: Naval Postgraduate School, Center for Contemporary Conflict, April 9, 2002.

Reimer, Dennis J. *Soldiers Are Our Credentials: The Collected Works and Selected Papers of the Thirty-Third Chief of Staff.* Washington, D.C.: Department of the Army, 2000.

Reliefweb. "Executive Summary and National Priority Projects." October 12, 2002. [Online.] Available: http://www.reliefweb.int/w/rwb.nsf/vID/1EB74FFA8B0155E4C5B002AAD79?OpenDocument. [December 6, 2002].

Rhem, Kathleen T. "Operation Mountain Lion Seizes Enemy Weapons." *The Pentagram,* June 21, 2002. [Online.] Available: http://www.dcmilitary.com/army. [December 8, 2002.]

Rogel, Carole. *The Breakup of Yugoslavia and the War in Bosnia.* Westport, Conn.: Greenwood Press, 1998.

Rohde, David. *Endgame: The Betrayal and Fall of Srebrenica, Europe's Worst Massacre Since World War II.* New York: Farrar, Straus, and Giroux, 1997.

Semonite, Todd T. *The Military Engineer as a Critical Peace Operations Multiplier.* Strategy Research Project. Carlisle Barracks, Pa.: U.S. Army War College, April 7, 1999.

Serafino, Nina M. *Peacekeeping: Issues of Military Involvement.* Washington, D.C.: Congressional Research Service, August 1, 2002.

Shalikashvilli, John M. *National Military Strategy*. Washington, D.C.: Department of Defense, February 1995.

Shinseki, Eric K. *The Army Vision: Soldiers on Point for the Nation*. Washington, D.C.: Department of the Army, October 1999.

Siegel, Adam B. *Requirements for Humanitarian Assistance and Peace Operations: Insights from Seven Case Studies*. Alexandria, Va.: Center for Naval Analyses, March 1995.

Silber, Laura, and Alan Little. *Yugoslavia, Death of a Nation*. New York: Penguin Books, 1996.

Sokolovic, Dzemal, and Florian Bieber, eds. *Reconstructing Multiethnic Societies: The Case of Bosnia-Herzegovina*. Aldershot, UK: Ashgate, 2001.

Solomon, Jay, Steve Levine, David Cloud, and Almar Latour. "Moving Targets: Now, It's the Alumni of bin Laden's Camps Giving Cause for Fear—Trained in Afghanistan, Many Have Since Fanned out to Spread Their Skills—Secret Site Outside Jakarta." *Wall Street Journal*, December 13, 2001.

Sortor, Ronald E. *Army Forces for Operations Other Than War*. Santa Monica, Calif.: RAND, 1997.

Steele, Jonathan. "How Bombing and Diplomacy Eased the Taliban's Grip on Kandahar." *The Guardian* (London), December 7, 2001.

Stevens, John. "Afghanistan's Hidden Killers: Land Mines." *State Magazine*, April 2002.

Tarnoff, Curt. *Kosovo: Reconstruction and Development Assistance*. CRS Report for Congress. Washington, D.C.: Congressional Research Service, January 16, 2001.

Tindemans, Leo, Lloyd Cutler, Bronislaw Geremek, John Roper, Theo Sommer, Simone Veil, and David Anderson. *Unfinished Peace: Report of the International Commission on the Balkans*. Washington, D.C.: Carnegie Endowment for International Peace, 1996.

Toft, Monica. Press briefing on terrorism. Kennedy School's Joan Shorenstein Center on the Press, Politics, and Public Policy. Washington, D.C. November 15, 2001.

Ullman, Richard, ed. *The World and Yugoslavia's Wars*. New York: Council on Foreign Relations, 1996.

United Nations. "Immediate and Transitional Assistance Programme for the Afghan People." New York: United Nations, January 17, 2002. [Online.]

Available: http://www.reliefweb.int/library/Afghan%20ITAP%202002_final.pdf. [December 7, 2002.]

————. *Report on the Fall of Srebrenica.* UN Doc. A54/549 (November 15, 1999).

United Nations Development Program/World Bank. "Afghanistan—Preliminary Needs Assessment for Recovery and Reconstruction." New York: United Nations, January 15, 2002. [Online.] Available: http://www.mineaction.org/countries/_refdocs.cfm?doc_ID=463&c. [December 7, 2002.]

United Nations Interim Administration Mission in Kosovo. *A Year and a Half in Kosovo.* Pristina: UNMIK, 2000.

————. *Kosovo 2001–2003: From Reconstruction to Growth.* Pristina: UNMIK, December 2000.

United Nations Interim Administration Mission in Kosovo/Mine Action Coordination Center. "Mine Action Program in Kosovo/Background." September 1999. [Online.] Available: http://www.mineaction.org/unmik_org/departments/hq/default.htm. [March 5, 2002.]

United Nations Mine Action Service. "Afghanistan." August 28, 2002. [Online.] Available: http://www.mineaction.org/countries/countries_overview.cfm?country_id=652. [March 5, 2004.]

————. "Bosnia and Herzegovina." November 30, 2002. [Online.] Available: http://www.mineaction.org/countries/countries_overview.cfm?country_id=692. [March 5, 2004.]

United Nations Office for the Coordination of Humanitarian Affairs, "Afghanistan: Interview with Reconstruction Minister Dr. Amin Farhang," October 7, 2002. [Online.] Available: http://www.irinnews.org/report.asp?ReportID=30262&SelectRegion=Central_Asia. [December 9, 2002.]

United Nations Security Council. Letter dated June 4, 1999, from the Permanent Representative of France to the United Nations, addressed to the Secretary-General, enclosing the Rambouillet Accords, "Interim Agreement for Peace and Self-Government in Kosovo," UN Doc. S/1999/648 (June 7, 1999).

————. *Report of the Secretary-General on the United Nations Interim Administration Mission in Kosovo.* New York: United Nations, 2000.

————. UN Security Council Resolution 1244, S/RES/1244(1999), June 10, 1999.

United States Army Corps of Engineers. *The History of the U.S. Army Corps of Engineers.* Alexandria, Va.: Office of History, U.S. Army Corps of Engineers Headquarters, 1998.

United States Army Corps of Engineers—Europe District. *Engineering In Europe, Special Edition, Kosovo: The Engineers' Story.* Wiesbaden, Germany: United States Army Corps of Engineers, May 2000.

United States Army Task Force Eagle Headquarters. *TFE Joint Military Commission Policies, Procedures, and Command Guidance Handbook.* Rodelheim, Germany: United States Army Printing and Publications Center, May 12, 1996.

United States Army Transportation School. *Division Transportation Officer's Guide, Reference 01-1.* Fort Eustis, Va.: Department of the Army, June 7, 2001.

United States Department of State. *Background Note: Bosnia and Herzegovina.* Washington, D.C.: Bureau of European and Eurasian Affairs, September 2001.

———. Bureau of Political-Military Affairs. Office of Humanitarian Demining Programs. "U.S. Humanitarian Demining Assistance to Afghanistan," July 30, 2002.

———. Office of Public Affairs. "Fact Sheet: International Contributions to the War Against Terrorism," May 22, 2002.

———. "The Rambouillet Agreement." n.d. [Online.] Available: http://www.state.gov/www/regions/eur/ksvo_rambouillet/text.html. [September 25, 2002.]

U.S. House Armed Services Committee. *Hearings of the Military Readiness Subcommittee of the House Armed Services Committee.* 106th Cong., 1st sess., March 22, 1999.

———. *Hearings of the House Armed Services Committee.* "Statement of General Tommy Franks, Commander, United States Central Command." 107th Cong., 2d sess., February 27, 2002.

"U.S. Strikes Terrorist Sites in Afghanistan, Sudan." *Air Force News,* August 20, 1998. [Online.] Available: http://www.af.mil/news/Aug1998/n19980820_981248.html. [February 6, 2003.]

Voice of America. "U.S. Military Shift Afghan Operations toward Reconstruction Efforts." December 6, 2002. [Online.] Available: http://www.reliefweb.int/w/rwb.nsf/9ca65951ee22658ec125663300408599/89c64eob53dc69d49256c8a0019fbb1?. [December 14, 2002.]

von Hippel, Karin. *Democracy by Force—U.S. Military Intervention in the Post-Cold War World.* Cambridge, UK: Cambridge University Press, 2000.

Walsh, Mark R. "Managing Peace Operations in the Field." *Parameters* 26, no. 2 (Summer 1996).

Wentz, Larry, ed. *Lessons from Bosnia: The IFOR Experience.* Washington, D.C.: National Defense University, 1998.

———. *Lessons from Kosovo: The KFOR Experience.* Washington, D.C.: DOD Command and Control Research Program, July 2002.

White, N. D. *Keeping the Peace: The United Nations and the Maintenance of International Peace and Security,* 2d ed. Manchester, UK: Manchester University Press, 1997.

The White House, *The Clinton Administration's Policy on Managing Complex Contingency Operations: Presidential Decision Directive.* May 1997. [Online.] Available: http://clinton2.nara.gov/WH/EOP/NSC/html/documents/NSCDoc2.html. [January 7, 2003.]

———. "The Global War on Terrorism: The First 100 Days." n.d. [Online.] Available: http://www.state.gov/s/ct/rls/rpt/6947.html. [December 3, 2002.]

———. *A National Security Strategy of Engagement and Enlargement.* Washington, D.C.: The White House, February 1996.

Williams, Michael. *Civil-Military Relations and Peacekeeping.* Adelphi Paper 321. London: International Institute for Strategic Studies, 1998.

Willis, G. E. "Army Leaders Seek More Funds for '98." *Army Times,* March 23, 1998.

Winslow, Donna. "Strange Bedfellows in Humanitarian Crises: NGOs and the Military." *Transnational Associations* 52, no. 5 (2000).

Woehrel, Steven J., and Julie Kim. *Kosovo and U.S. Policy.* Washington, D.C.: Congressional Research Service, July 3, 2002.

Woodhouse, Tom, and Oliver Ramsbotham, eds. *Peacekeeping and Conflict Resolution.* London: Frank Cass, 2000.

Woodward, David. *The IMF, the World Bank, and Economic Policy in Bosnia.* Oxford, UK: Oxfam, 1998.

Woodward, Susan. *Balkan Tragedy: Chaos and Dissolution After the Cold War.* Washington, D.C.: Brookings Institution Press, 1995.

The World Bank. "Afghanistan World Bank Approach Paper." Washington, D.C.: The World Bank, November 2001.

———. *Bosnia and Herzegovina: Toward Economic Recovery.* Washington, D.C.: The International Bank for Reconstruction and Development, 1996.

———. *Conflict Prevention and Postconflict Reconstruction: Perspectives and Prospects.* Washington, D.C.: The World Bank, August 1998.

———. "Reconstruction of Bosnia and Herzegovina." Press Release. Washington, D.C.: The World Bank Group, 1995.

The World Bank Group. *Reconstruction of Bosnia and Herzegovina: Priorities for Recovery and Growth.* Washington, D.C.: The World Bank Group, 1995.

———. *Transitional Support Strategy: Afghanistan.* Washington, D.C.: The World Bank Group, March 12, 2002.

Zartman, I. William, and J. Lewis Rasmussen, eds. *Peacemaking in International Conflict: Methods and Techniques.* Washington, D.C.: United States Institute of Peace Press, 1997.

Zimmerman, Warren. *Origins of a Catastrophe: Yugoslavia and Its Destroyers.* New York: New York Times Books, 1999.

Colonel Garland H. Williams, U.S. Army, was the military assistant to the assistant secretary of the army for civil works. From 1999 to 2001, he commanded the 16th Armored Engineer Battalion in Germany, which was deployed to Kosovo during 2000, for peacekeeping duties. As chief of contingency engineering for Allied Forces Southern Europe from 1996 to 1999, Colonel Williams served in Sarajevo as part of NATO's Implementation Force staff, coordinating the reconstruction of vital roads bridges, ports, and airfields damaged during the Bosnian war. He was a senior fellow at the U.S. Institute of Peace during 2002–2003.

Jennings Randolph Program for International Peace

This book is a fine example of the work produced by senior fellows in the Jennings Randolph Fellowship Program of the United States Institute of Peace. As part of the statute establishing the Institute, Congress envisioned a program that would appoint "scholars and leaders of peace from the United States and abroad to pursue scholarly inquiry and other appropriate forms of communication on international peace and conflict resolution." The program was named after Senator Jennings Randolph of West Virginia, whose efforts over four decades helped to establish the Institute.

Since 1987, the Jennings Randolph Program has played a key role in the Institute's effort to build a national center of research, dialogue, and education on critical problems of conflict and peace. Nearly 200 senior fellows from some thirty nations have carried out projects on the sources and nature of violent international conflict and the ways such conflict can be peacefully managed or resolved. Fellows come from a wide variety of academic and other professional backgrounds. They conduct research at the Institute and participate in the Institute's outreach activities to policymakers, the academic community, and the American public.

Each year approximately fifteen senior fellows are in residence at the Institute. Fellowship recipients are selected by the Institute's board of directors in a competitive process. For further information on the program, or to receive an application form, please contact the program staff at (202) 457-1700, or visit our web site at www.usip.org.

Sheryl Brown
Director

Engineering Peace

The Military Role in Postconflict Reconstruction

This book was set in the typeface New Century Schoolbook; the display type is Avant Garde Gothic Demi Bold. Cover design by Hasten Design Studio, Washington, D.C. Interior design and page makeup by Mike Chase and Kenny Allen. Graphics designed by Michael Sonesen. Copyediting and proofreading by EEI Communications, Inc., Alexandria, Va. Production supervised by Marie Marr Jackson. Peter Pavilionis was the book's editor.